MW00651180

"Just reading this made me want to dance! A reminder that women have built many revolutions, credited or not, and we will continue to revolt, innovate, and shine."

—LINDY WEST, AUTHOR OF *SHRILL: NOTES FROM A LOUD WOMAN*

"Somehow both appropriately broad and perfectly detailed, a beautiful, easily digestible book . . . You don't have to be a woman to enjoy it!"

—YASI SALEK, HOST OF *BANDSPLAIN* AND *24 QUESTION PARTY PEOPLE*

"If what neuroscientists tell us is true, that music is a social/ emotion-delivery device . . . truly a woman's voice, words, rhythms, and melodies are best adapted to express what it feels like to be a human. This welcome book reminds us of the many underappreciated musicians whose work found its way into our own self-images."

—SUSAN ROGERS, LEGENDARY PRODUCER, NEUROSCIENTIST, AND COAUTHOR OF *THIS IS WHAT IT SOUNDS LIKE: WHAT THE MUSIC YOU LOVE SAYS ABOUT YOU*

HOW
WOMEN
MADE
MUSIC

HOW WOMEN MADE MUSIC

A Revolutionary History from NPR Music

EDITED BY ALISON FENSTERSTOCK   INTRODUCTION BY ANN POWERS

National Public Radio, Inc.

HarperOne
An Imprint of HarperCollinsPublishers

Barbara Lynn

Contents page illustration: Stevie Nicks and Christine McVie *by* Jess Rotter

The credits on pages 333–34 constitute a continuation of this copyright page.

HOW WOMEN MADE MUSIC. Copyright © 2024 by National Public Radio, Inc. All rights reserved. Printed in the United States of America. No part of this book may be used or reproduced in any manner whatsoever without written permission except in the case of brief quotations embodied in critical articles and reviews. For information, address HarperCollins Publishers, 195 Broadway, New York, NY 10007.

HarperCollins books may be purchased for educational, business, or sales promotional use. For information, please email the Special Markets Department at SPsales@harpercollins.com.

FIRST EDITION

Designed by Janet Evans-Scanlon

Library of Congress Cataloging-in-Publication Data has been applied for.

ISBN 978-0-06-327033-6

24 25 26 27 28 LBC 5 4 3 2 1

CONTENTS

INTRODUCTION

by Ann Powers

What will it take for women in music to get their due? More to the point: Why do we keep having to ask that question? Since the days when the shouts and moans of the blues queens defined recorded music (and before that, but that's where this story begins), women have been musical pathfinders, innovators, and standard-bearers. Yet they have perpetually been treated as novelties, shiny and sweet but insubstantial, not truly essential to anything. So many women have tried to correct this error—as artists, historians, and fans, shouting "women matter" from the rooftops—only to be forgotten or actively erased. It's a cycle that needs to be broken. Women cannot only be appreciated as the Next Big Thing. They are fundamental, and always have been.

I'd spent many years working to help correct the record, only to see the old prejudices reinscribed. By 2015 I knew something serious would have to be done. That year, Jill Sternheimer, Alison Fensterstock, and I started a conversation while drinking beers in plastic cups one night in New Orleans. We'd met up to attend the Ponderosa Stomp, an occasional festival devoted to obscure elders from the golden age of garage rock and undercover soul. We regularly go to such retrospectives, which are now common, since writing music's genealogy is a major form of fandom and entrepreneurship: tribute shows, streaming documentaries, career-spanning playlists, and books like the one you're holding now. Jill, in fact, often organizes such events at Lincoln Center Out of Doors, where she has served as the director of public programs. Alison has curated music retrospectives for museums and for magazines, and in my writing I often focus on

Mexican American guitarist Lydia Mendoza was a star
on both sides of the border in the 1930s and '40s.

history, too, trying to tease out how artists' legacies form and expand or contract over time.

That summer night, we'd just seen the guitar player Barbara Lynn—then seventy-five years old—barrel and slide her way through a dazzling set of her R&B classics. Lynn was one of the genre's most elegantly fierce instrumentalists, yet she is hardly remembered now—and when she is invoked, it's as a novelty, that rare lady with an ax.

Why, we wondered together, doesn't Lynn get her due? We came to the obvious and oft-stated conclusion: that the general history of popular music is told through the great works of men, and that without a serious revision of the canon, women will always remain on the margins.

That night we asked ourselves: What can we do to stop the cycle? The answer: we developed a multiplatform series called *Turning the Tables*. Its very name contains the acknowledgment that the erasure or marginalization of women in music *is* cyclical, that it has happened again and again despite generations of feminists trying to stop it, and that a serious reset would be needed to make women visible and audible at the center of an art form where, without being fully acknowledged, they have always played a crucial role.

Turntables spin and a record plays out, as if it can sound only one way. But hip hop has taught us that the sound can change if a DJ puts her hand on an album and scratches. To turn the tables in music history, that kind of touch is necessary. Make a mark and ensure that it's heard, discussed, recorded. Change the way people think about the sounds and stories they've taken for granted. Redirect the music history; trouble its groove. *Turning the Tables* doesn't just put women and other marginalized people at the center of the narrative—it changes the tale.

In the months and years after that night that we watched Barbara Lynn rule on guitar, a group of women and nonbinary folk—writers, scholars, and other creative thinkers across the spectrum of popular music—expanded from three to nearly a hundred collaborators crafting the *Turning the Tables* project, including the live shows presented by NPR Music in partnership with Lincoln Center. With NPR Music's Marissa Lorusso, Paula Mejia, and Jacob Ganz added to the core team, we first produced an online list of "The 150 Greatest Albums Made by Women," focusing on what we determined was the album era—the early 1960s to what was then the present, 2016, when Beyoncé made *Lemonade*. You can find that list at the end of this book, on page 321, and commentary about some of the albums is included throughout each chapter, denoted with a record icon.

That list went viral because it was different from what had come before: it asked music fans to think about that era as belonging not to the Beatles and Bob Dylan and Prince (with the Ronettes and Joni Mitchell and Madonna clinging to some ever-so-slightly second tier), but as wholly defined by women's work.

The following year we created a playlist for the twenty-first century, two hundred songs that put aside Outkast's "Hey Ya!" and LCD Soundsystem's "Losing My Edge" in favor of M.I.A.'s "Paper Planes" and Adele's "Rolling in the Deep." We also declared Rihanna the most influential artist of the new epoch. (You can see this list on page 325 and other material from that season in these pages, too, denoted by music notes.) The following years saw us going deep on the women who invented twentieth-century music, from Bessie Smith to Celia Cruz, and considering the Indigo Girls as progenitors of queer pop fandom, Roberta Flack as a genius, Paramore's Hayley Williams as the embodiment of rock and roll liberation, and Tracy Chapman as an agent of queer awakening.

Seven seasons, many different approaches. Our team changed, and we continually expanded our roster of collaborators and advisors. What connects each iteration of *Turning the Tables* is a commitment to not merely reinsert women into already established hierarchies, but to reimagine those edifices when women define their foundations. This mission required—and allowed!—us to seek out others doing similar work across the spectrum of music writing, including critics who've emerged

Lena Horne *by* Dame Darcy

New York women rappers in the late 1980s. *From left, top row:* Sparky D, Sweet Tee, Yvette Money, and Ms. Melodie; *middle row:* Millie Jackson, MC Peaches, and unidentified; *bottom row:* Unidentified, Roxanne Shante, MC Lyte, and Synquis.

as leaders in a new era when women top mastheads and Black feminist scholars are building new bookshelves that look quite different from the ones available to me when I started my writing career more than thirty years ago. My greatest source of pride in this project is the virtual community we've built by placing vital current voices in dialogue with other voices uncovered from the archives.

In these pages, which expand the parameters of *Turning the Tables* to include excerpts from NPR's vast audio and digital library, you will learn how journalists, scholars, lyric essayists, and musicians themselves are all contributing to a sea change in popular music's present and our understanding of its past.

I want to believe this shift is permanent. When we founded *Turning the Tables*, I wasn't so sure. See, I'd been there before. As a fledgling music scribe in high school, I got my big break writing for the Seattle music monthly *The Rocket*—and was promptly assigned to the girls' beat, interviewing breakthrough stars like Joan Jett and the Go-Go's Jane Wiedlin about whether their gender hurt or helped in the boys' game of rock and roll. (The answer then usually added up to, "I don't wanna talk about it.")

I published my first official overview of "women in rock" in 1989 in San Francisco's alternative newspaper the *SF Weekly*; illustrated with a graphic that collaged together Debbie Harry's face and Madonna's, it showed me arguing that Madge's ascendancy might be as important as Patti Smith's had been more than a decade before. But the jury was still out.

By 1995 I'd been to grad school, moved to New York, and made the connection between the theory I read in my seminars, which taught me how perniciously embedded sexism is in the patterns of language itself, and the routine sexism I encountered in the supposedly progressive world of "alternative" rock, soul, and hip hop.

Through her own writing, my friend and colleague Evelyn McDonnell initiated a confrontation with that deep misogyny that resulted in the anthology we co-edited in 1995, *Rock She Wrote: Women Write About Rock, Pop, and Rap*. It was the first-ever collection of music writing by women alone. During that decade and beyond it, my fellow women music writers and I often joked that every year was dubbed "the year of women in rock (or hip hop or pop)"—a disruption of music's natural male-dominated order that might signal a new dawn, but which more likely wouldn't last.

Even as more anthologies and films and panels and compilations have been issued to show how vital the work of musicians who are not cishet men remains, it's been very hard to shake the idea that the place of women, nonbinary people, and trans people in music is provisional. Sure, another book about women in music hits the shelves (to paraphrase the great Kathleen Hanna, who decried the sexism of turning women into a trend in the Julie Ruin song "Crochet"). Does it change anything?

If you are a woman, queer, or nonbinary musician, or one who works in the music biz, or simply love music with all your heart, you've probably asked this question. If you identify as male but care about equity and justice in music, you likely have, too.

✳ ✳ ✳

Here's a scene from Joni Mitchell's days in Laurel Canyon, where she first became a rock star. Mitchell was working with David Crosby on her first, self-titled album, and they'd frequently attend parties at the houses of friends like Cass Elliot or the screenwriter Carl Gottlieb. Gottlieb later told music historian Barney Hoskyns that Crosby would have Mitchell wait in another room after they arrived. During a lull in the conversation he'd tell the crowd that he wanted to introduce someone. Mitchell would emerge, play a few songs, and retreat. "She goes back upstairs, and we all sit around and look at each other and say, 'What was *that*? Did we hallucinate it?'" Gottlieb said.

There were women at these parties, but most of the rising stars gathered in those jacaranda-filled backyards were men. Some soon became Mitchell's collaborators, some lovers—Graham Nash, James Taylor, Jackson Browne. They heard in Mitchell something they hadn't heard before: her unique guitar tunings, turning folk music toward jazz; her lyrics, often sharper in detail and riskier emotionally than their own. She really was an exception, the genius whose *Blue*, inspired by this period of her life and issued in 1971, topped the first *Turning the Tables* list. But there's also something off and sadly typical about this scene. In it, the female musician is a dream, a surprise, and a disruptor. She can claim the center of attention, but her rightful point of origin, and the place to which she returns, is a margin.

Now consider another scene, this one presented by the literary scholars Sandra M. Gilbert and Susan Gubar in their 1979 study *The Madwoman in the Attic: The Woman Writer and the Nineteenth-Century Imagination*. They recognized that women had, for a century, been reading an alternate history of literature into existence, a "canon that lived in the mind of every *femme moyenne intellectuelle* who spent her girlhood avidly devouring the classics of female imagination produced by Austen and the Brontës, Mary Shelley and George Eliot, and yes, if the girl liked poetry, Emily Dickinson."

Gilbert and Gubar's scenario of women trading worn paperbacks back and forth and having long discussions about *Pride and Prejudice* in comparison to *Wuthering Heights* doesn't isolate any one female writer as exceptional; instead, it

xii

INTRODUCTION

places them in dialogue across time and space, changing the idea of what great literature can be. Feminists then created a new canon of women's literature, in books like the 1985 landmark *Norton Anthology of Literature by Women*, which changed the game. More books by women were taught in college courses. Some titles lost to time, like Kate Chopin's *The Awakening*, were rediscovered. Arguments about these new canons ensued, and resulted in more change, including greater acknowledgment of women of color and women writing beyond North America. The changes stuck. A 2011 study found a direct correlation between the publication of the anthology and greater gender balance among authors considered central to world literature in general.

Despite the quantifiable effects of such work within the world of books, canon-making remains a fraught activity. The timeless aura that envelops anything called "classic" or even "best" arises in tension with the human work of placing art in that category, which is always connected to the particular time, place, and people affixing the gold star. When we launched *Turning the Tables*, we felt that our maverick attitude and our focus on the marginalized, overlooked, and undersung inherently solved that problem for us. In fact, that wasn't true.

From the moment we published that first list, we could see how it instantly froze in time; we slapped our foreheads, realizing just how many crucial voices we'd forgotten. We wanted to create a canon that lived and breathed, but we took years to really figure out how to do that. Facing the biases of a predominantly white original crew, expanding our contributors and really listening to them, confronting our errors in judgment, and trying out different formats—the essay, the podcast, the live performance, the video—made our series more like music-making itself, an activity that can be recorded but that exists most vitally in real time. In fact, as *Turning the Tables* continues to transform, we're still trying to make it as dynamic as possible.

This book inaugurates a new phase in our ongoing mission of infusing canon-making with life and, keeping it expansive, of imagining music history as a huge continuing conversation rather than as something solid, like a monument. It incorporates material from every *Turning the Tables* season and ranges far beyond that base to represent more than fifty years of NPR's coverage of women in popular music.

We did a deep dive into the NPR archives, finding rare gems pulled from on-air interviews, ranging from Joan Baez talking in 1971 about nonviolence as a musical principle to Patti Smith in 1976 describing the empowering effect of live performance to Nina Simone in 2001 explaining how she developed the edge in her voice as a tool against racism. We also sought out excerpts from other NPR projects that share the *Turning the Tables* spirit of challenging preconceptions and heralding the undersung, including *Alt.Latino*, the legendary vertical dedicated to pan-Latin music and culture and hosted by Anamaria Sayre and Felix Contreras; *The South Got Something to Say*, an epic survey of Southern hip hop edited by Briana Younger; and *Louder Than a Riot*, the groundbreaking podcast hosted by Sidney Madden and Rodney Carmichael.

Women musicians, as the chapter headings declare, are warriors, empaths, tradition bearers, and rebel scream queens. They are mothers, workers, technical wizards, and careful crafters. Nonbinary, gender-fluid, and trans musicians are all of these things, and lately also too often the bearers of the fears and misconceptions of a culture not catching up with itself quickly enough.

Readers will also learn much about how music is made and how musical lives are maintained. Women musicians are, after all, people, and while gendered definitions put them in certain positions, much of what they do involves their humanity beyond such categories.

That's one reason, I think, why so many musicians resist talking about themselves as women; too often, the discussion becomes exclusionary and unbalanced, with the aspects of their lives that are clearly tied to gendered experiences (like motherhood, sexual objectification and the beauty myth, or enduring and combatting sexism) blotting out equally or more important ones (like becoming skilled at playing an instrument, learning how to write, or navigating the dirty toilets and bad food of road life).

The very idea of "women in" music has shifted in the years that *Turning the Tables* has existed. Thinkers in the age of Black Lives Matter have made the phrase "intersectional," originated by the legal theorist Kimberlé Crenshaw and grounded in the crucial work of the feminist Combahee River Collective, central in discussions of power and identity. Intersectional thinkers demand the acknowledgment that the inseparable dynamics of racism, sexism, and homophobia (among other forces) form the systems that elevate some while denigrating others. Within music history, that has meant many things: that white women have sometimes been allowed into "boys' clubs" that would have never allowed in BIPOC women; that queer women and nonbinary or trans people have felt the need to hide their sexuality and gender in order to find any level of success; that Black women's innovations have been stolen and uncredited by white women as often as by men.

Turning the Tables has unfolded alongside—interwoven with—these crucial discussions. At the same time, mainstream pop has entered a period dominated by women—two, at least, the megastars Taylor Swift and Beyoncé. We have asked ourselves, at times, if our ultimate goal should be to help render our own project obsolete. Can we genuinely imagine a world in which a phrase like "women in music" would earn only blank stares? If that day comes, humanity will move in different ways; melodies and rhythms and vocal tones and fuzzed-out electronics may hit our ears differently, adding up to stories we can only half-imagine now. I actually think this is happening, right now. I still believe in the value of history, though—in the voices that echo forward from the past, and in those current and future artists who call back to those forebears; and in the one long song that is human experience, full of dissonance and breaks, bursts of cacophony and rhapsodic harmonies, crescendos that threaten to break the eardrum, and hushed passages that require the utmost attention to comprehend. I believe in trying to hear every note that matters. And that means every note.

Enya *by* Maggie Thrash

HOW

WOMEN

MADE

MUSIC

This is where *Turning the Tables* begins, with the mothers of rock and roll and the innovators who both echo and interrogate them now, showing that preservation is sometimes a demonstration of love— and sometimes an act of protest. The roots are very much alive, and still talking to the leaves.

TRADITION BEARERS AND BREAKERS

How Bessie Smith Influenced a Century of Popular Music

Singer Bessie Smith's recording career lasted only ten years, but during that time she created a body of work that helped shape the sound of the twentieth century. Her first single, "Downhearted Blues"—written by two women, pianist Lovie Austin and blues singer Alberta Hunter—was a major hit in 1923, selling hundreds of thousands of copies and helping her label, Columbia Records, out of a financial slump. With her subsequent recordings, Smith was one of the artists who propelled the fledgling "race records" market of music targeted to Black audiences that had launched a few years earlier in 1920 with Mamie Smith's hit "Crazy Blues."

Through the rest of the 1920s, Bessie Smith became one of the earliest stars of recorded music and a leading figure of what came to be called classic blues, a genre dominated by African American women. She was the highest-paid African American artist working in music and the first African American superstar. Bessie Smith's sound and her attitude, rooted in a distant era, are with us in the twenty-first century.

In that first hit record, "Downhearted Blues," you can still hear what won the hearts of her audiences. Smith sings about "being crazy about a man" who mistreated her and broke her heart. What sets the song apart is the attitude she assumes as she tells her story. In the opening lines she confronts the simple, terrible fact that "it's hard to love someone when that someone don't love you" and the pain that situation causes. But she also makes a commitment to avoid this kind of agony in the future. "The next man I get," she sings in a subsequent stanza, "has got to promise to be mine, all mine." The song's final lines express a confidence that suggests she might succeed in doing so:

I got the world in a jug, the stopper's in my hand
I got the world in a jug, the stopper's in my hand
I'm gonna hold it until you men come under my command

By the time she became the bona fide superstar whose influence earned her the nickname "the Empress of the Blues," Smith had been a singer for decades. Orphaned by age nine and raised by older siblings, Smith sang for spare change on the street corners of her hometown of Chattanooga, Tennessee, and went out on the road when she was sixteen. She learned how to hold the attention of an audience in the makeshift rural venues and city theaters where touring Black artists performed throughout the South in the early twentieth century. An all-around entertainer, she developed an act that consisted of songs, dances, jokes, and sketches.

Her onstage costumes of gowns, wigs, plumes, and elaborate headdresses communicated glamour and wealth, and she carried herself with a regal bearing that fit her nickname. But Smith's singing voice, of course, is the element that remains, the element that made her a legend. When Smith rendered a song, she tapped into her experiences of the hardships of poverty, racism, sexism, and, above all, the ups and downs of love. This gave her a down-to-earth quality that made it easy for her Black, working-class audience to connect with her. Whether she was singing the "Empty Bed Blues (Parts 1 and 2)" (1928), a ribald and humorous meditation on the sexual prowess of a lover, or expressing the terrifying experience of a flood in "Backwater Blues" (1927), Smith's authoritative delivery conveyed an authenticity that suggested she had actually lived through the things she sang about. She made prodigious use of her skills as vocalist, actress, and comedian to develop convincing and compelling performances, live and on record.

Decades before hip-hop artists rapped about the vicissitudes of Black working-class life, Smith sang about the everyday reality of wanting to live life to its fullest as a young, Black, poor woman—a category of person that the mainstream of America ignored with impunity, but a category that Smith insisted was important. Her voice reverberates with the tone and color of the South, and her lyrics, peppered with colloquialisms and turns of phrase associated with Black English, brought a distinctive perspective into the public conversation at a time when Black voices and Black experiences barely registered there. By singing about Black lives with care and conviction, Smith advanced the revolutionary idea that Black lives mattered—and specifically, that Black *women's* lives mattered.

To hear Smith's genius and to begin to understand the power of the blues, we need to slow down and adjust to her tempo so we can appreciate the skill with which she makes her vocal choices. Working within the framework of the blues, she varies her inflection and phrasing to convey an idea or a feeling. She stretches a note to emphasize a word, sings with varying degrees of roughness, or hits a high note at an unexpected moment to make us pay attention to her point. She stresses certain words while cutting others short; she deviates from the expected melody, offering an element of surprise. Smith teases meaning out of her lyrics, even the pedestrian ones, imbuing them with significance and using them to express her own unique personality and attitude. By turns Smith sounds confident, assertive, vulnerable, self-possessed, independent, and complex. The appeal of this persona and the vocal approaches that created it were powerful. Smith's artistry, communicative power, and public appeal anticipate that of Beyoncé, a singer whose capacity to articulate the longings, frustrations, and passions of African American women with tremendous vocal dexterity and onstage polish are a latter-day manifestation of the Empress of the Blues.

With their focus on intimate relationships, there's a timeless quality to many blues songs, but much of the material recorded in the 1920s was emphatically modern, responding to seismic cultural shifts. These were songs about and for women who were experiencing migration—either moving from rural Southern areas to Southern towns or Northern cities or experiencing the movement of those around them. The departures of lovers and the comings and goings of trains are frequent themes. In some cases Smith offers advice: "Pinchback Blues" (1924), a song that warns women about avoiding entanglements with good-looking, no-account men, opens with Smith's spoken word introduction, "Girls, I wanna tell you about these sweet men." At a time when American women of all races and classes were enjoying a considerable degree of personal freedom and mobility, this type of caution was an apt response to the rise of modernity associated with the Jazz Age. Migration brought Black women from the countryside to bustling cities where, earning their own money and often free from the surveillance of their families, they could experiment socially and sexually. Smith reminds her listeners to do so with their eyes open. Her catalog also includes observations about contemporary social inequities. In "Washwoman Blues" (1928), Smith sings about the day-to-day drudgery of being a laundress, about wishing for another option— working as a cook would be better, she sings, because she "could eat aplenty." In "Poor Man's Blues" (1928), a song she wrote, she addresses "Mr. Rich Man" and attacks him for being willfully ignorant of the way poor people live: "The working man's wife is starving, your wife is living like a queen," she assails. Smith's songs take seriously the psychic pain of being left by a lover, the urgent desire for sexual attention, and the brutal reality of poverty. Usually, Smith's protagonists demonstrate strength and independence; they are willing to seek other options, even when they don't seem easily available.

Smith's legacy began to take shape during her lifetime, and her sound has influenced some of the most prominent vocalists who followed in her wake. Smith made her final recordings in 1933 with producer John Hammond; three days later, working with Hammond in the same studio, Billie Holiday cut her first record. Over the course of her storied career, Holiday paid tribute to Smith; cited her as a formative influence; recorded "'Taint Nobody's Bizness If I Do," a song associated with Smith; and, most important, adopted Smith's approach to excavating and expressing the meaning of the lyrics she sang through ingenious choices of phrasing and inflection. The Depression and the growing preference for the swinging music of big bands and vocalists like Holiday made the sound of the classic blues women seem passé by the early 1930s, but the sound of Smith's resonant voice and her confident attitude reverberate in the popular music of the twentieth century, exerting a lasting impact on the vocalists who came after her.

When gospel great Mahalia Jackson was a child, she learned to sing by listening to Smith's records, and as a teenager she sang Smith's 1925 hit "St. Louis Blues" at church socials. In 1958, the release of *Dinah Washington Sings Bessie*

Smith and *LaVern Baker Sings Bessie Smith* indicated a continued interest in the Empress of the Blues two decades after her death. Washington, one of the leading lights of vocal music during the 1950s, and Baker, the first queen of rock and roll, located themselves in a musical lineage that Smith launched. So did Big Mama Thornton, a blues shouter who had been billed as "Bessie Smith's Younger Sister" on occasion during her touring years in the 1940s. She carried the imprint of Smith to white rock and rollers Elvis Presley, who covered Thornton's "Hound Dog" in 1956, and Janis Joplin, who covered Thornton's "Ball 'n' Chain" in 1968. In 1970, Joplin acknowledged her debt to Smith by contributing money to purchase a headstone for Smith's grave, which had been unmarked since her burial in 1937. Also in 1970, Columbia Records started the process of reissuing the 160 sides that Smith had recorded over the course of her career; the multivolume set affirmed her significance with the auspicious title *Bessie Smith: The World's Greatest Blues Singer.*

Even as the sound of popular music drifted away from the blues, Smith's persona, subject matter, forceful vocals, and fierce attitude were a presence on recordings released by succeeding generations of musicians. This was especially clear in the 1980s and 1990s, when women of the hip-hop nation such as Queen Latifah, Salt-N-Pepa, and TLC showed themselves to be inheritors of Smith's tradition. Their uncompromising attitude and their emphasis on chronicling the everyday aspects of Black working-class life offered updated versions of the blues spirit. It is no accident that Queen Latifah, who started the rap on her 1993 track "U.N.I.T.Y." by calling out men who disrespected Black women with the confrontational question "Who you calling a 'bitch'?," was tapped to portray Smith in Dee Rees's 2015 biopic *Bessie.* Queen Latifah's insistence on respect, her majestic demeanor, and the reference to royalty in her stage name connect her to Smith, the first queen of African American popular music. Salt-N-Pepa's "Let's Talk About Sex" and TLC's "Ain't 2 Proud 2 Beg," both released in 1991, opened up musical conversations about sexuality in relation to emotional fulfillment, physical pleasure, and sexual health. While the forthright approach of these songs and their direct address to women were in the mode of Smith's songs about the pursuit of sexual pleasure ("Nobody in Town Can Bake a Sweet Jelly Roll Like Mine" [1923] and "I'm Wild About That Thing" [1929], for example), they were also very much of their time: the exhortations to insist that male sexual partners use condoms were a response to the AIDS epidemic and part of "safe sex" campaigns that were coming into the mainstream but still controversial. Like Smith in the 1920s, these latter-day artists made the many dimensions of sexual intimacy part of a public conversation.

Nearly a century after Smith started her career as a recording artist, we can take for granted the presence of female singers who are at home laying claim to their needs—romantic and otherwise—and taking their voices to their limits without apology. The roots of these forthright articulations of womanhood were first sounded in the music of the classic blues women, and all of us—the singers and those of us who take pleasure in listening to them—owe a debt to Bessie Smith, the Empress of the Blues, the woman who, with a gorgeous, powerful voice, boldly sang the blues.

—Maureen Mahon, *Turning the Tables*, Season 3, "Eight Women Who Invented American Popular Music," 2019 (excerpt)

11. COAT OF MANY COLORS
Dolly Parton (RCA RECORDS, 1971)

For most of Dolly Parton's performing career, it's been impossible to separate the sequins and spangles of her outsize image from her humble, hardscrabble mountain roots, so intertwined are the two in the persona she's presented. Her 1971 album *Coat of Many Colors* was a formative moment both in the way it helped establish her artistic self-sufficiency—no longer viewed simply as TV star Porter Wagoner's "girl singer," she was making her mark on the country charts as a standalone singer-songwriter—and in how it sketched the contours of her enduring narrative. It's hard to overstate the importance of the self-penned title track; through the lens of plainspoken reflection, Parton's lilting folk-country ballad wove together a touching account of her mother's Appalachian ingenuity and her own alternative vision of beauty and glamour, grounding both in a homespun yet nonetheless aspirational ethic that would frame her music forever after. Released during a fruitful period in country's autobiographical storytelling tradition, during which peers like Loretta Lynn and hit songwriter Tom T. Hall were also doing important work, the song is one of the reasons that Parton came to be recognized as the tradition's archetype. With the remainder of the album, mostly written by her with a few Wagoner compositions thrown in, she laid out more of her musical template: her supple modernizing of ancient-sounding folk's gothic, modal melodies and pastoral sentimentality; her fabulously knowing backwoods wit; her amplifying of emotions shaken loose by adult heartbreak; her openness to pop's buoyancy. She was, it would become clear, a splashy, savvy, broadly appealing complete package like neither the country nor pop worlds had seen.

—Jewly Hight, WNXP, *Turning the Tables*, "The 150 Greatest Albums Made by Women," 2017

DOLLY PARTON
That country way

66 'Coat of Many Colors' is a true story that actually happened, and that happens to be my favorite song. There's just something about that song, it takes me back to home, it reminds me of the kind of parents I had, and just that country way. And it's got the spirituality and it's got the family in it, and so that's very personal to me, that song. 99

—*Morning Edition* with Bob Edwards, 2002

Dolly Parton

89. COME ON OVER
Shania Twain (MERCURY RECORDS, 1997)

Whether you love or hate today's mainstream country, you gotta give it up to Shania Twain for inventing its urbane sensibility and much of its forward-thinking sound. Her blend of country and pop, including big rock drums and dance-music synthesizers, revolutionized the genre—but only because her songs and delivery made those innovations feel right to country listeners. Instead of a nostalgically wistful cowboy in a turquoise belt buckle and ten-gallon hat, here was a modern woman in leopard-skin prints and pumps that she kicked off after a hard day conquering the workplace (which, in Twain's case, was the recording studio—she deserves credit as a true collaborator there with her then-husband, producer Robert "Mutt" Lange). Twain provided the worldview that made her and Lange's sonic innovations work in a tradition-minded genre. Her songs are about equality in marriage (her "9 to 5" update "Honey, I'm Home"), femininity that was never passive ("Men's shirts, short skirts, oh, really go wild," she sang in "Man! I Feel

Like a Woman!," perfecting the Southern gal-on-a-bender trope that persists throughout country to this day), and mutually satisfying sex ("If You Wanna Touch Her, Ask!," she sang, lending her trademark positivity to the feminist idea of consent). With *Come On Over*, Twain's third album, she and Lange got her balance of home truths and forward thinking totally right—and shipped forty million copies worldwide, making this the bestselling country album of all time.

—Ann Powers, NPR Music, *Turning the Tables*, "The 150 Greatest Albums Made by Women," 2017

LINDA RONSTADT
Some people don't realize who they're talking to

The '70s chart-topping country rocker looks back on her long and diverse career.

❝❝ The singer who had the most influence on my singing style was Lola Beltrán, who is sort of the Piaf of Mexico. You know, Mexican culture is often so taken for granted, it's sort of invisible in the United States—it's hard to get through that screen. It wasn't anything that I hid, but it was not as acknowledged as whatever else they were acknowledging. My vocal style is very influenced by Mexican singing—it's a belt style. I wasn't influenced by blues or [the] Black church as much as most rock and roll people were. I was much more influenced by Mexican music singers and rhythms.

I grew up in the Sonoran Desert, which is an area that exists on both sides of the border. In fact, my family was in that part of the world before this was a country, so to say that we're newcomers is a bit of a stretch. Even here in California, my family came here in '70, '69. So, you know, I resent anybody saying, 'Go back where you came from.' It's been easier for me because I'm light-skinned and I have a German surname, so I'm sort of a secret Mexican American. Some people don't realize who they're talking to, and they start making racist remarks. That happened to my father, too. He'd be at a cocktail party and somebody would start saying, 'These Mexicans that come in here . . .,' or some ethnic slur. It's not a good thing to do to my dad. 🙶

—*Weekend Edition* with Lulu Garcia-Navarro, 2020

JENNIFER LOPEZ
The Bronx shaped who I was

🙶 [The Bronx] really just informed and shaped who I was, walking those streets every day. Even the flavor of growing up in the hip-hop era there. The food that we ate, everything. All the traditions and the culture of growing up there, and with my family, formed and shaped who I am today. And I carry all of those sensibilities with me. . . . Growing up in the Bronx, I heard hip-hop music on the same street as you heard Latin rhythms, you know, and salsa, merengue. And you also heard pop music and R&B, and it was such a melting pot. It was such a mix of things going on. And even today, all of those influences are still there. 🙶

—*Weekend Edition* with Lynn Neary, 2014

118. I FEEL FOR YOU
Chaka Khan (WARNER BROS., 1984)

In the 1970s, Chaka Khan was the darling of funk as a central member of the Chicago band Rufus. But *I Feel for You*, Khan's first official album, released in 1984, had her standing front and center with zero distractions. (Rufus dissolved in 1983.) By that time, rhythm & blues had been largely overtaken by high-tech production tools that bent and reshaped traditional vocals and instruments, transforming them into something entirely new. That fresh landscape became the foundation for Khan's *I Feel for You*, a quintessential example of Black '80s pop. The album's title track was originally written and performed by Prince as a ballad in 1979. But Khan, along with Stevie Wonder on chromatic harmonica and Grandmaster Melle Mel and his "Ch-ch-ch-chaka-chaka-chaka Khan" intro, turned the song into an energetic marriage of hip hop and new-school soul that shot to number one on the *Billboard* R&B singles chart. Khan's impact on hip hop would later be felt via one of rap's leading men, Kanye West, who used *I Feel for You*'s standout ballad, "Through the Fire," as the base of his debut single "Through the Wire." This song would eventually become the blueprint of West's sample-heavy production style, which inspired scores of producers that came after him.

—Kiana Fitzgerald, *Turning the Tables*,
"The 150 Greatest Albums Made by Women," 2017

CHAKA KHAN
Funk is the mixture of blue and red

❝ I think funk is uniquely American Black music. Its mother was the music that the slaves sang when they came from the motherland, and thus came gospel. I think that mix of gospel and jazz and blues, it's probably what funk is. In my mind, when I sing it, I don't know what it is. You know—let's say that funk is the mixture of the color blue and red. ❞

—*Tell Me More* with Michel Martin, 2007

Willie Mae Thornton, Architect of Rock 'n' Roll

"I can't sing like anyone [else]," Willie Mae Thornton once said. "I have to do it my own way."

She told a New York City audience at the Museum of Modern Art in July 1971, "This is my own kind of soul."

Then, after a performance of her only chart hit, "Hound Dog," from eighteen years earlier, she forcefully evicted her drummer, replacing him behind the kit, for her country-Westernish "Swing on Home, Big Mama."

Thornton always did it her way, supporting herself as a working musician from the age of fourteen until she died at fifty-seven in 1984. "My singing comes from my own experience," she said. "I never had no one teach me nothin'. I never went to school for music or nothin', I taught myself to sing and to blow harmonica and even to play drums by watching other people. I can't read music, but I know what I'm singing. I don't sing like nobody but myself." She prided herself on taking someone else's song and turning it into her own inimitable style, her voice a magnificent instrument. Over her career, she also wrote nearly two dozen songs of her own.

A criminally unacknowledged architect of rock and roll, Thornton boasted a broad musical palette: she sang and recorded blues, R&B, country-soul, rock, funk, and gospel. Beginning in the '60s, Thornton donned clothing then considered transgressive for women performers—ditching her dresses for trousers with pockets for her harmonica, a jaunty porkpie or cowboy hat, and sometimes a three-piece suit. But she never discussed gender identity or sexual orientation. Her private life stayed private.

Willie Mae "Big Mama" Thornton

Willie Mae Thornton was born in rural Ariton, Alabama, about seventy miles from Montgomery, on December 11, 1926. She and her six brothers were the children of a Baptist preacher and "a Christian hardworking woman [who] sang Christian songs," as Thornton told Arhoolie records founder, Chris Strachwitz, who would release her music in the '60s, in an interview. But Thornton was inspired by the Empress of the Blues, Bessie Smith, later saying, "When I was coming up, listening to Bessie Smith and all, they sung from their heart and soul and expressed themselves."

Thornton was twelve when her mother died in 1939; soon after, she went to work in a Montgomery saloon, cleaning floors and spittoons. At fourteen, she sang publicly for the first time when the barroom entertainer didn't show up. Thornton then auditioned and won a spot in the Atlanta-based Sammy Green's Hot Harlem Revue. As one of the youngest members of the traveling troupe, she learned stage presence from the cast of singers, musicians, comedians, and dancers. She also picked up drums and harmonica. Her powerful vocals wowed audiences, and soon she was billed as "the New Bessie Smith," sometimes advertised as "Bessie Smith's little sister." Another influence was Memphis Minnie, whose "Me and My Chauffeur Blues" became part of Thornton's repertoire.

After seven years on the road, Thornton quit the revue after a stop in Houston, Texas. There, in 1948, she hired on at the Eldorado Ballroom. With the Harlem Stars, she cut her first record in 1950 for the tiny E&W label—"All Right Baby," a jump blues she wrote herself.

In 1951, Thornton signed with Peacock Records founder Don Robey, who ruled the local Black entertainment scene with an iron fist. Robey connected her with his client Johnny Otis, a Los Angeles bandleader who "liked the way I performed onstage," Thornton later said. At a stop with Otis's revue at New York's Apollo Theater, in 1952, theater manager Frank Schiffman added "Big Mama" to her name, referencing "her physical size and the magnitude of her voice," according to musicologist and NYU professor Maureen Mahon, in "Listening for Willie Mae 'Big Mama' Thornton's Voice" (*Women and Music*, 2011). Thornton would take ownership of her stage name on the 1954 track "They Call Me Big Mama."

On August 13, 1952, Thornton entered Radio Recorders in Los Angeles with Johnny Otis and his Louisiana-born guitarist Pete Lewis. Also in attendance: nineteen-year-old songwriting team Jerry Leiber and Mike Stoller, who'd penned tunes for the Otis revue's "Little Esther" Phillips. Otis requested a number for Thornton, and the day before the session, the duo came up with "Hound Dog," a bluesy song about a no-good gigolo sponging off his lover, who gets fed up and kicks him out.

Thornton took the song by the throat—howling, growling, and demanding, *"Wag your tail!"* Between Thornton's raunchy vocals and Lewis's propulsive guitar sound, the track inarguably set the blueprint for rock and roll.

With "Hound Dog" in the can, according to Thornton, "Don Robey put it on the shelf, and I went back on the road." Then while gigging with Peacock label mate Johnny Ace in Dayton, Ohio, in February 1953, her life changed forever, Thornton later recalled. She "turned the radio on in the car," en route to the venue, "and the man said, 'Here's a record that's going nationwide! "Hound Dog" by Willie Mae Thornton!'"

At age twenty-six, after twelve years on the road, Thornton was a star. "Hound Dog" stayed on the R&B charts for fourteen weeks; on March 28, 1953, it hit No. 1, where it resided for nearly two months. It eventually sold two million copies, but

Thornton only "got one check for $500," she said, "and I never saw another."

"Hound Dog" appeared on her aptly titled 1954 Peacock album *I Smell a Rat*. Thornton recorded numerous nonhits for Robey, and her sole smash was segregated to airplay only on R&B radio stations, with no television broadcasting. Black R&B singers were excluded from national TV until late 1955. (Of course, in 1956, Elvis Presley would famously sing his sanitized version of "Hound Dog" on *The Ed Sullivan Show*.)

By the end of the '50s, Thornton had fallen out with Robey and moved to the San Francisco Bay Area. In the early '60s, she recorded some tracks for an Oakland label, Baytone, including another original, "Ball 'n' Chain," which the indie never released. When she performed it at the Both/And club in San Francisco in July 1966, members of Big Brother and the Holding Company were in the audience. Janis Joplin, who'd just joined the band the previous month, had become a Thornton fan as a teen in Port Arthur, Texas, after discovering her "Hound Dog" 78.

That night, "Ball 'n' Chain" so moved Joplin that she scrambled to jot down the lyrics as Thornton belted out the tune. After the set, she and her mates approached Thornton backstage to ask permission to cover the song. Thornton gave the okay but warned, "Don't fuck it up." "Ball 'n' Chain" would become the highlight of Big Brother's sets, and Joplin's tour de force version at the Monterey Pop Festival in June 1967 would make her a star.

By 1967, Thornton had embraced a whole new audience, headlining San Francisco's Avalon Ballroom and Bill Graham's Fillmore. In April 1967, when Big Brother opened for her at the California Hall, Joplin was apparently terrified to sing "Ball 'n' Chain" with its composer present. She always introduced the song with kudos for its author, and afterward the two women bonded. Thornton later told a journalist, "That girl feels like I do." After Joplin's death in 1970, during performances Thornton would often dedicate the song to Janis's memory.

Amid the late-'60s blues revival, Thornton cut several records for Arhoolie, backed by Muddy Waters and other blues masters. She signed with Mercury Records for the 1969 album *Stronger than Dirt*, which skimmed the *Billboard* Top 200 album chart. Playing the Newport Folk Festival that year, she enthralled the crowds and made herself at home. Her then-manager Bob Messinger recalled: "Big Mama had her Cadillac in the backstage parking lot. She had her butane stove and cooked for the acts and sold them soul food. George Wein, who always demanded decorum and quiet backstage, never said a word."

Back in 1965, she had told Strachwitz that more than anything, she wanted to make a gospel record: "I'd like very much to do spirituals because I feel that I got the voice. I feel like I got the power." She finally did, in the early '70s, for the album *Saved*. In "Go Down Moses," with her voluminous chest voice, she proclaimed, "This is my world." Gospel music was the other side of the blues, just like, for her, rock and roll "wasn't nothin' but the blues speeded up."

Decades on the road and hard living took their toll, with Thornton suffering from chronic liver and heart problems. On July 25, 1984, after a poker game with friends, she was found dead at a Los Angeles boardinghouse. Twenty years later, in 2004, yet another generation of fledgling musicians began playing their own interpretations of her songs at the Willie Mae Rock Camp for Girls. Today, thriving year-round, the nonprofit continues to offer a safe space for girls and gender-nonconforming youth ages eight to eighteen to discover their own voices. Perhaps that is the best epitaph for this influential and boundary-busting musical pioneer.

—Holly George-Warren, *Turning the Tables* contributor

18

MC SHA-ROCK
"You gotta fight and fight and fight for your legacy"

The retelling of hip-hop history centers men, often excluding the women in the same frame, so if you haven't heard about MC Sha-Rock, original member of Sugar Hill's Funky 4 + 1, and the first woman MC, you're not alone. She was such a titanic force in early rap communities that even DMC, one third of the game-changing group Run-DMC, cites her as an influence. Yet she is not given her due as a trailblazer.

But Sha-Rock has receipts. Using her personal mementos, Sha-Rock takes us through her entry into early hip-hop culture as a B-girl, her emergence as a pioneering MC in her early teens, her groundbreaking (pregnant!) performance on *Saturday Night Live*, and her long-running fight to preserve her legacy, in her own words.

❝ The very moment [I got] my taste for hip hop is 1976 as a B-girl—you know, being out there, break dancing, watching young kids move around throughout the Bronx, traveling as nomadic B-girls and B-boys, just to hit those breakbeats. The MCing came in 1977. The first person that I saw breakdance was friends of mine that had went to junior high school with me. They taught me what it was to uprock, what it was to just hit the beats whenever you hear that certain breakbeat.

From there, you know, I used to travel and watch the famous twins perform—back then they were called the N—— Twins, now they are called the Legendary Brothers, Keith and Kevin. I used to travel around with them to B-girl, to every park jam, every DJ that played, every house party, every hip-hop venue. I traveled all over the Bronx just to be a part of the whole scene.

The circle was always male-dominated. It was a young male sport at the time. I was sort of like a tomboy growing up. But there was just a feeling that you knew you had to be a part of. Some of us was living in poverty, politicians always doing their own thing. So when we came within that circle, that was our way to get away from all the other negative stuff. I mean, just being out there in the street and just listening to some of this, the sounds and the music and the percussion—it just gave you a feeling like you could just take on the world. It just empowered you as a woman. **❞**

—Sidney Madden, Rodney Carmichael, and Mano
Sundaresan, *Louder Than a Riot*, 2023

The Detroit Cobras: Elemental

The Detroit Cobras *by* Nicole Rifkin

The story of Rachel Nagy and Mary Cobra, the women at the core of the Detroit Cobras, is so elemental it shouldn't raise an eyebrow. Like thousands of people before them, they got together and joined a band, and then kept that band going for almost twenty-five years. The Cobras were the kind of band where if you put them on the jukebox at a bar, everyone would immediately turn around and ask you who they were listening to. It felt like they were always playing live somewhere, and that somewhere would be dark and smoke-filled and smelling of stale beer and spilled whiskey.

With few exceptions, the Cobras only played songs originally performed by other artists. That does not mean they were a cover band. Mary Cobra would explain that cover bands are the ones playing "Don't Stop Believin'." "Elvis and Aretha didn't write their own music, but no one calls them cover artists," she told an interviewer. They played garage rock and Motown and girl group 45s (and more), and they executed everything with so much personality and style that an awful lot of people didn't know the songs weren't Cobras originals. The presentation and delivery of the Cobras' chosen material (it was always "the material") was every bit as earnest and dedicated as the endless line of white male supplicants to the blues on either side of the Atlantic, in any era.

The Cobras' mode of attack unintentionally mapped to their chosen moniker, sliding in stealthily behind a genius repertoire of songs that's obscure enough that it's unlikely more than a dozen people in the crowd had heard those songs before, rewired so that it fits them perfectly, and then executed with an aplomb that's a mixture of sweat and braggadocio and precision. Nagy was a born frontwoman (albeit one who never wanted to be a singer) with a voice that sounded like ancient stardust and felt like pieces of the closely furled knot of pain hidden deep inside your chest. Without exaggeration, Rachel Nagy carried a universe.

Alongside her, usually to her left, was her best friend, partner-in-crime, "life partner," as she often joked: Mary Cobra, guitarist, backbone, and muscle. Cobra is one of those musicians who merges with her instrument like it's part of her; she plays with authority and precision. Outside of the city, she is probably one of Detroit's most underrated musicians; on her home turf, no one would dare because they know better. She started playing guitar because there was a guy she liked on her street who played, so she convinced her parents to buy her one, and then walked up and down the street playing it. "Isn't that how everyone started?" she once asked an interviewer. Of course it is.

The first time I saw the Cobras live I was delighted because I had never seen two women together in that particular juxtaposition before, the blood brotherhoods like Mick and Keith, David Johansen and Johnny Thunders, even Steven Tyler and Joe Perry. These duos were still sitting in the tree house with the NO GIRLS ALLOWED sign. These pairings derived from the magic of the dyad, the intimacy of a never-ending inside joke, the deep vibes of nonverbal communication. I thought, *I didn't know we were allowed to do this.* It was intoxicating. It was not a feminist statement and yet it absolutely was. There is nothing more dangerous to cultural hegemony than two women conspiring.

Nagy and Cobra toyed with this mythology in their promotional photos. There were some full band shots with their cohorts, but primarily it was the two of them:

applying lip gloss in a dirty bathroom mirror; lying in swimsuits on chaise lounges poolside, swearing a pinky-promise to each other; Mary tying Rachel to railroad tracks, Snidely Whiplash and a damsel in distress. The images are hilarious but they're not a joke; it absolutely was planting a flag in the ground and claiming some territory. Image is not unimportant in rock and roll.

Nagy eventually decamped to New Orleans, home of her idol, Irma Thomas, but always came home to play shows and begin tours. It was before one of those tours in January 2022 that Rachel Nagy passed away at the age of forty-eight. Her hometown said goodbye at a tribute show later that summer, the proceeds of which were donated to Detroit Animal Care and Control in her honor. "We both loved animals," Mary Cobra said, talking to the *Detroit News*. "She, specifically, you know, she thought we were wolves, okay. She really did, and sometimes I wondered if we weren't."

—Caryn Rose, *Turning the Tables* contributor

139. ALL OVER THE PLACE
The Bangles (COLUMBIA, 1984)

The sunshine-y MTV world of the '80s was made for the Bangles, four talented women from LA who brought the girl group harmonies of the '50s and the psychedelic influences of the '60s into the decade of Rickenbacker guitars and power pop. We couldn't have asked for anything better than the slick production, well-crafted songs, and hooky choruses on their first album, *All Over the Place*. On the infectiously catchy album, Susanna Hoffs, Vicki and Debbi Peterson, and Michael Steele flexed their chops, sharing Beatles-worthy vocal harmonies and wielding jangly guitars like the Byrds. Like too many pop bands of the time, the Bangles became known more for videos with pretty faces and big hair than for the true Girl Power they brought to us all. Yet to allow the Bangles' success to overshadow the group's credibility and importance would be a shame.

—Rita Houston, WFUV, *Turning the Tables*,
"The 150 Greatest Albums Made by Women," 2017

9. BACK TO BLACK
Amy Winehouse (ISLAND, 2006)

Amy Winehouse
by Gabrielle Bell

The late '00s saw an explosive, cross-genre revival of retro-sounding soul music that continues to shape the pop landscape to this day. Arguably, that trend's catalyst was Amy Winehouse's earthshaking final album. Working closely with producers Mark Ronson and Salaam Remi, plus a then-little-known Brooklyn soul ensemble called the Dap-Kings, the young, beehived-and-tattooed London singer pivoted from jazz to the velvet musical vocabulary of '60s girl groups and Motown. Yet however smartly it evoked the sounds of an earlier era, *Back to Black* never could have been mistaken for anything but contemporary—or anyone but Winehouse. Funk and R&B grooves snapped through a post-breakbeat filter; her lyrics about lost love and self-destructive habits pulled zero punches; her delivery came fluid as exhaled cigarette smoke. Even "Tears Dry on Their Own," whose arrangement reproduced Tammi Terrell and Marvin Gaye's version of "Ain't No Mountain High Enough" down to the drum fills, sounded magnificently fresh with Winehouse's lead line—a romantic duet flipped into a frank, lonely rendering of a breakup's aftermath. This was a soul record that wouldn't forget that hip hop happened, a thoroughly modern tract on heartbreak whose bluntness made it believable.

—Rachel Horn, NPR Music, *Turning the Tables*, "The 150 Greatest Albums Made by Women," 2017

19. AMOR PROHIBIDO
Selena (EMI LATIN, 1994)

It's tough to overstate the impact and power Selena Quintanilla had across the United States and in Latin America as the Queen of Tejano music. Her humility, talent, and sense of style influenced generations of Latinos enamored of and overwhelmed with pride in their culture—a culture often perceived to be less than. With her music, she made the voices and experiences of Latinos in the United States visible. That's especially true of her album *Amor Prohibido*. Her last release before she was killed in 1995, *Amor Prohibido* is an ageless cultural symbol that was meant to transcend a moment in history. It did, to say the least. It became the bestselling US Latin album of all time, went platinum, had four No. 1 singles, and put Tejano music on the map. With *Amor Prohibido*, Selena was able to reach larger audiences with her more experimental and cross-cultural sounds, including a fusion of Mexican mariachi and Colombian cumbia sounds, and elements of R&B, techno, pop, and the ballads known as corridos. Writing about her is surreal, though. Growing up, I remember hearing my aunts and mom sing "Bidi Bidi Bom Bom." The floors would tremble when this song came on as everyone was pulled to the dance floor. In college, my friends and I would blast these songs to find some kind of familiarity when everything felt so different from us. Selena didn't break barriers with this album as much as she tore them down.

—Jessica Diaz-Hurtado, NPR, *Turning the Tables*, "The 150 Greatest Albums Made by Women," 2017

24

Mahalia Jackson: For Singers, There's No Going Back

Pope John XXIII blessed her twice at the Vatican and she wasn't even Catholic. The Reverend Dr. Martin Luther King Jr. preached with more pep in her presence, as did Black and white leaders of various Protestant denominations and churches worldwide. She captivated the king and queen of Denmark, the empress of Japan, four US presidents, Chicago broadcaster Studs Terkel, the city of New Orleans, Ed Sullivan, and Charlie Chaplin, among others. But musicians give the best compliments, and no one could praise her like the jazz pianist and composer Mary Lou Williams did at the 1957 Newport Jazz Festival. "That goddamn woman makes cold chills run up and down my spine," Williams reportedly said about the gospel great Mahalia Jackson. American popular music would never be the same without her.

Jackson had one of the great, big—maybe the biggest—gorgeous voices of the twentieth century, inducing hot and cold springs of unexpected feeling. Unlike many of her contemporaries, she followed an interior compass that kept her almost exclusively singing gospel songs. And she did so knowing that *what* she sang and *how* she sang informed most commercial music, from jazz and pop down through rock and roll. Her tone and timing and intensity not only rattled Black listeners like Williams, but—for the first time in history—inspired white listeners everywhere to appreciate American music with a Black gospel feel. By the early 1950s, when she made her television debut on Ed Sullivan's *Toast of the Town*, white Pentecostal worshippers already were acquainted with ecstatic revival singing. But her fiery runs, sensual moans, note-bending, and interpolations were something other, considered cutting edge for mainstream audiences. As were the New Orleans rhythms that she said put bounce in her music. Like most native New Orleanians, Jackson preferred singing and clapping on the 2 and the 4 of the beat.

By performing on television and radio almost exactly as she had in Black churches since the 1920s, Jackson was instigating a profound shift in the national aesthetic, says music historian Mark Burford, who in 2019 published *Mahalia Jackson and the Black Gospel Field*. Today, he says, nearly a century after she left New Orleans for Chicago, shouting her way onto records, world tours, and the national airwaves, "gospelized voices have become the *lingua franca* of popular culture."

Listen, for instance, to her Apollo Records release "Tired." She attacks the word "tired" like a dragon blowing fire. Sometimes she hits it with a single, solid note, and sometimes she adds more syllables, bending the sound up and up and up. Other syllables she'll throw away almost completely—like the word "trod." Volume and emotional density smother diction. Imagine the capitalized words below being sung with the ferocity of a blowtorch.

26

Lord, I'm TIRED, Lord
SO little resting
TIRED! [three syllables over three rising notes]
SO little resting
TIRED!
So little resting
Can't stop no-OW, Satan trod

Sounds like a classic blues, right? Most every music lover knows that Jackson adored the blues star Bessie Smith. In New Orleans, Smith's records were good company when Jackson was scrubbing and mending and minding other people's babies. That's when little Mahalia made the wallop in Smith's voice her own. "Mamie Smith, the other famous blues singer, had a prettier voice, but Bessie's had more soul in it," she said in a 1968 memoir co-written with Evan McLeod Wylie. "She dug right down and kept it in you. Her music haunted you even when she stopped singing."

Blues songs lacked the spiritual nutrition that a young Mahalia felt she needed in abundance. But Smith gave her hope. "When I used to listen to . . . 'I Hate to See That Evening Sun Go Down,' I'd fix my mouth and try to make my tone just like hers," Jackson wrote. "And I'd whisper to myself that someday the sun was going to shine down on me way up in the North in Chicago or Kansas City or one of those other faraway places that . . . Negroes that roamed away from New Orleans always talked about."

Some Black ministers in Chicago rejected Jackson's singing style, saying she was a rowdy jazzer masquerading in a choir gown. Others loved that she could draw a crowd. So "she would really toggle back and forth in her singing styles," Burford says. "In [more restrained] Methodist churches she'd sing one way. And in storefronts she'd sing another way." But Jackson's "toggling" could happen within the same performance. On an early Sullivan program, for instance, she looks queenly and composed in an elaborate choir robe with her hair glistening like a crown. But launching into the second half of "These Are They," she begins pantomiming washing her robe "in the blood of the Lamb," and marching in place, and clapping her hands, and shouting heavenward. As millions of uninitiated viewers watch from home, Jackson turns that show into a rocking Black church, and many, including Sullivan, are hooked.

At no time, however, was Jackson the only gospel phenom. She was surrounded by a contemporary crowd of talented Black artists—from the electric guitar-playing Sister Rosetta Tharpe, who dominated the 1940s rocking "Didn't It Rain" and other exciting arrangements, to the glamorous Ward Singers, who prevailed in a 1950s gospel singing contest that attracted two hundred thousand voters. The *Pittsburgh Courier* sponsored the contest and mega-concert, reporting more audience interest in the Ward-Jackson rivalry than in Dinah Washington versus Ella Fitzgerald in the jazz category. And yet, none of Jackson's rivals could sustain the interest of a mainstream white audience like she could. In 1954, she signed with Columbia Records and became the first Black gospel singer on that major label.

Back then, a hit gospel record might sell twenty thousand copies. But Jackson sold in the millions, which made her a valuable television asset. In addition to Ed Sullivan, she accepted invitations from Arthur Godfrey and the ever-popular

Mahalia Jackson

Dinah Shore. And with each national appearance, along with her history-making local television program in Chicago and her weekly CBS radio show, she was helping the sound of Black gospel cross over to other musical genres. Journalist Richard Kleiner said as much in 1954 in the *New York World-Telegram* and *The Sun*. "Mahalia Jackson, who's been a favorite in some circles for years, is widening her circle," he wrote. "Her highly individualized style—she uses her voice like a musical instrument—has been copied of late by many pop singers. Some critics claim the entire Johnnie Ray–Frankie Laine–Kay Starr–Sunny Gale school of singing is a direct result of Mahalia's vocal inventions. The similarity is startling."

Try listening to those artists today, and Jackson will *not* come to mind. "The influence is less in terms of sound than approach," Burford says. "In the 1950s, you get more of an extroverted performance—[white] singers singing with a full voice. There was more of an emotional commitment inspired by black gospel music and Mahalia Jackson."

For Starr and her pop contemporaries, Jackson's way of singing was a style choice. But for Jackson, her way of singing reflected her identity. She was, after all, an enormously talented zealot. Biographer Laurraine Goreau cites uncommon religious fervor, strong enough to break heels or topple wigs or lose a tooth in the middle of a song, as running through Jackson's entire life story. And yet, Burford contends that such ferocity was balanced by Jackson's piety. "There was a sense of reverence," he told me.

When Jackson died at age sixty in January 1972, she left an army of musical disciples, including jazz and gospel singer Della Reese, Aretha Franklin, and Mavis Staples, who were youngsters when she mentored them. They, in turn, have influenced countless performers, irrespective of race or genre. Jackson also made an impression on her keyboard accompanists, from Ruth Lee Jones, a.k.a. Dinah Washington, to a young Billy Preston, to her old newspaper carrier James Cleveland, whose Southern California Community Choir helped make the bestselling gospel record of all time. Franklin's live album *Amazing Grace* features her, Reverend Cleveland, and the choir at their best. The taping also took place in January 1972—a sign perhaps of Mahalia Jackson's fire passing from one generation to the next.

And yet, religious and secular music have continued to converge. Think Jesus metal and hip-hop artists making gospel rap. And for singers, especially, there's no going back. "Gospel techniques and practices have infiltrated the circulatory system of popular music," Burford says. "You can't attribute directly, but Mahalia was a watershed moment in that transformation in terms of what it meant for popular singing and what has come afterwards through soul music, through blue-eyed soul and R&B since then."

Anyone left unconvinced should watch a TV talent show. From Kelly Clarkson on, the big, bluesy, and gospel-y voices are the most thrilling. Or watch the national anthem sung at any recent Super Bowl. Whitney Houston's bouncy 1991 performance has a Black gospel feel that every subsequent singer has tried to match. It's no accident that Whitney's mother, Cissy Houston, who taught her to sing, led a pop-gospel group that provided backup for Jimi Hendrix, Aretha Franklin, Elvis Presley, and Mahalia Jackson.

The most persuasive example of the long tail of Jackson's influence may be a scene from *The Mike Douglas Show* that aired on July 31, 1970. She sings the Jackie DeShannon hit "Put a Little Love in Your Heart" with Douglas and Bobby Darin, and it's a weird trip.

Douglas, a former big band singer, has a swinging but reticent tone. Darin, sporting a mustache and open collar, is balding and lethargic. They defer to Jackson and at the same time seem a little afraid of her. She's wearing a pink Sunday dress and a wig the size of a birthday cake. Tossing in her dental plate, she gospelizes the lead on the chorus and they sing backup:

And the world will be a better place
This WHOLE WORLD will be a better place
For you (for you)
And me (and me)
You just wait (just wait)
And SEEEEEE!

After all these years—Jackson is the only one who sounds current. She rocks and syncopates, hums and interpolates, hollers and dances. She's the future. For you (for you). And me (and me). Just wait (just wait) and see.

—Gwen Thompkins, WWNO New Orleans,
Turning the Tables contributor

Rhiannon Giddens
Is the
21st Century's Revelator

Rhiannon Giddens is as bluegrass as they come. Raised in the North Carolina Piedmont by a biracial family, Giddens would listen to her uncle's bluegrass band, the Southeast Express. She remembers a childhood with Hank Williams refrains and old gospel numbers cooing through the radio.

Giddens's earliest memories of songs, of accents and upbringings, point to an intrinsic sense of self—an internal homing radar. She is a proud North Carolinian, someone who knows her roots down to the coordinates.

To this end, what has defined much of Giddens's career is her drive to calibrate that inner feeling with the perceptions of the outer world; to actively defy long-held assumptions that American banjo and fiddle traditions were invented by, and belong to, white people only.

"When I first got into string band music, I felt like such an interloper," she said in a keynote speech to the International Bluegrass Music Awards Conference (IBMA) in 2017. "It was like I was sneaking into this music that wasn't my own. . . . I constantly felt the awkwardness of being the raisin in the oatmeal." There was a cognitive dissonance for Giddens, a sense of "othering"—a pit-of-stomach suspicion that she did not *really* belong to the music she was interested in.

Giddens attended the legendary 2005 Black Banjo Gathering, held in Boone, North Carolina. While there, she met fiddler Justin Robinson and multi-instrumentalist Dom Flemons. Along with others, the trio met weekly to study

Rhiannon Giddens *by* Dame Darcy

with their mentor, Joe Thompson, a fiddler and the last of a long line of Black string band musicians from North Carolina (Thompson was in his late eighties at the time). After multiple band iterations, Giddens, Flemons, and Robinson formed the Grammy-winning Carolina Chocolate Drops.

When I first saw the Drops perform, at the Ottawa Folk Festival in Canada in 2007, I sensed immediately that I was seeing myself for the first time. During the concert, Giddens spoke about the banjo as a West African instrument, a descendant of the *akonting*, the *xalam*, and some fifty-eight other stringed instruments from varying regions. This was the first time I'd heard the true history told, and I rejoiced quietly in the audience.

With every performance, Giddens gently enters the listener's mind, whittling away at our fallacy of perception as reality. Her claims doggedly remain until we properly grasp that, though photographs and TV shows might have showcased only white string band players, musicians of color have always been there, slightly out of frame and focus.

As a guest curator of the Cambridge Folk Festival in the United Kingdom in July 2017, Giddens brought over Yola Carter, Amythyst Kiah, Birds of Chicago, and me. All of us are varying shades of black, all of us have decidedly different voices and creative styles, and all of us are worthy of an audience, a microphone, and a paycheck. And whether we've told her or not, most of us know that Giddens has influenced us in carving a path to our own reconstruction. "When we rise, we rise together," she told me backstage, "that's how it should be."

—Kaia Kater, musician, *Turning the Tables*, Season 2, "25 Most Influential Women+ Musicians of the 21st Century," 2018 (excerpt)

Why do we fight?
How do we keep going?
Music has always
been a mechanism to
inspire the battle for
freedom, safety,
humanity, and justice,
to keep feet marching
and fists in the air. It tells
the story of our world—
and changes its course
for the better.

WARRIORS

Mavis Staples

ODETTA
Addressing the fury and the frustration

❝ My personal experience was as a little Black girl growing up in the United States, a country that had Jim Crow in the South with signs and Jim Crow in the North without signs. And we knew where we were to go and where we should not attempt to go. And so growing up at that time, I studied classical voice, but when I got into the folk music area, I started addressing the fury and frustration that I had growing up and to deal with. In the '50s, there were people who were interested in improving the life situation in this country, and many of them heard of what my work was, and I was called upon to be of assistance to bring either attention or to do concerts in order to make monies for people to do the job that they had to do. This Christmas spiritual record, *Let My Little Light Shine* [the album was actually titled *Gonna Let It Shine*], to me represents the determination that me and my folks had and came through within this country while this country's foot was on our throat. We lived in spite of. We found ways to get over, around, through and to get stuff done. ❞

—*News & Notes* with Ed Gordon, 2005

MAVIS STAPLES
Sing a song to fix it

❝ Pops used to tell songwriters, 'If you want to write for the Staple Singers, read the headlines. We want to sing about what's happening in the world today, and if it's something bad, we want to sing a song to try to fix it.' ❞

—*All Things Considered* with Michel Martin, 2016

TRACY CHAPMAN:
Take a chance and do something

Tracy Chapman spoke with NPR after the release of her self-titled debut album, which included the Top 10 hit "Fast Car."

Tracy Chapman: People refer to me as a protest singer, and people have said things about being revolutionary and all that kind of stuff. And, you know, whereas I know that the kind of music I do is different than popular music, it's on the radio today. It isn't necessarily anything that's new. It's not new for a Black person to do. That's another thing people don't even think about—that Black people have a history of folk music, and that gets to be annoying.

NPR: What led you to write "Behind the Wall"?

Tracy Chapman: I was in college, I guess I wrote it while I was in school. And I was having a discussion with friends of mine about whether it's an individual's responsibility to help someone else, if they know that they need help. You know, take a chance and risk your own safety and security and do something to help someone else. And in the song, there's a specific incidence of a woman being abused. But the song really isn't about that. It's actually about the other person that's on the other side of the wall, and what they have to do.

I feel that I simply present things and people can then do what they want with that, and they will—they always do. They reinterpret and misinterpret and all those kinds of things, but I write first for myself. And if I'm happy with the song, then it's already served its purpose. But I think if it affects someone—if it makes them consider other people and the world around them, then I think I've done something good.

—*All Things Considered* with Margot Adler, 1988

100. IT'S MY WAY!
Buffy Sainte-Marie (VANGUARD RECORDS, 1964)

Buffy Sainte-Marie released her debut album, *It's My Way!*, in 1964. The cover
photo showed Sainte-Marie herself with a mouth bow—an image that was at once
foreign, innocent, and intense, and a mere foretelling of the depths contained
within the music. From the power of her warbling voice on "Cod'ine" to the
insistence with which she commanded the lyrics on "Now That the Buffalo's Gone,"
It's My Way! is an unusual, urgent debut oozing with an anger—at the scourge of
drug addiction, the ravages of war, and the historic mistreatment of Native
Americans—barely contained. Although the album didn't hit it big on the charts,
dozens of artists—including Janis Joplin, Glen Campbell, Roberta Flack, and Joni
Mitchell—covered her songs over the years. *It's My Way!* also launched Sainte-
Marie's remarkable career; she was an early experimenter with the possibilities
of technology with a groundbreaking electronic album, *Illuminations*, in 1969.
She continues to break new ground in thought, action, and sound, as the decades
pass, while maintaining steadfast roots in advocacy for Indigenous peoples of
the Americas.

—Jessie Scott, WMOT, *Turning the Tables*,
"The 150 Greatest Albums Made by Women," 2017

39

There Is Power
in a Song,
and There Is Power
in a Voice

I used to write love songs. Only love songs. I thought that that was what women were supposed to write. I wanted to be sweet, sexy, and palatable. I wanted to get onstage in a beautiful gown and a light-wash guitar and sing sweet melodies that made everyone love me. At least I thought that's what I wanted. In 2016, that all changed.

That summer, I was convinced I was going to quit music. I was broke, living in a bedbug-infested studio apartment with my then also-broke boyfriend in Sunnyside, Queens. I was waiting tables at the Bitter End and playing my love songs with my band at modest gigs or open mics on any night I had off. Donald Trump was running for office, and the world around me seemed bleak. Racist comments were ringing in my ears, and my blood was boiling on a daily basis. More than ever, I felt like an alien in my own country. Being the daughter of an Asian American immigrant and an Indigenous man of Akimel O'odham and Mexican heritage, I always knew I was an "other"—but during Trump's rise, I felt it more than ever. I felt a scarlet letter across my face. At the tender age of twenty-three, I felt like just another starving artist writing seemingly pointless songs as the world fell apart around me.

I decided to move back in with my dad in Los Angeles, quit music, and become an antigravity yoga instructor (yep). I was sitting on the same bed I slept on in high school when I opened Facebook. A couple of close friends on the Pine Ridge Indian Reservation in South Dakota had posted videos of security dogs attacking the peaceful protestors, the water protectors, at Standing Rock. I immediately gasped and sent a private message. I said, "Hey sis. I'm horrified. What can I do to help?" and she replied with, "Spread the word, rally folks to send supplies." Before these videos, I had heard whispers from my friends in the native community about the Dakota Access Pipeline, and how this pipeline construction was being moved from Bismarck, North Dakota (where the white city folk live), to right by the Standing Rock Sioux reservation, on sacred tribal land. At that moment, I finally understood that it was time for me to do something, anything, for my people.

I broke down in tears that night: I wept for the people who lived at Standing Rock; I wept for my great-grandmother, who was taken from her tribe; I wept for all Indigenous people who are treated like shit and have dogs sent to attack them, and for all people of color who are forced to live near pipelines and areas with bad water and air quality. I wept for mother earth and environmental racism. As clichéd as it sounds, I cried so hard until all I could do was write a song.

That night, I wrote "In the River." The day after that, I recorded it with my friend Justin Hergett. And the day after that, I made a video for it, with my then-nineteen-year-old brother, Román Zaragoza. We made a video with facts about what was happening at Standing Rock, and a call to action that included where to send funds. That night, we uploaded it to Facebook. And the next morning, I woke up to hundreds of thousands of views, and numerous messages.

Folks from around the world told me that they had no idea what was happening at Standing Rock until they saw my video. They sent funds to the places I suggested, and many people even traveled from all over the world to stand in solidarity there—one of those people being me. Standing Rock gave me newfound pride not only in being a musician, but in being an Indigenous woman. It showed me that there is power in a song, and there is power in a voice. I don't feel that my efforts as a musician can compare with the tireless work of those who were on the front lines, in the medical tent, or on the ground for months at Standing Rock— but the movement changed the course of my life and reminded me that I am enough, and that one ripple of an idea or a song can spread awareness and can help create change.

Months after Standing Rock, I was performing in New Mexico and a sweet young woman kindly drove me to the coffee shop where I had forgotten my wallet. She was nervous and finally spoke, saying, "I lived at Standing Rock for four months working the medical tent. We listened to your song every day before going to the front line. It reminded us to stay peaceful."

During the Standing Rock movement, we used to say "Standing Rock is everywhere." The front line is everywhere. Every stage is a rally. And I carry that legacy with me at every show. Every performance is an opportunity to speak the truth. Every time you have a mic is an opportunity to speak truth to power and stand up for ourselves, each other, and mother earth.

—Raye Zaragoza, singer-songwriter, *Turning the Tables* contributor

JOAN BAEZ:
A creative act, a forceful act, and a positive act

Joan Baez, the legendary protest folk singer and mentor to Bob Dylan, considers where her activism has been and how far it has to go.

Joan Baez: There's a lot of potential energy. I don't think things are as messy [now in 1971] as they were a couple years ago. I think there's a general veering away from violence as the major tool right now. I mean, if we can develop tools other than armed struggle bullshit at this point, then there might be a lot to come out of that. But that means a lot of hard work. And I think it's a good time. Out of the last five, ten years that I've been speaking and traveling around and watching stuff, this is the first time I've felt as though there's a possibility, by doing a lot of work, that the human race would survive. But I think it's going to take the kind of organizing that—it depends on how serious people are going to be willing to be, whether you're willing to live and die for something or whether you're willing to do it just on a weekend, you know?

NPR: Do you think that there's still room for creative nonviolence of the kind that you were involved in what seems to be a hundred years ago now?

Joan Baez: Oh, I don't think that, frankly, there's room for anything else. I mean, I think either we create, or we destroy, you know? And if you want to destroy, then we've probably got a few years left to do it in, and you could enjoy it or whatever. But I'm really more of a creator. I mean, my mind runs more along creative lines, and I think that either we build something new, which has little to do with destruction, you know—I mean, if you build something that's good enough, then the things that are rotten are going to just crumble by themselves anyhow, you know?

—Joan Baez with Jeff Kamen, *All Things Considered*, 1971

66. PATA PATA
Miriam Makeba (REPRISE, 1967)

In 1967, the South African singer and songwriter Miriam Makeba was living in exile when the US audience first heard modern African music—Afropop—with her album *Pata Pata* (Touch, Touch). Sung mostly in Makeba's native Xhosa language, the unforgettable melody of the title tune is perhaps known by most everyone. But exactly, what is it?

Pata Pata is the name of the dance
We do down Johannesburg way
And everybody starts to move
As soon as Pata Pata starts to play—whoo!

Though melodically and harmonically jubilant, the music on Makeba's album challenged serious social themes like apartheid and land reclamation. Forbidden to return to South Africa for more than thirty years, Makeba, dubbed "Mama Africa," said in a 2006 NPR interview: "In life you make choices. You say, 'Okay, are you going to sit here, Miriam Makeba, and say, I'm a star and forget about home?' Or do you decide to say, 'I'm a South African, and this is what is happening to our people' and so on. And I made that decision. And from then on, I was branded that artist who sings politics."

—Suraya Mohamed, NPR Music, *Turning the Tables*,
"The 150 Greatest Albums Made by Women," 2017

MIRIAM MAKEBA
I'm not lying

❝ Now, I'm always branded as this political thing, I'm singing politics or mixing music with politics. I don't. All I do is tell the truth about how we live. Because when I say to you today that we are a colonized people, I'm not lying. When I say to you, we Black South Africans cannot vote in our own land, I'm not lying. It's a fact. And if it becomes political, then there's nothing I can do about that. ❞

—All Things Considered with Lynn Neary, 1988

DIAMANDA GALÁS
Active mourning

In 1986, the writer Philip-Dimitri Galás, the brother of the fearsome and unclassifiable avant-garde vocalist and pianist Diamanda Galás, died of AIDS.

❝ I mean . . . if there were a religion, I would say that he was it for me and he was my greatest inspiration. I think a passive mourning would—would be very dangerous. This is an active mourning. I think as long as I keep the work going, then I can live with his absence. I can live with that. ❞

—Morning Edition with Andy Lyman, 1992

13. LIKE A PRAYER
Madonna (SIRE RECORDS, 1989)

In 1989, AIDS was ravaging cities everywhere, particularly New York, Los Angeles, and San Francisco. The Supreme Court had begun to chip away at abortion rights. Activists were handing out condoms in the streets and fighting the indifference of the Reagan Administration, which instead supported the abstinence-only policies of fundamentalist Christians and the Catholic Church. Madonna's album *Like a Prayer*, released that same year, daringly takes on the struggles of a generation that refused to accept spirituality without sensuality. Through interweaving gospel, funk, soul, and pop, the album's songs raise questions about religion, sexuality, gender equality, and interdependence. For one thing, the title song opens with a few seconds of a hard rock guitar that stop abruptly and make way for a gospel choir and an organ. The lyrics suggest a girl who might experience God as a lover—or is it a girl who loves a man as if he is God? While "Oh Father" was in many ways about Madonna's own father, it goes beyond her relationship with him and instead alludes to someone who abuses power. And when all those activists weren't agitating in the streets, they were dancing to "Keep It Together," Madonna's tribute to her family. While most critics saw this as the album where Madonna went from bubblegum pop to true artistry, that wasn't the only thing she did with *Like a Prayer*. With this album she also led the way for a new generation of top female pop stars to express themselves.

—Laura Sydell, NPR, *Turning the Tables*,
"The 150 Greatest Albums Made by Women," 2017

45

SINEAD O'CONNOR:
I knew there would be trouble

NPR: Back in 1992, Sinead O'Connor made a now-infamous appearance on *Saturday Night Live* during which she sang an a cappella version of the Bob Marley song "War." Toward the end, she substituted the word "racism," from Marley's original lyrics, with "child abuse," and she sang it twice. Her words were supposed to draw attention to allegations of sexual abuse in the Catholic Church, but it's what she did at the end of this song that shocked America. She held up a picture of Pope John Paul II and ripped it to pieces. Afterward, O'Connor was vilified. Crowds burned her records. But the revelations of widespread sexual abuse among some Catholic priests have brought Sinead O'Connor back into the spotlight. She's recently emerged as one of Ireland's most passionate defenders of the faith, and an even more powerful critic of the Vatican.

Sinead O'Connor *by* Maggie Thrash

Sinead O'Connor: I think the problem is that people don't really realize that we knew about this back in 1987, here in Ireland. And it didn't become an issue in the States until about '95, if I'm correct. But in 1987, the Catholic Church in Ireland took out an insurance policy in every diocese to cover them against claims, which they foresaw would be made by victims and their families, and the first people that began, in 1987, to start coming out and saying that this had happened to them . . . I think the reason people were so shocked in the States, I mean, quite rightly, no one could imagine that something like this could be happening.

NPR: At the time, what was it like to endure that anger and hatred, particularly from America?

46

Sinead O'Connor: It was grand, to be honest. I mean, I'm an intelligent woman. I knew how people would react. I consider myself a spiritually, intellectually developed woman. I knew there would be trouble. I was quite prepared to accept that. To me, it was more important that I recognize what I will call the Holy Spirit, and that I acted out of respect for that. And I would have more fear of disrespecting that than I would of causing difficulty for either myself or anyone else. I knew what to expect, and I knew what would happen, and I was perfectly willing to deal with the consequences.

—*All Things Considered* with Guy Raz, 2010

14. HURRAY FOR THE RIFF RAFF, "PA'LANTE"

Hurray for the Riff Raff's Alynda Segarra spent much of their youth hopping trains in search of America. Their sixth album, *The Navigator*, follows the story of a young girl, Navita, as she does the same. "Be something!" goes the rallying cry of the American by-your-bootstraps dream—and also of "Pa'lante," Segarra's ode to the working-class Puerto Rican community they grew up with in the Bronx. "Colonized and hypnotized / Be something," they sing in their piercing, wavering alto over a slightly out-of-tune piano. "Sterilized, dehumanized / Be something."

After an interlude drawn from Nuyorican poet and playwright Pedro Pietri's poem "Puerto Rican Obituary"—first read in 1969, the same year the Young Lords of New York City adopted *pa'lante*, or "forward," as their motto—Segarra's "be something" resolves into that familiar phrase pointing forward. They urge *pa'lante* to the same "millions of dead Puerto Ricans" that Pietri did—and add to that as well civil rights and independence activist Julia de Burgos, transgender rights activist Sylvia Rivera, and now, the estimated 4,645 dead [at the time of writing in July 2018] after 2017's Hurricane Maria, whose homes continue to collapse in their absence and whose ghosts inhabit the music video in New York and on the island like silent flags. A call to keep moving with unwavering memory because we must, "Pa'lante" is Hurray for the Riff Raff's strongest anthem of resistance to date.

—Stefanie Fernández, *Turning the Tables*, Season 2,
"The 200 Greatest Songs by 21st-Century Women+," 2018

SOLANGE
Still fighting for our voices to be heard

Solange discusses her number-one album *A Seat at the Table*, against the backdrop of the Black Lives Matter movement.

Solange *by* Rashida Chavis

48

❝ I think that right now, this generation—we've been through a lot. We've been through a lot, and we are still going through it. And we are still fighting against these internalized messages. We are still fighting for our voices to be heard. And then we're fighting for action to happen after our voices are heard, after we're documenting these incidents, after we're speaking out about them, we're fighting for action. And I think that it was important for me, throughout the duration of this album, to also feel active in working this stuff out and not just having a platform to vent and cry and mourn. ❞

—*All Things Considered* with Ari Shapiro, 2016

Abortion Songs Hit Different When Heard in This New World

Heralded underground emcee Jean Grae's video for "My Story (Please Forgive Me)" (2008) is shot in black and white—if only it were that simple.

Accompanied by a track from producer 9th Wonder, the young woman we follow throughout the five minutes of visuals is tortured by the choices she is forced to make. Isolated and under-resourced, she has an abortion that she relives again and again in detailed flashbacks and daytime hauntings that lead her to doubt and self-harm. Lyricism takes us from the home to the clinic to the woman's adult career, and yet we never fully arrive anywhere.

Grae's protagonist lives a life in demonstration of the wicked 1945 bar by the intrepid poet-author Gwendolyn Brooks, "Abortions will not let you forget." Written with acute clarity, this dense opening sentence from Brooks's poem "the mother" describes the ongoing struggle for reproductive justice and the songs created alongside it. Forgetting these conditions, experiences, and rights is not an option. The awful and defiant stories epitomized by the symbol of the wire hanger in a pre–*Roe v. Wade* world continue to mark the dangers of a post-*Roe* world. When a pregnant and abandoned woman threatens to "end it" in Dolly Parton's "The Bridge" (1968), listeners are faced with a quiet, personal dilemma made public. That shift became a mission in the decade that convinced us that the personal is political. Roberta Flack's "Compared to What" (1969) dares to accompany the word "abortion" with a bouncing bass and set of funky horns.

Reproductive justice has always been about more than the right to not have a child. It's also about the right to have a child and the right to parent with dignity. The humor and despair of parenting beyond one's desire or means is the theme of Peggy Seeger's "Nine Month Blues" (1979), in which the children continue to come despite her best-laid (contraceptive) plans. Undoubtedly cued by the women around her, Seeger plainly announced the dreams that don't involve (more) children.

A career, we're told, is one of those dreams regularly compromised by—if not pitted against—parenting, and that tension appears powerfully in the popular musical record as first-person narrative. R&B singers Jhené Aiko and Lauryn Hill both discuss the strong cautions from the people around them when they became pregnant as young stars. Hill's iconic lines in "To Zion" (1998), "'Look at your career,' they said / 'Lauryn, baby, use your head' / But instead I chose to use my heart," announce the cold calculation and misogyny of the music industry as well as women's rebellion against it. Hill was responding twenty-five years after *Roe v. Wade* but in the wake of other policy disasters: Reagan-era conservatism emboldened public harassment and violence against reproductive justice advocates through abortion restrictions while also rolling back the social safety net.

Intersectional vulnerability produced by the dismantling of public services and protections, plus the active HIV/AIDS epidemic, continued with the presidency of George H. W. Bush. Those factors led to the rise of the Rock for Choice benefit concerts, which, thanks to journalist Sue Cummings, the Feminist Majority Foundation, and punk band L7, were for a decade semiregular reminders that shit wasn't okay. Joined along the way by Nirvana, Bikini Kill, Pearl Jam, Rage Against the Machine, Sarah McLachlan, Salt-N-Pepa, and others, Rock for Choice precipitated other collectives, including 1993's Rave for Choice with longtime abortion rights advocate and Deee-Lite frontwoman Lady Miss Kier at its helm.

In a world already primed for charity rock, these concerts were distinct for their roving locations in cities where abortion providers had been assaulted or murdered. Singer-songwriter Ani DiFranco offered her own site-specific tribute in "Hello Birmingham" (1999). In it, from her native Buffalo, New York, where an anti-choice sniper killed a local doctor one year earlier, she offers greetings to the

Alabama city shaken by a clinic bombing. It's telling that this fever pitch moment of violence occurred while abortion was legal.

The streets demonstrated what the courts debated, as challenges to the 1973 ruling moved their way from local contests to the conservative-majority Supreme Court of the United States. It was there, on the eve of the decision's fiftieth anniversary, that those rights would die. In the summer of 2022 Reina del Cid marked the occasion with a trip back to the nineteenth century. Her adaption of the patriotic hymn "America" ("My Country 'Tis of Thee [Land of Inequality]"), which announces SCOTUS as "six robed dinosaurs / [who] conspired to wage a holy war / over our bodies," summed up the devastation of the reversal.

Other song adaptions after the SCOTUS decision were less about changing the song than about changing its use. Pop star Olivia Rodrigo went viral at the 2022 Glastonbury Festival in England when she and guest Lily Allen performed Allen's "Fuck You" in dedication to SCOTUS. Megan Thee Stallion, whose "Plan B" was fresh on the charts, led a chant from her Glastonbury stage, repeating, "My body, my muthafuckin' choice." The songs hadn't changed, but the times had. Songs hit different when heard in a new world, one where, as Rodrigo said in the introduction of her performance, "So many women and so many girls are going to die because of this [decision]."

Because we believe this to be true, songs like Lesley Gore's "You Don't Own Me" (1963) and Loretta Lynn's "The Pill" (1975) return to us and linger, anew. Abortion playlists are blooming like wildflowers all over the internet. Generations of songs before, during, and after rights live on, and grow in size when disturbed. Paired with the struggles that give them meaning, these songs will never let us forget.

—Shana L. Redmond, *Turning the Tables* contributor

Ani DiFranco:
We're Really Gonna
Sing About This

When I first started writing about abortion I was nineteen. And I had just had my first one and that was very hard, because I was very ashamed. And it was not something that anybody talked about in public. So like a lot of things at that time in my life, I had to really break that membrane, like, oh, we're really gonna go and stand onstage right now and sing about this and talk about this. And you know, it's scarier in the beginning. My experience was that you get a lot of judgment, and you get a lot of pushback, and you get called a lot of things. But that tends to come from that sort of greater voice of the Overlord, you know, from the superstructure that never got you to begin with and never affirmed you in this way that you know yourself to be, so that didn't hurt me or dissuade me. The other responses, which came from around me, at my level and in my terrain, when it came to the subject of reproductive freedom and abortion, it was other young women saying, Oh, my God, thank you, thank you, thank you. Me too. Me too.

I had been putting things in my songs and messaging the world and talking about my experience as a female in a way that made so many other females, or queers, or people who just look at things differently. . . . I heard so many me-toos and thank-yous over the years for sort of giving voice to a lot of people's thoughts who don't feel they have a voice. It's gotten easier, in some sense. This process of saying the unsayable in public has definitely gotten easier over the years.

It's always been super important to me, and super fundamental to me, to talk about reproductive freedom because—and this is where I start sounding like a crazy person to many—I see reproductive freedom as step one for solving all these social problems. So, so long ago in human society we turned toward patriarchy—a human culture which does not recognize even the full sentience of half of its members and does not include their sensibility with equal weight and airtime, so you can't come up with viable solutions and you can't strike balance. So you have to sort of address the fundamental imbalance of patriarchy, which I think begins with reproductive freedom.

You just can't come from patriarchy and solve sociopolitical crises of any kind. I think climate change, racism, classism, all of the hierarchies and imbalances stem from a fall. If the body politic is riddled with the disease of patriarchy, you just can't get to a healthy place—you have to go back and address that. . . .

I remember learning in Feminism 101 at the New School about the feminist continuum. And it made total sense to me, because I've experienced it: women who came before me unlocking my voice or my own understanding of myself, like awareness of my own voice, like being able to even fucking hear it, you know. For the "Lost Woman Song," it was very specifically a poet named Lucille Clifton, who is also from Buffalo, an African American feminist poet who I discovered when I was very young, eighteen. She wrote a poem called "The Lost Baby Poem." I was like, you can talk about this. I can talk about this. You just affirmed my hope that I'm not evil and irresponsible. And this is not something I should just carry silently in shame to be used against me. It's something that I can take ownership of, and I can help other women to feel ownership of, just like Lucille did for me, you know? I read that poem by her. It made me sob and it unlocked something in me that said this is important to talk about, you know.

I've written a way better song, I think, about reproductive freedom since then, and that's the one I play. I've written several. That song, the "Lost Woman Song" I mean—I use the word "tragedy." "A relatively easy tragedy." The fifty-two-year-old me looks at that, and I can feel the weight of the judgment and somebody else's perspective. You know, that was 1990. When [Bill] Clinton was elected—"Abortion should be safe and accessible and rare." We would long for that now, but still, in that statement, there is judgment. It's very easy, and very common, for women to shoulder all the responsibility and all of the judgment for how and why abortion should be rare, and to think that it's their own personal defects and character flaws and weakness and irresponsibility and all of that that leads to an abortion.

So now when I look at "Lost Woman Song," I can feel the distance I've come from

Nina Simone

the girl who wrote that song, and I would never use a word like "tragedy." The idea that abortion is tragic didn't come from me. I wrote "Lucille, your voice / still sounds in me / Mine was a relatively easy tragedy." She, Lucille Clifton, had a self-administered abortion, not in a medical facility, and lived to tell the tale. So I was comparing my experience to hers—at least I had Planned Parenthood to go to in Buffalo. But the word "tragedy," there's no way I would stand on a stage and sing that now in reference to reproductive freedom. It's the opposite of a tragedy in my mind.

—Ani DiFranco, as told to Alison Fensterstock, New Orleans, 2023

NINA SIMONE:
Singing songs of deep, deep resentment

Nina Simone: Well, it's very simple, my dear, I worked hard. I started out as a pianist when I was three. I studied twenty-two years, classical music. And then when I was rejected at Curtis Institute of Music to be a classical pianist . . . I then went into show business, to a bar, because of the rejection, and I learned all types of music. So I call my music Black classical music.

NPR: I'm wondering, why were you rejected?

Nina Simone: Because I was Black, my dear.

NPR overvoice: Her voice has been described as haunting molasses vinegar—and, like her personality, has both sweetness and edge, sometimes in the same moment. Nina Simone describes how this creative tension and vocal style emerged in personal and social terms.

Nina Simone: Well, I developed it because of racism. First of all, you have to understand that I still sing and play for the American Blacks and the Third World Blacks. So I have an edge, because I deeply regret what has happened to the Blacks in this country and the Third World people. So you see me singing songs of sweetness and tenderness and you see me singing songs of deep, deep resentment of what has happened here, and I don't think it's gotten any better.

—*All Things Considered* with Nick Spitzer, 2001

Do songs ever hit you as hard as they do in your teens, when you're discovering some planet-shaking musical meteor from the past or the sound of right now? They mark our milestones, they jolt our bodies, and they stick with us forever, like a tattoo or the first time you felt like you knew who you were.

TEENAGE KICKS

Alanis Morissette *by* Margaret Flatley

LAURA NYRO
Teenage folk wisdom

66 I think that teenagers are in touch with a very primal truth in life. Sometimes someone will say, Well, you were so young, to write a song like that. Yet, I think that there is a folk wisdom in the song that a lot of teenagers have.99

—*Weekend Edition* with Scott Simon, 1989

29. JAGGED LITTLE PILL
Alanis Morissette (MAVERICK, 1995)

Every teenager is expected to be angry at some point over the course of her adolescence. But not every teenager manages to shatter expectations surrounding women worldwide, as well as their access to and expressions of that anger. At age nineteen, the Canadian pop star Alanis Morissette started work on *Jagged Little Pill*, the 1995 record that would ultimately sell forty million copies and that offered an unprecedented lyrical vocabulary for processing and experiencing young womanhood. A generation of listeners smashed plates to this record, and then gathered up the pieces and built something better. *Jagged Little Pill* contains flawless angry songs, but it also contains perfect songs of introspection and self-belief, radically centering the narrative on (female) self instead of (male) other. Often miscast as a breakup album, Morissette's blockbuster is really a fully formed exploration of being a person feeling their way through the world. It broke ground by giving equal space and value to emotions that women are expected to express publicly, as well as those they aren't.

—Katie Presley, *Turning the Tables*, "The 150 Greatest Albums Made by Women," 2017

ALANIS MORISSETTE
Anger is a powerful life force

❝ If there were to be a quality that I'd become a poster child for, I'll take anger—because as a woman, the main emotions that we are, quote-unquote, not allowed to feel are anger and sadness. That anger is such a really powerful life force. And I think it can move worlds, you know, it is behind every activism and every serviceful move that I do. Anger feeds it. So for me to think that anger can go away is naive. But the form that that anger takes and the degree to which I'm responsible for it—and that I don't allow it to be destructive—you know, ideally, that would be how I operate with it, but sometimes it has its way. ❞

—*All Things Considered* with Guy Raz, 2012

20. PRESENTING THE FABULOUS RONETTES FEATURING VERONICA
The Ronettes (PHILLES RECORDS, 1964)

The British Invasion hit American shores in February 1964, changing the course of American pop for the foreseeable future—but three girls from Spanish Harlem invaded the British first. Twenty-year-old Veronica Bennett, her sister Estelle, and their cousin Nedra Talley arrived at Heathrow that January with a *Billboard* No. 2 hit, "Be My Baby," under their belts, and when they met the Beatles, the four mop tops were already their adoring fans (so was their opening act—the Rolling Stones). "Be My Baby"—the centerpiece of the trio's debut album—would hook millions more, rock royalty and commoners alike, with its heart-thumping kick drum, plaintive *whoah-oh-oh*s, and dense production, courtesy of Phil Spector's Wall of Sound, which dependably takes the listener's breath away by filling every available molecule of air with music. The studio work is wizardly, but it's Veronica—the future ex–Mrs. Phil, and the forever Ronnie Spector—who is the magic element, switching between rock and roll swagger on the loose-hipped "(The Best Part of) Breakin' Up" and demure teen yearning on "I Wonder," plus a loose, muscular, full-throated take on Ray Charles's "What'd I Say," all stamped with her indelible sweet-tart voice. Everything about the Ronettes always teetered on the blissful edge of too much—too-tight dresses, too-bountiful beehives, too-heavy eyeliner drawn to a razor-sharp wing, and *Fabulous Ronettes* is an overflowing platter. But *whoah-oh-oh* is what passion sounds like, when it transcends the capacity of language.

—Alison Fensterstock, *Turning the Tables*,
"The 150 Greatest Albums Made by Women," 2017

JOAN JETT
I've never been able to figure out who is threatened

❝ It was very exciting. We [the Runaways] were very naive, you know, so we thought we were going to seriously change the world and that everybody would embrace us and love it. And we had a rude awakening, you know. And I was quite shocked, actually, even as a teenager, to see what we ran into. People say girls can't play rock and roll. I was like, well, what do you mean? Women play cellos and violins in symphony orchestras. They're playing Beethoven and Bach. What do you mean they can't play rock and roll? You're not saying they're not physically capable. What you're saying is they're not allowed to, socially, that rock and roll by its nature—the 'roll' in the word 'rock and roll' implies sexuality. That's why they wouldn't show Elvis from the waist down or, you know, everyone thought Chuck Berry was going to steal their sixteen-year-old daughter, you know, and run off—you know, rock and roll is that threatening thing. And so a girl playing rock and roll, it's saying I own my sexuality and I'm going to tell you what I'm going to do. And I think people just find that threatening. I'm not really sure why. I've never been able to really get an answer or quite figure out who is threatened. **❞**

—*Day to Day* with Madeleine Brand, 2006

Lorde Is the 21st Century's Author of Adolescent Evolution

Given the fully unselfconscious swagger that carries Lorde across the stages of stadiums today, one might almost have repressed the memory of the twitchy, bushy-haired, sixteen-year-old singer who seemed to convulse more than dance at the 2014 American Music Awards and looked like she'd have preferred being set on fire to the unexpected attention involved in winning a Grammy.

The distance between expectation and reality is an optical illusion at the crux of inhabiting the teenage world. As I watched Lorde's graceless, passionate movements, I realized it doesn't really matter if you're fooled by that gap. Secure in her art, Lorde wasn't beholden to the opinion of the outside world or the pressure to be embarrassed by her own dancing.

It was glorious.

Before her debut, *Pure Heroine*, Ella Yelich-O'Connor was just a teen from suburban New Zealand, searching for a reconciliation between the glamour of pop culture excess and the mundane grace of the waiting-for-your-life-to-begin period for an ordinary high schooler. Lorde was trying to kill time and instead she snatched the mic, became an unintentional spokesperson for the day's youth, and ushered in a sonic shift toward minimalism and dark pop.

"I'm little but I'm coming for the crown," Lorde warned on *Pure Heroine*. A self-fulfilled prophecy, "Royals" hit commercial US radio in the summer of 2013. By October, the sleeper hit knocked Miley Cyrus's "Wrecking Ball," a much

HOW WOMEN MADE MUSIC

buzzed-about pop culture behemoth, right out of the No. 1 spot of *Billboard*'s Hot 100. Lorde would sit on the throne for nine straight weeks to become the female artist with the top-selling single of 2013.

"Royals" was a fresh look at the ambition for material wealth that traditionally flooded bars of braggadocious hip hop. In the song, Lorde uses a teenager's pointed skepticism to critique extravagance while giving a send-up of the genre that worships the lifestyle. It found Lorde stepping into complicated questions of race and appropriation—questions a sixteen-year-old New Zealander might not have considered when lambasting the pervasiveness of American pop cultural ideals. Some criticized the song for deploying negativity toward the materialistic hallmarks of rap while employing hip-hop beats; Lorde later apologized for her limited perspective.

But undeniably, "Royals" dripped with a resonant specificity (the oft-quoted "everybody's like Cristal, Maybach, diamonds on your timepiece"), an aficionado's kiss-off performed with precision and style. Her affected cool on the verses cracked on the chorus: one part longing, one part resignation, as if to say, *I can't change who I am, but wouldn't it be nice?*

When she sings "Baby, be the class clown / I'll be the beauty queen in tears," her voice translates the words in my head: *That's all they want from us, to be stereotypes of ourselves. Play along.*

This theater is at the heart of teenage life, taking a magnifying glass to the script of social interaction and trying on all the costumes to see what fits, how the power dynamics shift in response. On "Tennis Court," Lorde calls the process of donning and shedding these archetypes "a new art form showing people how little we care." It's a thesis for the conflicting themes of her work: the vacillation between the insecurity that accompanies desire and the practiced aloofness that conceals an eagerness to experience adult life and all its flaws.

What's continuously remarkable about Lorde's work is her insistence on speaking to the experience of her age as it is lived. America loves its young stars but historically denies them the opportunity to sing authentic songs. And when we take for granted the tradition of underage singers performing dramatic tunes about adult love—songs like "My Man—He's a Lovin' Man," "Want You Back," or even ". . . Baby One More Time"—it's harder for us to seek out art that captures the voices and perspectives of the young people actually singing the songs.

Using preternaturally mature talent to tell mature stories and priming these kids to be effortless performers denies their peers from the same age demographic an opportunity to see themselves reflected onstage. Lorde's work is distinctive in that it is written by her and for her—a document of the nuanced fabric of one adolescent's reality that has resonated universally.

—Cyrena Touros, NPR Music, *Turning the Tables*, Season 2, "25 Most Influential Women+ Musicians of the 21st Century," 2018 (excerpt)

THE GO-GO'S:
We changed possibilities for girls

The Go-Go's debut album, *Beauty and the Beat*, is celebrated as the first album by an all-woman band whose members played their own instruments and wrote their own songs to top the *Billboard* 200 albums chart. It's also a harbinger of what rock would become, and a bridge between punk, the movement whose rebelliousness had quashed the excesses of classic rock, and the genre-fusing music of the 1980s. If groundbreakers like the Ramones, the Buzzcocks, and Blondie had shown that pop and punk were not mortal enemies, here was a band that showed how the two styles could merge with certifiable success.

NPR Music spoke with the Go-Go's to take a closer look at how these punks changed pop. "Here's the thing we always say: You can take the girl out of punk, but you can't take punk out of the girl," says Charlotte Caffey, lead guitarist. "Honestly, to this day, we're all in our sixties, we're still those same bedraggled little ragamuffins that we were. It's in us; it's part of who we are."

Jane Wiedlin (guitar, vocals): I've actually gotten in arguments with trolls online about it, like, twenty-year-old white guys: "Go-Go's aren't punk!" Like, oh my *GOD*, shut up! I'm real happy to clear that up, because being a part of the Hollywood punk scene is one of the most important things to ever happen to me. I'm not happy when people dismiss it.

Belinda Carlisle (vocals): In London, you had a big, political, angry scene, very macho. In New York, you had sort of a dark underground, with Johnny Thunders and the Ramones, that kind of thing. LA was more about *art*. There wasn't a whole lot for a kid in Southern California to be angry about. It's a different kind of city; it's open; you have the beach.

Gina Schock (drums): I drove my dad's pickup truck across the country with my friend from high school. I pulled into Los Angeles on Valentine's Day of 1979, and I was so knocked out by the size of the freeways. When I saw the Hollywood sign, it was mind-blowing. The punk scene there was RAGING. It was the perfect time to be arriving there.

Kathy Valentine (bass): The women were not competitive; you took notice of each other. There was a silent affirmation of sorority. That's what it felt like.

I really credit punk rock for opening the door, in that you *could* do it. It was very inclusive—not only gender-wise, but in musical format. The energetic pop bands, the hardcore punk bands, the artsy bands, the rootsier bands, like the Blasters— there was a broad spectrum of music. I don't think the Go-Go's would've existed without that kind of openness and anything goes.

Gina Schock: People thought that we were a put-together band, or America's sweethearts, all the same old crap we heard for years and years, when in fact we were down and dirty like the boys. We were just a fucking rock band—young women happening in a big way.

Jane Wiedlin: We were five really strong, kind of bull-headed women, together, and I think the energy we created—it was so pro-women and so powerful. At the time, we discounted it, and it was important. We changed things for hundreds of thousands of girls. When I think about that, that's probably what I'm most proud of: we changed possibilities for girls.

—Interviews by Hilary Hughes,
Turning the Tables, 2020 (excerpt)

Hayley Williams Is the 21st Century's Pop-Punk Prophet

Hayley Williams
by Margaret Flatley

Paramore were just kids: in the depths of YouTube, a grainy video montage from 2005's iteration of the mall-punk caravan Warped Tour finds the band green, awkward, at the starting line. Paramore, fronted by powerhouse singer Hayley Williams, came from small-town Franklin, Tennessee. They had formed only a year before—Williams was fifteen—but already you'd never heard someone face the void or holler a "wh-o-oa" with such vigor and aplomb.

Even in corporatized bubblegum mutations, punk subcultures are, for kids, a means of finding fellow outcasts, of feeling less alone. Community is at the heart of that. When Paramore spent 2005 writing on its LiveJournal about bands, it was asserting connections with peers and establishing a lineage with emo forebears. Those ties are emboldening and life-affirming. Of course, girls have always been crucial fans and consumers of rock—emo and pop-punk included. But for too long, they were denied that highest level of participation: the stage, the mic, the name and face. By insisting to her major label, Atlantic, that she keep her band—not become an Avril-style solo artist, as they would have preferred—Williams carved out a radical new space. She became a center.

Mall-punk was misogynist by design: boys were centered onstage, girls were consumers, lyrics were for so long sexist and unchecked. Williams herself was no exception. Paramore's unstoppably catchy 2007 single "Misery Business" was one of the smuggest and most spiteful hits of that era. Williams sings bitterly about hating a girl who stole her boyfriend, just as she is here taking him back. There is one especially egregious line that critics fixate on, where Williams uses the word "whore," but the toxicity of the song is present in its whole vindictive tone. "Misery Business" is a logical conclusion of third-wave emo's hostile attitude toward women: after years of keeping girls off stages and dehumanizing them in evil lyrics, it finally just pits them against each other.

Paramore had already started excising the song's most problematic lyric before announcing, earlier this month, that they will step away from playing "Misery Business" live for the foreseeable future. With that, Williams sets another precedent. Artists can change, can admit their faults, can create discourse.

In 2018, though, nothing about Paramore's early sound threatens to disappear completely. Traces of its scene's emotional openness, raw diaristic detail, and cleanly carved hooks can be found across pop's power centers.

Williams's influence has left a bold mark on the zeitgeist. Grimes cited Paramore as a primary inspiration on 2015's *Art Angels* and included "That's What You Get" on her list of the greatest songs of all time. As a child, Soccer Mommy's Sophia Allison played the same song at rock camp. Not long after Lil Uzi Vert shared a clip of himself singing "Ain't It Fun," he called Williams the biggest influence on his labyrinthine sense of melody. Only recently embraced by more discerning corners of the music-critical establishment, Paramore has resonated with vanguard artists across genres who are unafraid to earnestly think for themselves. The band's fans, willing to seem uncool, have recast definitions of "cool" in the process, bringing Paramore with them.

—Jenn Pelly, *Turning the Tables*, Season 2, "25 Most Influential Women+ Musicians of the 21st Century," 2018 (excerpt)

64. SPICE
Spice Girls (VIRGIN, 1996)

Twenty years ago, the sound of platform sneakers scuttling across the floor hit American airwaves, giving way to the laugh heard round the world. Those three seconds before the beat drops serve as the introduction to "Wannabe," Spice Girls' first single from their debut album, *Spice*. They are so universally recognizable that "Wannabe" was ranked the catchiest pop song since the 1940s in a recent study. Ushering in a new wave of zealous pop, Spice Girls knew what the world really, really wanted—and delivered. "Wannabe" topped the *Billboard* Hot 100 for four weeks and became the bestselling single by a girl group in history. The rest of *Spice* followed suit, borrowing from R&B, hip hop, and even disco to relay messages about safe sex ("2 Become 1") and female solidarity ("Love Thing"). Scary, Sporty, Ginger, Baby, and Posh influenced a whole generation of women (even Adele is a fan), and last year, Project Everyone's #WhatIReallyReallyWant campaign repurposed "Wannabe" as a call for women's rights internationally.

While riot grrrl champions Bikini Kill released a zine titled *Girl Power* in 1991, the Spice Girls were the first to peddle the concept to the mainstream. Despite the complicated implications of their commodified feminism, their overarching message of empowerment and strength in numbers was one to get behind. And as a unit, they were a multifaceted force to be reckoned with. *Spice* was a manifesto by women who ditched their management team in search of more independence and evenly split song royalties among the group, and its endurance is palpable; *Spice* is still the bestselling album ever released by an all-female group. Now, *that's* girl power.

—Desiré Moses, WNRN, *Turning the Tables*,
"The 150 Greatest Albums Made by Women," 2017

Beyoncé Is the 21st Century's Master of Leveling Up

Bey Hive, forgive me, for I have sinned: I used to despise Beyoncé.

But it's complicated. She's been a part of my life for as long as I can remember. I was all of eight years old when she made her official debut at sixteen as the lead singer of Destiny's Child in 1997 with the single "No, No, No." As the frontwoman, Bey sparkled, but she wasn't fully illuminated—even so, it was clear as day that a star was on the horizon.

In the beginning, it almost felt like Bey held back. As a member of a teen R&B/pop group, she didn't seem focused on rocking the boat. She was merely hoping to be welcomed into the industry. And she was, much to my chagrin. Which brings me back to my sin.

Beyoncé and I come from the same state, Texas, but our cities of origin couldn't be more different. She's from Houston, with all of its culture and influence; I'm from a small town, Seguin, hundreds of miles away, with its striking similarities to a black hole.

Coming from a place that had a Walmart as its central point of entertainment, my main escape was television. Seeing Bey's face on the TV screen was easy enough to roll along with. To be frank: she was a Black woman singing pop songs for the masses. Nothing could be more appealing to a young Black girl. It was inspiring.

It was obvious to me where Bey was headed, and why. She was surrounded by dark-skinned faces—LaTavia, Kelly Rowland—plus the medium-toned LeToya

Destiny's Child

Luckett and eventually Michelle Williams. But Bey was always in the middle, always the lead. It wasn't lost on me that this central figure passed the brown paper bag test, and the others around her did not. I, myself, did not. Because no matter how well you sing, no matter how beautiful you are, if you're not of a certain color, a certain skin tone, there's a commercial barrier that you just can't climb over. So when Bey stepped out to go solo, it was expected. I saw it as the closest chance a Black woman had to being an international pop star.

As exciting as the thought of that possibility was, it wasn't enough to make me roll with Beyoncé into this new stage of her career. Instead, I hated, mightily, from afar. Going through puberty while Beyoncé was in the midst of her glow-up was . . . trying. Mostly because the town I grew up in didn't exactly lift up dark-skinned

Black girls, like me, in their beauty. Bey was #goals, before #goals was a thing. She was like a fair-skinned princess in the fairy tale of life, the kind that would get rescued by the perfect Prince Charming. There was just one issue: she was so badass that she didn't need rescuing.

I felt like I did. I was the youngest of three, raised on Section 8 by a disabled single mother. To say that money was tight was a severe understatement. Meanwhile, Bey—one of two children raised in a two-parent, upper-middle-class home—was making her own money, paving her own path in both music and pop culture. On top of her otherworldly beauty, her light skin, and blond hair, I felt like it was simply unfair comparing her life to mine. So I shifted my personal frustrations onto her. Anytime anyone tried to exalt her in my presence, I was quick to shoot them down. With an eye roll, I'd ask: "Is she *really* that talented? Or is she just light-skinned and good enough?"

The honest truth is, I disliked Beyoncé because I wanted to be her, flaws and all. It would take years before I understood the internalized colorism that affected my perspective of Beyoncé. And it was Bey herself who would teach me this lesson.

The first breakdown of my wall against Bey came through her embrace of women while preparing for her 2007 The Beyoncé Experience tour. The year prior, she put out a call for musicians to try out for her all-female band. Ten women eventually made the cut after a grueling audition process, becoming an essential part of Bey's intricate and demanding live experiences. At the time of this grand undertaking, I felt myself morphing from adolescent to young woman, and with that conversion came a more cemented understanding of the dynamics between men and women in any given occupation—in this instance, the dominant presence men held over women in the music industry. With this experiment, Bey was deliberating stepping beyond the lines of normalcy.

Seven years later, during the Mrs. Carter Show World Tour and at the 2014 MTV VMAs, Bey would stand in front of the word "FEMINIST" emblazoned on a large screen in all caps. But she was my introduction to feminism before I even knew the word existed. From "Upgrade U" to "Irreplaceable" to "Run the World (Girls)," Beyoncé has continuously spoken direct words of encouragement to women and maintained a strength that she's sought to pass on to her fans—and nudged her listeners toward the concept of intersectional feminism. With a careful hand, she has taught her listeners how to love not just her, but also love and understand people who aren't like them. When Beyoncé sings, it sounds like she has a word of advice that she genuinely feels could change your life, if only you took heed.

She built a voice that was sellable to every radio station, every TV channel, every market—and she found a way to cater to audiences across the board. Her music never strikes directly in any genre, but she has made it a point to move closer and closer to her Black audience. Closer to me.

In particular, recent years have illustrated a most obvious prioritizing of Bey's Blackness; it came to a head with "Formation" in 2016, with lyrics like "I like my negro nose with Jackson Five nostrils" and visuals that notably featured Black women dancers wearing Afros, and Bey herself in waist-grazing cornrows. With *Lemonade*, for which "Formation" was the lead single, she reclaimed genres birthed by Black people—rock with "Don't Hurt Yourself" and country music with "Daddy Lessons"—and presented us with a twenty-first-century Black female perspective.

The visual album *Lemonade* in particular centered Black women and their lack of visibility. It was made especially clear when she included an excerpt from a 1962 speech by Malcolm X: "The most disrespected person in America is the Black woman. The most unprotected person in America is the Black woman. The most neglected person in America is the Black woman." In that moment, I felt seen. In that moment, it felt like my sister and my aunts and cousins and friends were seen. The veil of separation between me and Bey was lifted and I realized (or perhaps remembered) that no other popular artist on Beyoncé's scale had ever positioned us as a priority.

Embedded on the *Lemonade* album itself was one small detail that stood out as one of the most significant steps toward centering Blackness she's taken thus far as a pop artist. On the album's second single, "Sorry," she delightfully says, "I ain't sorry / N——, nah." She says it casually, as if it's the most-used word in her vocabulary. This is a global superstar with millions of fans, many of them non-Black. This is a person who has built her brand on inclusivity. And yet here she is, using this very particular piece of exclusively Black slang. It's a word that has long frolicked in her husband's lexicon but had seldom presented itself via Bey herself.

The context of "Sorry," about Bey going out to spite Jay, heightened this usage to a moment of conscious liberation.

Bey's ability to have laser-focused attention on the Black experience didn't happen overnight: It took years for her to amass a following first. She then constructed a platform strong enough from which to make such bold statements. And since *Lemonade*, Bey has continued to make a concerted effort to put Black bodies in her visuals, and call attention to the importance of Black women and Black love. The album cover for *Everything Is Love*, for example—a photo of her Black dancers, Jasmine Harper and Nicholas "Slick" Stewart, in the midst of an intimate hair maintenance session in the Louvre—is an intentional decision. It's not for fun; it's to make a statement that putting her own spotlight on Blackness is her foremost goal with her career at this point. An event as recent as #Beychella established her undistracted focus on the Black experience. By invoking an invented HBCU campus, complete with a backing marching band, Bey literally stepped her way into strongly identifying with her Black fans. She even went so far as to sing the Black national anthem, "Lift Every Voice and Sing."

On the surface, Bey might seem like the closest thing we've had to a perfect pop star. But the title doesn't fit anymore: Bey has weaved together an entirely new matrix of celebrity. She continues to catch us off-guard by delving further into her personalized elevation of Black people, and Black women specifically. Our issues have become her issues. She represents me, us. Her arrival at this point was a slow build. And it's given us all time to recognize that belonging to the Bey Hive means accepting Beyoncé's journey to the heart of what it means to be Black in 2018.

—Kiana Fitzgerald, NPR Music, *Turning the Tables*,
Season 2, "25 Most Influential Women+ Musicians
of the 21st Century," 2018 (excerpt)

FIONA APPLE:
Turning the truth into something beautiful

NPR: Your first album, *Tidal*, came out in 1996 when you were still a teenager. Everyone knows that, everyone talks about that. What do you wish you could tell your teenage self now, as a woman in her forties?

Fiona Apple: Well, that teenager that started, I would tell her: "You are on the right track, and there's going to be a lot of people who are going to tell you that what you're doing is stupid. And they're going to be people of authority, and they're going to be the people that you love and they're going to be the people that you trust. Please do not believe them. As genius, or as wonderful, or as loving, or as smart, as worldly, as experienced as they may be, they don't know you. *You* know you. You're doing great. Don't let them stop you."

I would tell her that. But I'm glad that I don't have the chance to tell her that, because I think the experience that I did have is worth it. It's not a totally happy thing, it's just like I wouldn't have it any other way because I like what I did with my life. That's how I've always wanted to live. I've always wanted to live facing the truth, taking the truth and turning it into something beautiful. That's a wonderful way for anybody to live. And so I like that the truth of all my life isn't all happy and perfect and no obstacles anywhere, because it's what I did with all of that that makes something that now can maybe help other people.

—*All Things Considered* with Ailsa Chang, 2020

99. FEARLESS
Taylor Swift (BIG MACHINE RECORDS, 2008)

No listenership is cast aside with the same fervent damnation as young women— their interests are frequently written off with complete critical derision. Challenging that notion is best accomplished by being too damn good (and confident in that excellence) to ignore. So goes the success of the then-teenage Taylor Swift, a Nashville-via-Pennsylvania talent whose ideation reached its full

fruition on *Fearless*, a self-written country-pop album of immeasurable catchiness. In "Fifteen," she writes from a place of newfound maturity, adopting a big sister role for those most affected by being young and vulnerable (everyone). In "Love Story," fantasy is grounded in intimate reality, a *Romeo and Juliet* metaphor imbued with restraint—she avoids grandiose gestures and instead offers timeless confessions. *Fearless* manages to play to Swift's admiration for her female pop forebears (Sheryl Crow is mentioned in interviews), the narrative songwriting of the country music she grew up on, and her own personal hybridity. At its simplest, *Fearless* displays Swift as a brilliant songwriter. At its truest, the album shines with an explosive voice, an ineffable gift. No one can question Swift's success now, and *Fearless* proved it then. Just ask a girl.

—Maria Sherman, *Turning the Tables*,
"The 150 Greatest Albums Made by Women," 2017

TAYLOR SWIFT
Come back when you're in your twenties

❝ I was never convinced I was going to make it. And I look back—my mom and I reminisce about this all the time because we had no idea what we were doing. My parents bought books on what the music industry was like. They had no idea what the music industry entailed and what was involved with it. Something that was said to me early on was, 'Teenagers don't listen to country music. That's not the audience. The audience is a thirty-five-year-old housewife. . . . How are you going to relate to those women when you're sixteen years old? You should come back when you're in your twenties.' And I kept thinking, 'But I love country music and I'm a teenager! There have to be more kids out there like me.'

I've written all my songs on every single one of my records, and that's what's been fun about looking back. My first album is the diary of when I was fourteen, fifteen, sixteen. My second album, *Fearless*, was from sixteen to eighteen, and so on, and so on. So you have my life being recorded in journal entries from these two-year periods of my life since I was sixteen. I like to write about love and love lost because I feel like there are so many different subcategories of emotions that you can possibly delve into. I've never missed two people the same way—it's always different for me. I've never fallen in love with someone and had the same exact kind of feeling come over me. **"**

—*All Things Considered* with Guy Raz, 2012

93. . . . BABY ONE MORE TIME
Britney Spears (JIVE RECORDS, 1999)

Oh baby, baby, how were we supposed to know that 1999 would birth one of the most lasting pop albums of the millennium (and beyond)? The combination of Britney Jean Spears's vocals and stellar production work from Max Martin made for an incredibly prescient record, one that still sounds pristine and poppy nearly two decades after its original release. This record broke through the boy band molds and showed me, as a seven-year-old growing up in West Virginia, the power of an independent woman on a single mic. But not everyone felt the same way. At the time Spears dropped her debut, critics immediately wrote her off as a Madonna rip-off and a Lolita-type with no discernible talent, complaints that tend to follow achieving young women with unique voices. And yet, . . . *Baby One More Time* went on to become one of the bestselling records of all time, the bestselling album by a teenage solo artist, and a multi-platinum Grammy-nominated release for Spears, not to mention an international pop model for artists like Ariana Grande, Nicki Minaj, Grimes, and South Korea's Girls' Generation. Teen pop is typecast as being irrelevant or shallow, but Britney Spears's debut is a multigenerational time capsule that's proved to be as relevant then as it is today when dealing with broken hearts, finding light in dark places, and navigating the ups and downs of adulthood. Starting with that one record, Spears redefined pop music (and she drove us crazy) with her showwomanship.

—Joni Deutsch, *Mountain Stage*, *Turning the Tables*,
"The 150 Greatest Albums Made by Women," 2017

17. CONTROL
Janet Jackson (A&M, 1986)

There would be no *Rhythm Nation*, *Janet*, or *Velvet Rope* without *Control*. This was the breakout album for then-nineteen-year-old Janet Jackson, who until then was fondly known as Michael Jackson's little sister, Penny from *Good Times*, and Willis's girlfriend on *Diff'rent Strokes*. She fired her dad as her manager, got with producers Terry Lewis and Jimmy Jam from the Time, and made an album that clearly said "I'm a grown-ass woman," in case anyone was confused. The album, released February 1986, took on important issues such as sexual harassment, safe sex, and abstinence, and we sang right along with her, making hits out of "What Have You Done for Me Lately," "Nasty," "Control," "When I Think of You," "Let's Wait Awhile," and "Funny How Time Flies (When You're Having Fun)." But Jackson did something especially pivotal with the video for "The Pleasure Principle," another single from the album. She walked alone into an empty loft with kneepads on, kicked over a chair, cabbage-patched, and clarified for those in the cheap seats that she was as great a performer as her big brother: "Ba-by you can't hold me down! Ba-by you can't hold me dow-ow-own!"

—Tanya Ballard Brown, NPR, *Turning the Tables*,
"The 150 Greatest Albums Made by Women," 2017

107. LEADER OF THE PACK
The Shangri-Las (RED BIRD RECORDS, 1965)

The girl group boom of the late 1950s and 1960s cast the voice of the American teenage girl squarely into the spotlight. But the Shangri-Las, with their tough-girl personas and blue-collar Queens accents, tapped into its darker side, with dispatches from the more haunted part of the adolescent psyche—where every broken date or fight with mom is weighted with potentially apocalyptic significance. Neither of the two sets of sisters—the Weisses and the Gansers—that comprised the group were over seventeen when they recorded the *Billboard* chart-topper "Leader of the Pack," the melodramatic apex of the teen-tragedy genre that gave their 1965 debut LP its name (and which, it turned out, wouldn't even be their only song in which a young lover dies blinded by tears). The revving motorcycles and breaking glass on the title cut, co-written by Brill Building hit-makers Ellie Greenwich and Jeff Barry alongside producer George "Shadow" Morton, along with the Morton-penned, mournful "Remember (Walking in the Sand)," set the tone for the Shangri-Las' most memorable recordings. More often than not, these were abstract, eerie radio plays as much as pop tunes. The Shangri-Las would release only one more album, but their aesthetic would reverberate for generations, through endless covers and name-checks by acts ranging from Bette Midler to Blondie to Amy Winehouse. In particular, their frequency of danger and doom resonated with the men of hard rock and punk—they've been referenced and cited by the Jesus and Mary Chain, Twisted Sister, and maybe most famously, the New York Dolls—who not only quoted them on the song "Looking for a Kiss," but also put Morton at the helm of their 1974 album *Too Much Too Soon*.

—Alison Fensterstock, *Turning the Tables*,
"The 150 Greatest Albums Made by Women," 2017

The Shangri-Las *by* Nicole Rifkin

MARY WEISS OF THE SHANGRI-LAS
Everything was black and white

"I think teenagers for the most part have an intensity that we seem to—I don't think we grow out of it, but there's variable shades of gray added. When you're a teen, for me anyway, everything was black and white. **"**

—*Fresh Air* with Terry Gross, 2007

149. SONGS IN A MINOR
Alicia Keys (J RECORDS, 2001)

Alicia Keys graduated from high school at age sixteen with a scholarship to
Columbia University. But she decided to pursue a future with a different Columbia
instead—Columbia Records, the label that signed her at age fifteen. Like many
Black women artists who came before and after her, she had to contend with
people who lacked respect for her as a creator and a person. As she told the *New
York Times* in 2002: "So I'm working with them, and them being not receptive to
the fact that I play. 'Little girl, sit over there in the corner.' Them being attracted to
me, whatever, 'Little girl let's go to the movies, let's go to dinner.'" Keys couldn't
work under those conditions, so she found a Queens basement and made her own
studio there. When she took her finished records to Columbia, they didn't like
them. So she left and released *Songs in A Minor* with J Records. It reached No. 1
on the *Billboard* charts and secured Keys's position as one of the most visionary
composers of her time. A classically trained pianist raised on hip hop in Hell's
Kitchen, Keys took varied influences—including Chopin (her favorite composer),
Marvin Gaye, Billie Holiday—and, with them, crafted a distillation of her spirit.
The album's most enduring songs, "Fallin'" and "A Woman's Worth," are perfect.
And when we listen to them, we should take care to remember the story of the
young woman who made them. She taught an entire generation of us to persevere,
to know our stuff—and yes, to know our worth.

—Jenny Gathright, NPR, *Turning the Tables*,
"The 150 Greatest Albums Made by Women," 2017

How Donna Summer and Debbie Harry Taught Me to Embrace My Inner Bad Girl

It was the fall of 1979, and I was ten. I was standing in my family's small bathroom, studying my face in the mirror. I held my head at a slight right angle, staring at eyes stuck behind the glasses I abhorred—the glasses I had been wearing in different sizes and styles since I was in the second grade. I attempted to gather my long, thin cornrowed braids into a high ponytail, but it didn't look at all like the ones my white prep-school girlfriends wore. Not just because of the texture, but because of the way the cornrows lay flat against my scalp. I couldn't casually pile all my hair on the top of my head, absentmindedly securing it with a hair band to "get it out of my face." My friends were always playing with their hair. Flipping it. Twisting it. Pulling it into a bun. Taking it out again. I longed to have hair like theirs. I wanted to tuck my hair behind my ear as I leaned over alluringly, gazing into Cheap Trick singer Robin Zander's eyes—his lyrical Caroline come to life— "Oh Caroline, my life shined when you walked in." My friends' hair wasn't merely straighter. It offered a pathway to the kinds of experiences that I could only hear about in the rock songs I adored and in the rock magazines I devoured.

I flipped my braids and took another long, squinting look, hoping to see a version of myself that never appeared. I wasn't pretty, but I didn't feel ugly either. Not exactly. I just saw a girl existing in some awkward, unattractive in-between

category that made it easy to look past her. The type of girl unworthy of attention, particularly from boys. Especially the white ones. And really, more than anything, I wanted attention. I was extremely, painfully, paralyzingly shy. But there was something deep and unexplainable inside of me that wanted the world to look at me. I spent untold hours focused on hazy daydreams where I danced or sang or acted my way into my peers' consciousness. Where I would do something so unexpectedly interesting that, as if turning on a light switch, I would come to school the next day, reborn a star. But really, I wanted to be like Donna Summer and Debbie Harry.

I was a child during the 1970s, but like my mother, who was born in 1946 and felt a strong connection to 1950s popular culture, I embraced the latter part of the "me" decade like I was grown. I lived with my mother, grandmother, and occasionally my uncle, in a two-bedroom apartment in the Breukelen Houses, a housing project in the southeast section of Brooklyn, New York. Every morning, I took the L train to Packer Collegiate Institute, a K-12 college prep school in tony Brooklyn Heights. During the day, I battled my invisibility among my peers. I was a good student, but outside of the classroom I felt like an outsider. My skin color and social class kept me at a distance from my classmates. No matter how much fun we had together at school, or during our occasional playdates at my friends' houses in the Heights or Park Slope, they never really knew me. In all my years at Packer, not one school friend visited me at home. This is not because they declined my invitations. The profound shame I felt about where (and how) I lived made inviting my friends home *feel* impossible.

On a warm spring night in 1979, my mom brought home *Bad Girls* by Donna Summer. As soon as I saw the album cover, I knew it was for adults. My mom played the title track, "Bad Girls," over and over, so when it was my turn to listen to records on the living room turntable, I played it, too. I loved the hypnotic beat, and the women who sang "toot-toot, hey, beep-beep," simulating the sounds of the cars slowly cruising up and down Sunset Boulevard, sounded sexy, cool, and seductive. My mom never censored my popular culture consumption, so while I only had a vague sense of what a sex worker did, I knew that it was something talked about in

Debbie Harry

83

hushed tones and not something I was supposed to know about, let alone want to be. Even so, when I heard Donna Summer's refreshingly nonjudgmental lyrics, "Now don't you ask yourself who they are. / Like everybody else, they want to be a star," and when she offers, "Now you and me we're both the same, / but you call yourself by different names," that really resonated with me. I wanted to not just be seen by my classmates. I wanted to be a *star*. So maybe it was okay to be a Bad Girl after all.

"Heart of Glass" from Blondie's 1978 release *Parallel Lines* offered the ideal combination of rock and disco, with its quasi-disco flavor and Debbie Harry's candy apple–sweet voice, guarded by teeth that could bite if you were not careful. When I heard it on the radio in early 1979, I was hooked. Although I had already heard "Heart of Glass" on the radio, I was not prepared for the reaction I would have to hearing "Hanging on the Telephone" for the first time. I had listened to Beatles and Rolling Stones songs before, and I had been exposed to other 1960s-era rock bands through my mother, but "Hanging on the Telephone," a cover of the 1976 Nerves tune, was the first modern-era rock song I paid close attention to. Not only was I immediately engaged by Blondie's bouncy, energetic power pop, but being a somewhat precocious prepubescent, I was even more intrigued by the lyrics:

I had to interrupt and stop this conversation
your voice across the line gives me a strange sensation
I'd like to talk when I can show you my affection.

The connection between rock and roll and sexuality was hardly lost on me, even at age nine. And although I couldn't yet articulate those confused sexual feelings to others, or even make good sense of them in my own head, I knew it was cool that Debbie Harry not only had enough attitude and pluck to front an all-male rock band, but she also wasn't shy about letting a "boy" know she was interested. This was extremely important to me because a few months later during the fifth grade I had difficulty doing just that. I could *never* tell the popular Irish American boy in class that I *liked* him. So it would naturally follow that Debbie Harry, another Bad Girl, would become my hero.

Debbie Harry and Donna Summer—contemporaries who were just three years apart in age—on the surface could not seem more different: one a rocking singer-songwriter-actress from the NYC punk scene, and the other a singer-songwriter-actress who would become known as the Queen of Disco. But these artists share much in common. Summer's 1977 track "I Feel Love" would inspire Blondie's "Heart of Glass" and later "Atomic" from their 1979 album *Eat to the Beat*. And later still Summer and Harry would share Giorgio Moroder as a producer—he was at the helm for both Blondie's 1980 six-week No. 1 hit single "Call Me" and Summer's 1980 release *The Wanderer*. But most importantly for me, these two iconic women known for their beauty and a particular brand of 1970s-era glamour and sex appeal also felt unattractive as girls, turning to 1950s / early 1960s actress Marilyn Monroe as an aspirational symbol of female glamour. In Summer's 2003 memoir *Ordinary Girl: The Journey*, she says that she channeled Monroe's voice for "Love to Love You Baby," and in 2012's *Blondie: Parallel Lives*, Harry shares, "I always thought I was Marilyn Monroe's kid. I felt physically related and akin to her long before I knew she had been adopted herself. . . ."

In Summer's memoir, she talked about her struggle to love her hair: "The problem for me was that I didn't really like the way I looked with my hair braided. She [Summer's mom] braided my hair so tight it made my eyes slant. I'd see myself in the mirror afterward and wonder who was that little girl staring back at me. Being braided and not liking it was one source of my low self-esteem." Summer also cut her face at seven, leaving a large, noticeable scar: "The scar on my cheek became the focal point for everything I hated about myself. I was convinced that I had ruined myself for life and would never be attractive to anyone, especially a man."

Harry, too, felt ugly during her girlhood: "I hated the way I looked growing up. I had this blonde hair, pale-blue eyes and these jutting cheekbones. I didn't look like any other kids I grew up with and I felt very uncomfortable about my face. I hated looking in mirrors and I definitely didn't think I was pretty. . . . When I was a baby I was real pretty, but in between I was a real mess. I was very ugly. I just grew up weird." Reading these words now, I am sad for all of us, but I also feel a retrospective gratefulness. I was not alone in these painful feelings. Even girls who grow up to become world-renowned symbols of beauty and sexiness can feel ugly.

Summer's and Harry's infectious, eternally singable and danceable, chart-topping music; sexual freedom; and fierceness of spirit helped me to imagine a more passionate and confident way of being. It didn't happen right away. That feeling of invisibility stayed with me throughout most of high school, but they planted seeds in me that would flower by the time I began college. Donna Summer and Debbie Harry showed me that women could be fierce in their lyrics and in their stage personas. And I welcomed a fierceness that was not born of violence (as it was with the two key women in my life), but of sexual independence. They were both *Bad Girls*. And when I listened, I got to be one, too.

—Kimberly Mack, *Turning the Tables* contributor

DONNA SUMMER
How would Marilyn sing this song?

" Well, the vocal [on 'Love to Love You Baby'] was very breathy and airy, and basically I was a theater singer, so I had been, you know, much more of a belter. And it was really different and difficult for me to tap into who this person was. And so I imaged Marilyn Monroe and just began to think, 'Well, how would Marilyn sing this song?' And she would be very soft. And then, you know, I started playing with the thought in my mind, and so as I began to sort of think of it her way through her, I began to understand who the song was for and who the song was about and the girl singing it. And I tapped into it and recorded it. "

—*Fresh Air* with Terry Gross, 2003

 ## 63. KATY PERRY, "TEENAGE DREAM"

While this era's faux-woke, grill-sporting Katy Perry has taken a nosedive into a cyclone of dystopian kitsch, there was a time when her appeal was simple: her nostalgic pop singles were silky and pristine, like a soft swirl of vanilla ice cream. At a time when pop can feel overstuffed with spectacle—multiartist guest features, visual drops, strategically planned Twitter beef—listening to "Teenage Dream" provokes wistful reconsideration of a classic formula, one whose subtlety and nuance can be easily overlooked. The song is a blissful memory encased in glass: "We can dance until we die / you and I," Perry sings, promising to stretch the ephemeral. The beauty is in stasis, sealed with a declaration: "We'll be young forever."

—Cat Zhang, *Turning the Tables*, Season 2, "The 200 Greatest Songs by 21st-Century Women+," 2018

 ## 47. AVRIL LAVIGNE, "COMPLICATED"

Like the Frankie Valli classic "Can't Take My Eyes Off You," "Complicated" isn't a slow love song and it isn't a poppy dance song—it's a ballad with an edge. At a time when tweens seemed obsessed with dressing alike, Avril Lavigne busted onto the scene and taught young women that it was okay to be different. In embracing her uniqueness, she told us all that being ourselves is way less complicated.

—Lisa Famiglietti, WXXI, *Turning the Tables*, Season 2, "The 200 Greatest Songs by 21st-Century Women+," 2018

 ## 21. CARLY RAE JEPSEN, "CALL ME MAYBE"

The best thing about the "song of summer 2012" is that it is exactly what it purports to be: a candy-crush teenybopper pop hit about meeting a cute guy (crazy) and working up the courage to ask him to call you (maybe). It's fun and it's flirty and it makes you want to dance. It's not trying to be super-deep or sexy—it's just reveling in the feeling of being young and happy and taking big risks, like talking to a guy at the pool while wearing Hollister jeans and a lot of lip gloss. If translated into emoji, at least half the lyrics would be hearts—with some kissy faces and sunshine thrown in for good measure. This is a song that will always sound best heard blasting from a radio somewhere. With a sparkly disco beat and an urgently catchy chorus, "Call Me Maybe" succeeds because of its ability to immortalize the feeling of summer through the mood of blushing teenagers.

—Alyssa Edes, *Turning the Tables*, Season 2, "The 200 Greatest Songs by 21st-Century Women+," 2018

Gender. Lust. Color. Size. Health and sickness. Clothes. The human body is a lot, from the heart to the hips and the pleasure and pain both can bring. Sound waves interact with cells, blood, and muscle, and beats and lyrics move your ass and stab or fill your heart; our bodies are fodder for indelible songs and battlegrounds for the women who put their own on the stage and in the studio.

Joan Jell

JOAN JETT
I just do it

❝ I don't wait till stage to use my sexuality. My zipper's down right now. I mean, I use it all the time. I'm always attacking, you know? I'm not the passive girl, you know. It's just, I don't think about it. It's not that calculated. I just do it. ❞

—*Day to Day* with Madeleine Brand, 2006

MADONNA
Trying to see what the boundaries were

❝ I was raised in a very kind of conservative household. Where, you know, the idea was, you know, my father didn't go around telling my brothers they had to be virgins when they were married. He just told my sisters and me and I kept thinking, Well, wait a minute. There's something wrong with this picture. How come my brothers don't have to restrict themselves sexually, but we do? And there seemed to be a lot of restrictions put on women when it came to sexuality and none on men. And as I became more famous, and started to see what people were writing about me, I noticed that people were writing and making comments about the way I looked. And then I would compare it to what they would write about men. They wouldn't comment so much about the way a man looked. And then I also noticed that if you were perceived as being sexy or attractive or pretty, the idea that you had something of value to say was also taken away from you. And so I think I kind of got angry and reactive about all of that. And I decided to take it all the way over the edge and say, Well, wait a minute, that's not true. You can actually be very sexual and very intelligent at the same time. And watch this. And here, I'm going to do it. And not only that but there's more to life than the male turning a female into an object, a sex object. I'm going to turn *myself* into a sex object. You know what I mean? I was just playing with convention and sexuality and trying to see what the boundaries were. I was kind of trying to work it out not only in my own head, but trying to understand why men and women were perceived differently and treated differently, only to realize and understand now that in fact, women and men are different. And that's all there is to it. You know, male energy and female energy is indeed very different. And that is why we're on a very primal level, we have the reactions that we do. So it was a sociological study for me. 🍂🍂

—*Fresh Air* with Terry Gross, 2004

69. SHE'S SO UNUSUAL
Cyndi Lauper (PORTRAIT/SONY 1983)

She's So Unusual helped usher in the sound of a decade—specifically, the "I Want My MTV" 1980s. The album—Cyndi Lauper's first—burst out in 1983 with a synth-pop confetti cannon and that little earworm "Girls Just Want to Have Fun." Yet the album is sprinkled with other hits, like "Time After Time" and "All Through the Night," and went platinum six times. Lauper unabashedly sang about female empowerment all over the album, but on "She Bop," a song about masturbation, she really drove the message home. Heavy panting punctuates the song's upbeat synths and features lyrics like:

Cyndi Lauper

Well I see them every night in tight blue jeans
In the pages of a Blue Boy magazine
Hey I've been thinking of a new sensation
I'm picking up good vibrations.

The song was a hit on the charts but also made its way onto a different sort of chart: "She Bop" landed on the Filthy Fifteen list, a list of songs deemed inappropriate by the Parents Music Resource Center that ultimately played a role in the creation of the parental advisory label (Lauper was in good company, with the likes of Prince, Madonna, and AC/DC). Controversy aside, the album manages to touch on heavy topics (her powerful cover of the Brains' "Money Changes Everything," for example) while still staying true to its joyful core. The cover art and synth sounds root this album firmly in the '80s, but Cyndi Lauper's *She's So Unusual* transcends time.

—Lauren Migaki, NPR, *Turning the Tables*,
"The 150 Greatest Albums Made by Women," 2017

 ## 10. PEACHES, "FUCK THE PAIN AWAY"

Pop has always used sex as a vehicle, but nobody knows how to hot-wire that energy like Peaches. The Canadian artist released *The Teaches of Peaches* in 2000, and it opened with what would become her signature anthem and electroclash's calling card. Over sparse, farting bass and jubilant hi-hats, Peaches doesn't just tell us what feels good to her—"Suckin' on my titties like you wanted me"—she demands sexual release with a cool stare, while also advocating for education and contraception. Her vocal was recorded live, and the song's brilliance owes much to the way she delivers explicit lyrics with punk insouciance—an attitude that continues to inspire conversations around gender and sexual expression. Early critical reception often cast Peaches's frank sensuality as "smutty," a reductive move that feels prudish at best. However, twentieth-century morals could never hold Peaches or "Fuck the Pain Away" back; both artist and song are of this new millennium, and still as potent as ever.

—Ruth Saxelby, *Turning the Tables*, Season 2,
"The 200 Greatest Songs by 21st-Century Women+," 2018

Celia Cruz:
The Voice of Experience

By the time I saw Celia Cruz in concert, she had already released more than forty albums over the course of a career that spanned nearly half a century and had long established herself as the reigning Queen of Salsa. It was the spring of 1995 at the Aragon Ballroom in the Uptown neighborhood of Chicago, and the city was just beginning its muddy thaw.

She was sixty-nine; I was twenty-four. One of us managed to sing and dance until the early morning hours without a break.

I was joined that night by a handful of other twenty-something-year-old friends, fellow graduate students who hailed from far-flung points on the diasporic map. Some of us had grown up listening to our parents play Cruz records, while others of us had only recently come to recognize her voice as we sang along to her iconic version of "Guantanamera" (first recorded in 1968) on the 1992 *Mambo Kings* soundtrack.

During our time in Chicago, we'd all forged a bond through the rituals of intellectual debate, frequent huddling on blustery elevated train platforms, and above all, regular salsa dancing. One of us was a Puerto Rican raised in California and shaped by years of Jesuit education who'd traveled to Cuba to cut cane during the Special Period; another was a Chilean *conguero* whose family was forced to leave Santiago after Pinochet's coup in 1973 and who grew up in Indiana. One of us was a Hampton-educated Black American military brat born on Guantanamo Bay Naval Base when her father was stationed there in the early '70s; and then there was me, a Tejana with flimsy Spanish who'd learned how to gallop along to a Mexican *cumbia* long before I'd ever learned to catch the Caribbean clave beat.

Salsa, a musical genre that has long defied classification and a singular origin story, is generally understood to have developed in the 1960s and 1970s in New York City during a period marked by the generative contact among growing numbers of Latinx immigrants from throughout Latin America and most especially from across the Caribbean. Nationalist sentiments inform the long-standing debates about salsa's origins. There are some (like Cruz herself) who claim that salsa emerged primarily from Cuban musical styles like *son*, *guaracha*, and *rumba*. Others trace its roots to the confluence of Latin American styles like Puerto Rican *bomba* and Colombian *cumbias* as well as Cuban traditions. Some of us agree with all of the above; salsa scholar Frances Aparicio defines salsa as "a conjunction of Afro-Cuban music (*el son*) and rhythms of Puerto Rican *bombas* and *plenas*, and of African American jazz instrumentation and structures."

Salsa's Afro-diasporic rhythms keep your center of gravity low as you move across space, and its Spanish-language lyrics keep your mind moving from romantic love to commentaries about the social and political conditions of Latinx life. Rhythmically, lyrically, and kinesthetically, salsa carries in it and urges us to move within the traditions of survival and innovation among communities historically subjected to plantation slavery and the forces of migration across the Americas. In other words, salsa is quintessentially American music.

Cruz's voice is synonymous with salsa. It is earth and star, the iron heated until it glows and struck until it curves, a warm and deep contralto that melts the boundaries of gender. Rich as molasses but agile as the hand wielding the knife that cuts the cane. A voice whose sonorous tones and dexterous enunciations capture both the toils and virtuosity of Black Cuban labor and the delight in the fruit it bears.

It's hard to overemphasize the significance of Cruz's presence as a Black woman, of the sound of her voice resounding within and hovering above the overwhelmingly (and indeed, at that time, exclusively) male-dominated and hypermasculinist realm of salsa. Sure, there was Cruz's contemporary, La Lupe, a woefully underappreciated and ultimately ostracized female vocalist, but the salsa industry made room for only one woman in that era, and that woman was Celia

Celia Cruz

Cruz. Luckily for me, her voice carried past that moment in time, carried within it lessons in presence and stamina.

Salsa experienced a resurgence in popularity during the 1990s due, for better or worse, to the widespread commercialization of the genre. But even as salsa and countless other "Latin" products were discovered and marketed as part of a larger cultural "Latin Boom," many of us continued to mark out a hallowed space for ourselves on the rapidly commodifying dance floor. For Aparicio, and for those of us who spent the better part of the 1990s dancing to its rhythms, salsa was in many ways "the quintessential musical marker of *latinidad* [Latinx identification] in the United States and in Latin America." The salsa from this period, generally referred to as *salsa romántica*, is often derided for its lack of musical sophistication or lyrical gravitas that marked salsa music of the golden era in the 1960s and 1970s. And while this claim is not entirely wrong, it fails to account for the feminist interventions in the genre made by salsa artists of the 1990s like La India and for the enduring presence and contributions of Cruz herself.

By the time my friends and I arrived at the Aragon Ballroom, we'd endured winter by making the rounds to several of the thriving local salsa clubs or to each other's living rooms where we'd clear the furniture to make space for dancing. In regular rotation that year were songs like the title track from Cruz's 1993 album *Azucar Negra* and La India's 1994 feminist salsa anthem "Ese Hombre." In Cruz's song we could hear the pronouncement of Black diasporic blood memory—"Mi sangre es azucar negra" ("my blood is black sugar")—and an insistence that salsa would carry us through the everyday and the holy days—"Soy calle y soy carnaval" ("I am the street and the carnival"). Her song reminded us that the rhythms to which we moved were drawn from the source of our people's long laboring and were, as well, its exalted product—"Soy la caña y el café" ("I am the cane and the coffee").

For us, Cruz's longevity created a space for the arrival of La India, a Puerto Rican–born, Bronx-bred *salsera* from our generation who got her start in the Latin freestyle music scene in the mid-1980s. In La India's songs (frequently played on repeat at home and always requested of the club's DJ), we rejoiced in her rueful subversion of the *romántica* trope and structure of *salsa romántica*. Her lyrics begin, "Ese hombre que tú ves ahí / que parece tan galante" ("That man that you see over there / who seems so gallant"), and then just as the horns blare and your body launches into its first sequence of moves, she turns generic convention on its head with the chorus, "Es un gran necio / un payaso vanidoso" ("Is a great fool / a vain clown").

Both Cruz's and La India's songs played on the same dance mixes that we made or DJ setlists that spun at the clubs during that time. For us, Cruz was not just an emblem of salsa's grand past but a relevant and vibrant force that continued to charge its present and shape its future. She continually reinvented herself over time while maintaining an immutable sense of her signature divinity like a classic diva. So, sure, we flocked to her concert that spring because we wanted to be in the presence of a living legend, to bow (and turn and glide and shuffle and spin) before the Queen. But, mostly, as twenty-something-year-olds, we came because we wanted to dance to rhythms that resonated with our current lives. We understood that as a true diva, Cruz was of her time and capable of transcending it. We came because we had faith in her power to transport us along with her across this continuum.

By the time Cruz took to the Aragon Ballroom stage in her custom-made, gravity-defying shoes and called out to us with her signature shout—*¡Azucar!*—it was 1 a.m. By then, I'd already broken a sweat warming up to the opening acts and had even taken a brief disco nap on the bench of a booth while the ice melted in my cocktail. Cruz opened her mouth, the band lifted their horns, and we came together on the dance floor.

Some of us danced "on the 1" (*step-step-step-pause*); others, "on the 2" (*pause-step-step-step*). To those who were perhaps more sophisticated (or maybe just more rigid) than we were at the time, what you danced on, or where you took the pause, in salsa was often regarded as a defining measure of authenticity. The pause, as dance scholar Cindy Garcia observes, "is the most crucial component of the dance—potentially sensual and volatile." Maybe because we were naive or maybe because we knew we'd never measure up or maybe because of our developing feminist consciousness, we just took turns taking the lead. Whether on the 1 or on the 2, for us, it all added up to a sum greater than our individual parts. To learn how to salsa was to learn about your relationship to time, about how to measure it and move to it and dwell in its pauses.

That night at the Aragon, Cruz sang out, "La rumba me está llamando" ("The rumba is calling me"), the opening lyrics of her signature 1974 hit "Quimbara," and we answered the call. I danced to the song with my girlfriends, sharing the lead, feeling for the pause and trying to keep up with Cruz's vocal gymnastics and the tempo's wild acceleration. Salsa dancing was how we were coming to know who we were in relation to one another as fellow Black and brown women. And dancing to "Quimbara," with its impossibly fast rhythms and tumbling lyrics, not only offered us a source of deeply embodied pleasure but trained us to outmaneuver and outspeak and outrun any foes who sought to hunt us down.

The year after her concert at the Aragon, Cruz recorded a duet with La India called "La Voz de la Experiencia." The song, written by La India, is at once an homage to Cruz as *La Reina de La Salsa* and an enactment of the crowning of La India, *La Princesa de La Salsa*, as the successor to the throne.

Watching the footage of it now, when I am exactly twice the age I was when I first saw Cruz at the Aragon, what I find moving is how the duet showcases two women of some experience—neither of whom are what anyone would call thin or young or fair-skinned—publicly performing their mutual adoration and encouraging each other's virtuosic capacities, their voices barreling across time and space, their bodies catching the clave as they dance *cucaracha* side steps in sync with one another. Knowing who they are in relation to one another as fellow Black and brown women.

By the time I write this, it's the last days of a summer marred by the targeted massacre of Mexicans and Mexican Americans in El Paso, migrant refugees dying in detention along the border, continued governmental disregard of recovery efforts in Puerto Rico, and ICE raids targeting undocumented workers in the Midwest, and I'm not much in the mood to talk about singing and dancing. But then, hasn't salsa always ever been in some ways about the struggles embedded in and transformed through its lyrics and rhythms? Isn't Cruz's voice made of the soil on which we've toiled, the earth and the harvest our people have culled from it? *¡Azucar!*

At the end of the performance of their duet in 1999, La India falls to her knees at Cruz's feet in a grand diva successor act of worship. Cruz immediately responds matter-of-factly with the command, "¡Levántate! ¡Levántate!" Get up, she instructs. It's time to get to our feet. Time to rise. There's work to be done. New movements to learn and to join. *Tienes que estar en control. Ten control control.*

—Deborah Paredez, *Turning the Tables*, Season 3, "Eight Women Who Invented American Popular Music," 2019 (excerpt)

ANGELIQUE KIDJO
Celia Cruz gave me that strength

In 2019, Afro-pop legend Angelique Kidjo released the tribute album *Celia* and talked to NPR about Celia Cruz's influence on her work and life.

" I never wanted to be Celia. I wanted to give back what Celia gave me— the strength for me to be a woman in the music business. She gave me that strength. She gave me the endless possibility that what we women decide to do, we can do. We're still talking about the #MeToo movement today, we're talking about women's rights, we're talking about women's empowerment. We're our own worst enemy, because we're always doubting of our capacity, our possibilities, our challenges, and our skills. Men don't question twice when you give them a high position; they embrace it and take it. We're still in this position because we have been raised like that, to be subdued, to be wise, to be the one that cares, but never to think about ourselves, to be at the forefront of any decision, of any managerial position, or just to lead the world. We're always doubting our own power. And Celia has said to me, by going onstage and saying '*azucar*,' by the way she dresses, everything about Celia is self-determination and self-affirmation. You can be whoever you want to be. You just have to have the courage to embrace yourself. "

—*Alt.Latino* with Felix Contreras, 2019

Gaga: Bringing Vulnerability and Self-Care into the Modern Pop Universe

Throughout her career, Lady Gaga has carried herself like a supernatural being, building her performance persona on elaborate choreography and staging that feels like a fantasy world. Offstage, she's known for carrying herself like an otherworldly creature, one fond of wearing out-of-this-galaxy outfits and impractical footwear. She drapes herself in the accoutrements of a pop star, exuding larger-than-life glamour and effortless confidence.

But Gaga has also led the way in bringing vulnerability and self-care into the modern pop universe: shunning the spotlight when she needs to focus on her health and talking openly about living with a disability. Around the release of the 2017 documentary *Gaga: Five Foot Two*, she revealed on Twitter that she lives with fibromyalgia, a chronic health condition that causes muscle and joint pain as well as symptoms like fatigue and even brain fog. She also canceled European tour dates while she worked on her health.

These revelations loom large in *Gaga: Five Foot Two*. In one of the film's most intimate moments, the camera pans to Gaga lying on a couch in her apartment, a blanket wrapped around her, as she's sobbing from what she describes as intense pain on the right side of her body. Clearly in agony, she expresses empathy for people who may still be trying to figure out their chronic pain, and gratitude that she can afford help to navigate her health challenges.

But even this privilege doesn't protect her from mental anguish. As a team of people work together to try to assuage her pain, she wails, "Do I look pathetic?" and covers her face with her hands: "I'm so embarrassed." From there, she starts spiraling, talking about the potential physical impact of childbirth on her body and what might happen to her hips. "I'm not afraid of those things, like getting pregnant and becoming older with my fans," she says. "I'm excited. I want to become an old rock star lady."

This declaration shouldn't be radical. But Gaga self-identifying as a rock star *and* as someone with a disability subverts deeply held societal biases. In general, the description of rock stardom (or pop stardom, for that matter) rarely includes disability; instead, the terms are synonymous with superhuman performances and inherently ableist job requirements. Rock and pop icons are expected to be in pristine physical and mental shape, possessing enough stamina to execute marathon-length shows night after night perfectly. Aging is no excuse, and the standards are impossibly high: when Beyoncé didn't appear to be dancing as much as usual on the opening night of her 2023 Renaissance Tour, many blamed a foot injury—an unfounded rumor—instead of calling it a deliberate aesthetic choice.

However, Gaga has pointedly and consistently incorporated disability references into her art. In the video for 2009's "Paparazzi," Gaga portrays a successful starlet who is tossed off a balcony by her lover. Cue to newspapers with inflammatory headlines ("Lady Gaga Is Over," "Lady No More Gaga") and her exiting a limo to a red carpet and a waiting wheelchair. At first, she seems to lean in to the trope that disability equals helplessness, as she's carried to the chair by other people and holds her body very still.

But Gaga soon upends stereotypes: sporting first a red jewel–encrusted neck brace, she then strips down into gold metallic lingerie with a matching helmet, neck choker, and arm sleeve. Looking sleek and robotic, like her fall transformed her into a bionic being, she grips crutches, stands up, and twists into some contorted dance moves. The cynical take is that Gaga's embracing inspiration porn, the idea that able-bodied people lionize and find motivation in disabled people's lives and triumphs; the richer interpretation is that she's reclaiming the invasiveness of paparazzi photographers and demanding that people look at her disabled body.

The latter scenario seems more likely given Gaga's subsequent advocacy for disability. The lyrics to the 2011 LGBTQIA+ anthem "Born This Way" are intersectional: she specifically encourages anyone living with disabilities who has been mocked or alienated to brush off criticism and feel proud of who they are. Her visual embrace of disability also became more nuanced and striking. During a performance that same year in Sydney, Australia, Gaga also assumed her mermaid persona Yüyi and performed the power ballad "You and I" onstage sitting in a wheelchair.

Disability activists and organizations criticized her Australian performance amid accusations of appropriation, with Jesse Billauer, founder of the Life Rolls On foundation, saying, "I invite [Gaga] to learn more about the 5.6 million Americans who live with paralysis. They, like me, unfortunately, don't use a wheelchair for shock value." At the time—before Gaga revealed her fibromyalgia diagnosis—such a critique felt valid and even warranted. Disability isn't just a fashion choice or an outfit to take off at the end of the day.

Gaga's performance did have precedence, however: decades before, Bette Midler created and performed as the boisterous mermaid character Delores De Lago, who spun around onstage in an electric wheelchair doing choreographed dances. (Memorably, a 1983 performance found her joined by fellow chair-using mermaids dubbed the De Lago sisters for a raucous cover of Gloria Gaynor's "I Will Survive.") Midler wasn't thrilled with Gaga's homage, although Gaga pleaded ignorance to knowing about Bette's creation.

In a case of life imitating art, paparazzi snapped Gaga in two separate wheelchairs after she had hip surgery in 2013. The first chair, which was custom-designed for her by Ken Borochov, founder of the high-end jewelry and headpiece brand Mordekai, boasted luxe padding and 24K-gold-plated spokes and a frame. The other chair featured fabric printed with Louis Vuitton's trademark logo. These photos dominated the tabloids, making mobility devices into couture fashion and daring people who are uncomfortable being confronted with disability to recalibrate their responses.

Disability visibility within the music world continues to increase. Linda Ronstadt, who retired from singing because of progressive supranuclear palsy, has continued to make documentaries and tell her life story in other ways. Years after a 2015 brain aneurysm, Joni Mitchell returned to the stage, cane in tow, to reinterpret her rich catalog once again. Actress and musician Selena Gomez has been frank about having a kidney transplant owing to complications from lupus. Artists and disability activists such as Gaelynn Lea and Lachi have been advocating for accessibility while carving out unique niches within music.

Yet not every artist living with a disability can have the show go on; for example, Céline Dion had to step away from the stage in 2022 because of the rare condition stiff-person syndrome. In the wake of her diagnosis, Gaga herself has run into skepticism. "I get so irritated with people who don't believe fibromyalgia is real," she told *Vogue* in 2018. "For me, and I think for many others, it's really a cyclone of anxiety, depression, PTSD, trauma, and panic disorder, all of which sends the nervous system into overdrive, and then you have nerve pain as a result. People need to be more compassionate. Chronic pain is no joke. And it's every day waking up not knowing how you're going to feel."

That lack of understanding cropped up again in mid-June 2023, when Gaga shared a sponsored Instagram post with the migraine medication Nurtec ODT. On the medication's website, she shared a long testimonial detailing her decades-long history with debilitating migraine and how Nurtec helped her. The partnership did not land well with a portion of Gaga's fan base: instead of expressing sympathy, many instead wondered why she hadn't yet released a video of her Chromatica Ball tour.

The vehement response was disheartening. Seemingly in response, Gaga shared a lengthy note on Instagram a few days later explaining what she had been up to offline, which did include prepping a film. The interactions didn't just illustrate the toxic side of fan culture, and the weighty expectations placed upon pop icons, but also how even being famous doesn't insulate people from a lack of understanding about disability.

In another scene from *Gaga: Five Foot Two*, Gaga visits a doctor to discuss her chronic pain and devise a treatment plan. As the cameras roll, she receives trigger point injections in her back while getting her makeup done and lamenting the fact that her 2016 album *Joanne* has leaked online, disrupting the promo cycle. The juxtaposition is striking—even as doctors are working, she's working even harder.

—Annie Zaleski, *Turning the Tables* contributor

LIZZO:
But are you only saying that because I'm fat?

Lizzo

Terry Gross: Sometimes when I see somebody who's nude or who's half-nude, largely nude on their album cover or in a photo and it's a woman—it sometimes bothers me 'cause I think like, oh, are you making yourself into a sex object for men? When you're doing it on your album cover, I think it's a really bold statement, and it's a statement for women. Because you are trying to break the mold of what beautiful is.

Lizzo: Yeah, but are you only saying that because I'm fat? You know what I'm saying? Because I feel like if I were a thin woman, maybe that wouldn't be the case. I feel like women who are smaller aren't really given the opportunities to be body-positive or role models either because we've been conditioned to believe that women are using their bodies for the male gaze. And I think if I were slimmer, I don't think people would look to me with the same type of like, oh, wow, she's so brave, she's doing this and representing everyone—that they would—you know I'm saying?—because I'm big.

—*Fresh Air* with Terry Gross, 2019

106

LORETTA LYNN
I've shocked a lot of people

66 Like I've said, I've shocked a lot of people about the things that I've recorded like 'The Pill' and 'One's On the Way' and different things. But I went to radio stations, and I'd say, 'Hey, is there any women in here?' And they'd say, 'Yeah.' I said, 'I bet you five bucks they're on the pill, too.' I was the only one that didn't take the pill and I didn't have to have it. My old man took care of that a long time ago. 99

—*All Things Considered* with Melissa Block, 2004

Megan Thee Stallion, "Simon Says"

Birthed in New Orleans, twerking is fundamental to Southern hip-hop culture—
a physical expression of sexual freedom and a way for Black women to embrace
the agency that's been stripped away due to centuries of marginalization.
In theory, it's a visual representation of a liberated Black woman in motion.
In practice, it's Megan Thee Stallion's commanding:

Simon says put your hands on your hips, huh
Simon says put your hands on your knees, ayy
Simon says put your hands on your feet, ayy
Simon says bust it open like a freak, ayy.

Adored and objectified for her "stallion" frame—a Southern euphemism for
tall and fine Black women with ass—the Houston rapper collaborated with
Juicy J, one of the region's twerk anthem architects, for "Simon Says." Megan's
lyrical style is an addition to an evolving body of hip-hop feminism in unison
with lineages that stretch back to the likes of Diamond, Eve, and Trina, whose
musical contributions implicitly address misogynoir in hip hop. She exists
among a current generation of Black women rappers who have become dominant
forces in contemporary hip-hop culture and will shape the genre's evolution.

"Simon Says" represents the transformation of women's bodies as subject to women's bodies as speakers unto themselves. The old ways are dead. Let them be reborn in the image of a twerking Black woman from the South.

—Taylor Crumpton, NPR Music's
The South Got Something to Say:
A Celebration of Southern Rap, 2020

MERCEDES SOSA
Proud of my heritage

Mercedes Sosa is a Grammy-winning Argentine folk superstar.

" The more I live and travel, the more I feel I've come to appreciate my face and my Indian features. They have allowed me to open up to all sorts of audiences and I think to communicate and change people. I'm proud of my heritage and my connection to an ancient America and to a new America. "

—*Morning Edition* with Elisabeth Perez-Luna, 1991

Whether you're plugged into a stack of amps, sweating in the front row (or lurking in back), or even behind the scenes putting it all together, the energy of a live show can both shake up the world and build a new one. There's no way to edit or do another take, and sometimes, in the high-wire act of live performance, familiar songs take on new meaning.

LIVE

PATTI SMITH
I feel like a real human

❝ The thing that performance has done to me is you're dealing with the moment, you know, because that's it. You don't get no second chance when you're on a stage. That's it. If you're daydreaming and you're not thinking about it or you can't get into it, you don't get off. Most of the thing I like about being onstage is I'm right there with everybody. If I'm doing bad, I'm experiencing the same pain as they are. It's not a shell. Most of my life I've been sort of like, my soul or my consciousness is hovering over me like a little spaceship. And there's this shell, this body. And it's like with performing, I feel really integrated. I feel like a real merging of this part of me that wants to express myself artistically or re-create nature, whatever it is with my body, you know, it's all one. I'm really grateful. Rock and roll, and being a performer in rock and roll, has really solidified me as a person. Everything is better. I feel when I love somebody, I love them for real. Everything feels more real. It's like I feel like a real human. ❞

—NPR's *Voices in the Wind* with Bob Malesky, 1976

113

Patti Smith

The Pretenders:
"The Reason
We're Here Is to
Take Care of Each Other"

Or is it? It was fair to ponder whether this formulation from the Pretenders' 1981 "Message of Love" entered into the minds of the promoters of 1983's US Festival, which took place in late May at the sweltering venue Apple cofounder Steve Wozniak had carved out of property adjacent to the 16 and the 216 in sweltering San Bernardino, California. Wozniak's stated goal for the festival was to promote the relationship between technology and rock 'n' roll, which is sort of like saying your goal is to promote the relationship between a starving lion and a lazy gazelle. Oh, they made a relationship alright.

In both years the concert took place—1982 and 1983—temperatures soared into the 90s, which, combined with traffic fumes and overall poor air quality, made for a modified respiratory hell. And yet, seduced by the incredible array of talent booked at exorbitant rates, the two US Festivals attracted more than a million attendees and still managed to lose twenty-three million dollars. Already the tech sector was exhibiting its uncanny capacity to make the music industry unprofitable.

In 1983 Chrissie Hynde and the Pretenders are big stars, but everyone is on this overstuffed bill. Monday's lineup includes—and this is a *Monday*—Los Lobos, Joe Walsh, Stevie Nicks, and David Bowie as headliner. The Pretenders are on well before sunset, and afternoon slots at summer festivals are notoriously awful, a microwave-baked dead zone of sun-addled zombies, stretching ten thousand rows back. If you start them up, they'll probably eat you. Oh and what else? They'll be following up a young and feral Irish group named U2. What fresh hell is this?

Here is how dressed-in-white Chrissie Hynde handles it, alongside her dressed-in-white band mates: sheer molten force. Towering Marshall stacks. Ten great songs of such overpowering resonance and character that it would fill a nuclear blast crater with a foreboding, sonorous quality. The opening earthquake rumble of "My City Was Gone," thrilling audiences long before it became ubiquitously recognizable as the theme from Rush Limbaugh's toxic drive-time AM radio show. The mercury danger of a song which flagrantly doubts that America, in the weird warm bath of its Morning in America glow, has the remotest idea of what it's actually doing.

The band behind her is tremendous. But is the band behind her the Pretenders or pretenders? The irony of the band's name took on new resonances in the face of so much loss. Hynde, the gifted Ohio-transplant to London, working in McLaren and Westwood's infamous SEX shop on King's Road, had shuffled through potential band mates including Mick Jones from the Clash and Steve Jones from the Sex Pistols. And then she found the perfect band. And then she made the perfect record.

The Pretenders' self-titled debut album (1980) introduced an entirely novel female character into the established fabric of rock music. Hynde is rash, vulgar, romantic, sensitive, and quick to offense. As a singer and songwriter, she is immensely talented of course, the equal of the heady London cohort she was then spending time with, but her insights and her anger vibrate on a different and distinctly feminine frequency.

The album is an instant classic. And then everyone starts dying. First the genius lead guitar player James Honeyman-Scott by cocaine toxicity, and then bassist Pete Farndon from a heroin overdose. She remakes the band, and the band never stops being great. Something they share with AC/DC and the Rolling Stones. The barely tolerable burden of sole survivors. Each new iteration is a monument to a high-functioning individual managing a survivor's guilt too steep and acute and unscalable to be reckoned with. The miraculous *Learning to Crawl* (1984) is a masterpiece that outstrips the debut. Some of the studio players can stick around, and some have other gigs.

So the new backing group at the US Festival are strongmen for hire. They are hard, physical specimens playing an aggressive style. A strange thing about playing in the rotating cast of the Pretenders is that you *must* think about the band name, it's in the job description. Hynde takes painstaking time to introduce them. They are: on drums, Martin Chambers; on bass, Malcolm Foster; on keyboards, Chris Thomas (the great producer!); on guitar, Robbie McIntosh. They are beautiful and totally anonymous. It may be the finest live group Chrissie Hynde has ever convened. Every terrible loss, an addition by subtraction. Every waking nightmare, an unwanted opportunity.

This is Chrissie Hynde, who won't be denied. When she launches into a triumphal "Brass in Pocket," she has somehow accomplished both seduction and transcendence. The teenage wasteland audience goes insane, as Hynde dutifully manifests the scarlet outlaw of her most famous song. She is Johnny Cash, dressed in white. A set-closing rip-through on the gold-digging standard "Money" intended to tweak the festival organizers for their greed just ends up predicting the next forty years of American life. Her city was gone. She was never pretending.

—Elizabeth Nelson, musician, *Turning the Tables* contributor

SLEATER-KINNEY'S JANET WEISS
The thrill of playing live

"As a drummer, I think it's the best place to be heard. A practice space is just brutal for the people who have to listen to the drummer. The studio can be very difficult—with headphones, and you're sort of trying to make things sound a certain way and it's very challenging. But live, where there is air and there is energy from the crowd, I think that energy can elevate what I do to a new level. I'm sort of re-creating that in my mind, I think, when I play on a record or when I play at practice. In the right situation onstage, I feel more like a superhero than any other time in my life. "

—*Morning Edition* with Leah Scarpelli, 2015

48. ROCKS THE HOUSE
Etta James (ARGO, 1963)

On September 27 and 28, 1963, Etta James howled her way through juke-joint blues, soul, and R&B numbers at the New Era Club in Nashville. These performances comprise her first live album, *Rocks the House*, released the following year. Hailed as one of the greatest live blues records ever captured, *Rocks the House* showcases an equally magnetizing but different side of James, whose strength as a balladeer was already popularized on stunning studio tracks like "A Sunday Kind of Love" and "At Last." Onstage at the New Era Club, which James handpicked specifically for these recordings, the twenty-five-year-old attacks each song with the perfect storm of fire and grit. From the crowd's beckoning on the opener "Something's Got a Hold on Me" to the call and response on the raucous "What'd I Say," James's performance is a testament to the power of the human voice. With a backing band led by guitarist David T. Walker, she unabashedly delivers the blues and embodies soul in its rawest form. After all, she knew what it meant to experience the messier parts of life and to come out on the other side. (The ACE bandage covering her wrist on the album's cover was meant to hide the track marks from her heroin usage—an addiction that would interrupt her career off and on throughout the years.) With her captivating rasp and sass, Miss Peaches got a hold on the world and never let go.

—Desiré Moses, WNRN, *Turning the Tables*,
"The 150 Greatest Albums Made by Women," 2017

Etta James

ETTA JAMES:
I want to sing real stuff

On *Fresh Air* with Terry Gross, blues screamer Etta James talks about pop vocalist Georgia Gibbs's cover of her "The Wallflower," also known as "Roll with Me, Henry"—"Roll" as in the already euphemistic term for sex that makes up half of "rock and roll."

Etta James: Yeah, well, you know, during those days, you weren't allowed to say "roll." Because roll was like a vulgar, vulgar word. You know what I mean? Think about it—they would probably have burnt Prince at the stake. But you couldn't say "roll," so they banned my record from the air. And what happened? What we had to do was sell it underground. And not only that, change the title to "Wallflower." And then when Georgia Gibbs did it, she just made it "Dance with Me, Henry," so that all the kids could go buy it and take it home and listen to it, because their parents weren't gonna go for no "roll." Are you kidding? Roll with me. How do you roll with somebody?

NPR: Do you think there's a difference between what a song means to you now and what it meant back then, or how you sing it now and how you sang it then?

Etta James: I really understand, you know what I mean? I understand what I'm singing about, you know. Songs that I get, any song that I decide to sing or a song that someone sends to me or recommends, I like to be able to relate to that song, not just have a song there that talks about "come fly me to the moon, let me dangle on the stars." That's not my cup of tea. That's not real. I want to sing real stuff. I want to know what I'm saying. . . . And I think that's what I can do now. I think that's what I definitely do. Matter of fact, I know I do.

—*Fresh Air* with Terry Gross, 1994

119

Looking Back at Whitney Houston's 1991 National Anthem

For its thirtieth anniversary in 2021, critic Danyel Smith discussed Whitney Houston's 1991 Super Bowl national anthem performance, which took place in the early days of the first Gulf War.

———————

I couldn't believe when I saw it. I was like, that's what she wore? Is this a rehearsal? There's a lot of things that Whitney Houston was known for in her career, but showing up to stuff in a sweatsuit and a zip-up jacket is not among them. And she did in fact look like she might be going to choir rehearsal at her church in Newark. But that was the energy that was needed. Because honestly, declaring war is a kind of insanity that it was very difficult for me to wrap my head around, but I do know this is not the kind of thing that you need to celebrate with diamonds and furs and in heels, and it seems very much like that outfit that she wore was almost out of respect for the fact that a lot of people were pulling on uniforms and going to put their lives on the line. And she sang it like that.

It's a massive deal for a Black woman to be as visible as that. It wasn't like she was just chosen, because oh, my God, there's this Black woman and she has an amazing voice. When you're the kind of person who has seven consecutive No. 1 pop hits—you have to realize when you have a No. 1 pop hit, that means everybody pretty much knows who you are in the United States of America. So then you're going to times that by seven consecutive. She was selling millions and millions of records. She was never, never not on the radio. Man, believe me, the National Football League knew that they were hiring a person who had the experience of moving masses of people.

She's such a picture in that moment of preparation and grace. My favorite part of her performance . . . when she sings the word "free," right, you have to go up really high for that note, and so many people falter at that space. They shorten it. It kind of goes thin at the top of their voices, where she not only sings it strong and big and rich and lush all the way through it, she's building up to the high note. But then just to let you know how dope she is, she adds like a two- or three-note flourish.

Whitney Houston

That was a moment when she didn't care if everybody could sing along with her. That was the moment when she's like, I'm giving y'all me. Right here. It just reminds me, as I walk through life—yes, we're all here to be in service to each other for a better world. Right? That's our best-case scenario on this planet Earth. But every once in a while you have to remind people who you are. And that's when she did it.

—Danyel Smith, NPR's *It's Been a Minute*, 2021 (excerpt)

Janis Joplin: Holes in Her Soul

Janis Joplin
by Nicole Rifkin

Janis Joplin burst into this world like a flaming comet. She burned brightly, felt deeply, and disappeared in a flash, but the mark she left on music blazed a trail like a Western pioneer. The lawless rebel, the misunderstood schoolgirl, a pariah and a protestor with progressive ideals and a love for Black music, she was rock and roll's own version of Calamity Jane. Janis had a God-given undeniable talent for conveying pure electricity on the stage. She was a visionary of live performance and had the unique ability to express the raw emotion and elusive pain of the human experience through her art.

To me, Janis is not only a fearless portrait of what a feminist could and should look like, but should be hailed as an early queer icon. She was fluid in her sexuality in a time when that wasn't really accepted. She was a singular force; so powerful and so dangerous, she almost seemed supernatural. She was a mystic, a romantic, and a hazard to herself and others, but she was also fragile and vulnerable in a time when that wasn't considered a "superpower."

In her youth, she was raised on a steady diet of Beat poetry, Bessie Smith, and Chuck Berry as she cruised from town to town late at night, drinking beers and smoking cigarettes—"Doin' the Triangle" driving between Port Arthur, Beaumont, and Lake Orange. She stood up for equal rights and pushed for desegregation in a time and place like Beaumont, when that simply wasn't done. When she heard Elvis's version of "Hound Dog," she went and dug up the original by Big Mama Thornton and proclaimed it better.

By the time I was born, Janis was already dead and probably off in another galaxy somewhere far away. But the tales of her talent and her fatalist myth and the weight of her heavy and beautiful soul are all twisted up in cosmic blues, and suspended in time through the grace of what she left us through her records.

I was in my early twenties when I walked into Tower Records and rented a copy of D. A. Pennebaker's documentary on the Monterey Pop Festival. I had just moved to Nashville to pursue a career as a musician, and in just five minutes and forty-six seconds, my entire musical world was flipped upside down. I've never had such a visceral reaction to watching a live performance by a musician. As I sat there watching Janis perform Big Mama Thornton's "Ball 'n' Chain," I started bawling my fucking eyes out. I simply couldn't control myself, it was such a mix of emotions: excitement, joy, pain, sorrow, and awe. I imagined it was like when people weep while watching an opera. I was moved. I was also angry. Angry I couldn't be alive at the same time as Janis because I wanted to know her. Why did she have to die so young? I was angry because I simply wanted to *be* her and I knew I couldn't. I had heard Janis's songs my entire life and I'd listened to some of her albums before, but this was one of the first times I truly saw her perform.

"Oh tell me why?" She drags this line out and reaches up into the strength of her high-chest voice. Her delivery is bold and her voice is on the edge of breaking, until she finally screams with such conviction and fearlessness—*"Why has everything gone wroooooong?"* I knew, in that moment, I never believed the words someone sang more than the way Janis just did. That performance was earth-shattering to me in the best way. I could feel the very fiber of her being as she stood there with her eyes closed, shaking like a preacher in a pulpit. Janis became my idol in that moment—along with all of the self-destructive behavior that came with it.

I studied her style. I studied her delivery, the way she moved, the way she breathed, the way she screamed, the way she exhumed the holes in her soul and transformed it back into rock and roll. I studied her facial expressions, her unkempt hair and her jewelry—her heavy beads and bracelets and witchy rings. I studied her clothes—or the lack thereof. She wore no bra, and that was obvious through her sheer, knitted gold pantsuit. As she stood in the sun, nipples showing and arms raised outstretched like a topless singer in the front of the choir of lost, stoned flower children, she looked as close as it gets to being free.

I went back to Tower Records and checked out anything else I could find with her in it. I followed the red and fuchsia trail of her feathered boa for five days in the summer of 1970 as she rode the "Festival Express" through the Canadian night on a private train. There she was, just three months before her death, alive as can be on film, riding on the club cars full of musicians who were drinking, partying, and playing with wild abandon. I pored over the free-flowing stream of consciousness monologue in the middle of a ripping rendition of "Cry Baby," where she talks about all the dudes in her life always "wandering off to find themselves in Africa or New York City or Casablanca or somewhere like that." The footage gave me chills and brilliantly captures one of my favorite versions of Janis in all her energetic, enigmatic, self-effacing glory.

I often wonder what albums we would have been gifted from Ms. Joplin had she gotten to live out the days that were robbed from her. I speculate that she would have bestowed on us an Appalachian bluegrass album—or perhaps she left behind some unmined country gold from her sometimes-buried Texas roots. The simple feel of her original songs "Mercedes Benz" and the brilliant "What Good Can Drinkin' Do" could easily be classified in that country-funk vein, or that swampy, Southern jug band sound, with a Leon Russell or Willie Nelson swagger to them. I used to cover the latter, and it's such a great mix of Texas swing and Bessie Smith barroom boogie. The words cut like a knife:

My man he left me, child, he left me here
Yeah, my good man left me, went away and left me here
Lord, I'm feelin' lowdown, just give me another glass of beer

I get a sad, sinking feeling when I hear the lo-fi demo of her on acoustic guitar singing her ex-lover Kris Kristofferson's "Sunday Morning Coming Down," thinking about the interpretations and incarnations of songs and entire albums we missed from Janis in her thirties and beyond. How incredible it would have been to hear both her singing *and* her writing voice grow and age, to find even more depth and more meaning.

Honestly, when I was very young, in my early twenties, I longed for the kind of tragedy that would give me the depth that Janis Joplin had. I too lived in a very reckless manner, sometimes barreling through life a little carelessly, following Janis's lead even though I knew where it ended. I know what it's like to ride a steam engine off the track, flirting with death because it's what musicians do to further legitimize their pain and spin a tall tale. Something about it was both thrilling and terrifying. I look at Janis a bit like a cross between a patron saint and a cautionary tale. I can imagine very easily how Janis felt tethered to her bad girl image, because for a very long time, I was completely lost in living out mine. I began drinking at the age of twelve and fell into a fable I created of myself. I was this wild, wounded, and wasted party girl. My career was in the toilet, and I had lost a child, and I was in a lot of pain. If I hadn't been numbing myself with music and men and cocaine and booze, I might not have made it out alive either. Maybe it was fate, or maybe it was luck.

Janis was so good at spinning the story for the press and making herself into almost a caricature. A character in the film *The Man Who Shot Liberty Valance* says the famous line, "When the legend becomes fact, print the legend." It's easy to let your persona become you. But I believe if Janis would have found the tools to help her, she would have been able to lean in to her true self and shed the weight of carrying around her fame and her outlaw image and her name. She was making an attempt at doing just that during the making of her final album, with the endearing new moniker "Pearl." We know from her diary entries and letters home that were so beautifully woven into Holly George-Warren's brilliant book *Janis: Her Life and Music* that she was trying to take time off the road to be domestic and care for herself. She wanted to be happy and healthy and take walks in the woods and become a wife and a mother. She was even taking long, extended breaks from the alcohol and the drugs, but she had little support. I believe those things could have happened for her, and maybe they are in some alternate reality. Janis Joplin lives outside of space and time, because her voice still echoes everywhere, ahead of her time.

Janis was fearless and made a lot of tough choices, but she is not a victim. We are the victims because she isn't around to share her art. I can look back now and see how easy it would have been for me to end up where Janis did. But truly, Janis went out on top, and that's where she belonged. What she accomplished in her sweet, short life is nothing short of a miracle. It's hard not to daydream about where the muse would have taken her next. Like the heat of a meteor that translates into light and leaves a trail behind it, Janis's soul did, too. What she left in her wake was like a faded constellation, and I feel like I've been trying to decode it my entire life. Janis is one of those rare and multidimensional cosmic artists who shine brighter than a solar eclipse. You can't look directly at them, or you'll burst into flames.

—Margo Price, musician, *Turning the Tables* contributor

SHERYL CROW:
Just be in the room with people

NPR: I think one of the things live that's really powerful about what you do is, you're such a storyteller. And somehow when you bring your songs live to an audience . . . you have to get that story into the heart of your audience. . . . How do you do that as a performer? Because you have choices, you have the vocal skill to go for the big note. You could dance and flash, but you're sharing the story. How do you do it?

Sheryl Crow: Flashy, I'll never do. Well, you know, I always welcome the opportunity to just be in the room with people. And I will say things changed for me after I had breast cancer, and I wanted all the lights on all the time, I wanted to look at everybody, I wanted to have that connection. . . . And now I have to keep breathing. . . . It grieves me that it's almost impossible now, particularly for young people, to just *be*, to be quiet and just to be in the room together and absorbing each other's energy and being comfortable with being in their bodies, you know, in a place and experiencing something collectively. So I don't care if it's five people, I mean, I'm happy to just sing to you, if you don't mind. And if it's ten thousand or a hundred thousand, I mean, to me, it's all the same. Because I can always see people and feel something, you know, and isn't that—I mean, that's what life is, it's feeling and it's breathing.

—NPR's Tiny Desk Fest with Ann Powers, 2019

126

HOW WOMEN MADE MUSIC

Are You Loving This As Much As I Am?

Jill Sternheimer, the cofounder of *Turning the Tables*, has worked in music since she was sixteen: at radio stations, box offices, record labels, festivals, and most recently as director of public programming for Lincoln Center Out of Doors, where she booked three concerts celebrating *Turning the Tables'* first three seasons in 2017, 2018, and 2019. Here are five of her favorite live music moments.

———————

She's Got the Power: A Girl Group Extravaganza, Lincoln Center Out of Doors, 2011

The instantly recognizable drumbeat echoed out, and the audience knew what was coming as Ronnie Spector sang the first lines of "Be My Baby," the girl group national anthem. Her perfect, raspy Noo Yawk voice led a choir of her contemporaries: Lesley Gore, LaLa Brooks, and members of the Cookies, the Chantels, and the Jaynetts, plus rock and roll veterans she had inspired from the E Street Band, Patti Smith Group, and Yo La Tengo. "Be My Baby" is a song you crank loud if it comes on the car radio, and we were hearing it live with both the audience and stage full of musicians all in heavenly bliss joining in.

If a stranger had walked by, they would have seen a stage full of grandmothers and very grown-up musicians, but if they closed their eyes, it was a group of teenage souls singing, pleading, swaying, and praying "Say you'll be my darling." It was the indescribable magic that is made only when audience and band come together to worship the songs that are in our collective DNA.

NPR Music's *Turning the Tables*, Lincoln Center, 2017

Ann Powers and I turned around and Roberta Flack, a gorgeous vision in sequins, was being wheeled to the piano next to her dear friend, and icon in her own right, Valerie Simpson. We had had no idea whether Ms. Flack, who was recovering from a stroke, was going to feel up to coming onstage. All we could have was an "If you build it, she will come" mentality, and leave the rest up to the universe. Not a scenario a concert producer ever wants to be in. But every once in a while, we take a wild chance and wait for the miracle.

Simpson looked at Flack, nodded, and hit the first notes on the piano. By the third line Flack's rich, sultry voice was in the center of the song, battle-scarred, but unmistakable. The clearly moved audience kept silently on their feet, as if to lend their energy in solidarity.

Ann and I stood on the side of the stage weeping for joy. It felt like we had gotten to give a truly special thank-you for a brilliant career.

Madonna, the Virgin Tour, Cleveland, 1985

When I was sixteen, I got my first job as a gofer with the big concert promoter in Cleveland. My entrance to the glamorous world of live concert production was to blow up hundreds of balloons that said "Dreams Come True," to fall from the ceiling into the audience at the end of Madonna's show. But my labor was part of the event everyone was dying to be at, and I couldn't be more proud or excited.

When Madonna changed into her wedding dress for the finale, thousands were watching her, mouths agape, taking in every thrust and roll around the stage. When every teen heart in the auditorium was open, six thousand balloons fell from the ceiling. Dreams Come True—it sure was one of the first days mine started to.

Laura Nyro, Newport Folk Festival, 1989

Sun in my face, boats in the harbor behind me, I was on hallowed ground—the Newport Folk Festival—for the first time in my life. As soon as the woman at the electric piano opened her mouth, I was riveted. I'd learned from my books and liner notes that Laura Nyro had written many of the hit songs that rang out in the backseat of our family station wagon, recorded by acts like the 5th Dimension and Barbra Streisand. But I had never seen her or heard her own renditions of the famous songs she wrote. I was completely swept up! I realized that day that a huge part of popular music revolved around the axis of a solo woman at the piano. I looked at the stranger next to me in her hippie dress and smiled, thinking, hey, are you as excited as me to be here? Are you going to go to a record store tomorrow and buy a Laura Nyro record? Are you going to put a song of hers on the next mixtape you make for your best friend? Are you loving sitting here in the grass on your blanket as much as I am?

Hurray for the Riff Raff, New Orleans Jazz and Heritage Festival, 2012

Alynda Lee Segarra played a few covers, like Irma Thomas's classic "Time Is On My Side," as a hometown nod. But it was her original songs that really slayed me. When she sang "There must be somewhere in this whole world," the opening line of "St. Roch Blues," she hushed the New Orleans party crowd down as she cracked all of our hearts open with sad tales of violence in that beloved city. When the song got to the line "Ooh, I keep on crying," it was a collective moment of sorrow and mourning for the dead. There's something that changes you at a cellular level when you're in a crowd singing an anthem together. In these fraught political times, it feels so good and safe to be among others also being transformed.

—Jill Sternheimer, *Turning the Tables* cofounder

129

Fashion, Statement: The Legacy of Marian Anderson's Fur Coat

As one of the twentieth century's most venerated vocalists, Marian Anderson performed in stately concert halls and grand opera houses around the globe. But the site of her best-remembered concert was a wooden platform erected on the steps of the Lincoln Memorial. On April 9, 1939—a chilly Easter Sunday afternoon—Anderson performed there, after she was barred from singing at Washington, DC, venues that enforced "whites-only" policies. The concert was carried live by NBC radio, so that far-flung listeners could tune in to hear Anderson's majestic contralto in a program that ranged from "America" to Schubert's "Ave Maria" to African American spirituals.

Although many activists had worked to secure the Mall for Anderson's concert, the most iconic images of the day show her as a solitary figure, bravely lifting her voice on behalf of her fellow Americans. In these images, Anderson stands before a hedge of microphones, the white marble colossus of a seated Abraham Lincoln rising up behind her. The viewer's eye is drawn to the visual parallels between Anderson and the Great Emancipator, both of whom look out upon the crowd. Even the styling of their attire is similar. Lincoln is portrayed in an unbuttoned frock coat, while Anderson wears a full-length mink opened to reveal an embellished jacket and matching skirt.

Anderson's fur coat has always drawn me to this image. The weather was chilly that April afternoon—*The Washington Post* put the high temperature of the day at 47 degrees—so it was hardly unreasonable for her to wear mink to stay warm for her performance. And it was Easter Sunday, an occasion for women and men of all stations to dress up and be seen in their festive attire. A society columnist for the Baltimore *Afro-American* even noted that "Marian's minks" set the tone for holiday parades that saw many women wearing fur toques instead of spring bonnets.

And yet even as it might have served practical purposes, Anderson's mink was also richly symbolic. At a moment when she was singing in the national commons, Anderson chose to dress in a way that emphasized her regality as an internationally renowned artist. The coat was also a tangible reminder of the conditions that had caused organizers to seek an outdoor venue for Anderson in the first place. Addressing the audience before her performance, Secretary of the Interior Harold Ickes used the concert's outdoor setting to make a political point, declaring, "In this great auditorium under the sky, all of us are free." But his lofty words did not change the fact of racial segregation as it was practiced in the nation's capital. Nor could they change the ways that Black women experienced racism as an affront to their value and standing as women. When Anderson wore fur that day, she presented a figure of Black female beauty and elegance that would have resonated with Black audiences, especially Black women.

Anderson's coat links her to other Black female entertainers who, in the decades before consumers and manufacturers began rethinking the use of animal pelts, used fur garments to express important aspects of their public personae as Black women. Of course, fur has long been a staple of celebrity fashion, and both men and women have worn it as an expression of extravagance and indulgence. But wearing fur had particular resonance for twentieth-century Black female stars, who used fur jackets, hats, and stoles to fashion themselves as women who were worthy of respect and admiration—and sometimes even to question the class and race assumptions that defined female respectability.

Fur was also aspirational. At mid-century, it was marketed to American women as a commodity linked to middle-class marriage—as something husbands bought for their wives to display their prosperity. Anderson took a different tack, representing her many fur garments as elements of her "working uniform." "I like

131

simple, tasteful clothes," she observed in her 1956 memoir, *My Lord, What a Morning*, which devotes a full chapter to describing the seriousness with which she approached the labor of creating a pleasing visual "impression" for her audiences: "I do not go in for things that dazzle, for I am not a dazzler, and pay much more attention to my concert costumes than to my everyday clothes."

Not all Black female musicians took as practical an approach to the work of image-making as Anderson, who was known for taking an iron and even a sewing machine on tour with her. For blues singers like Bessie Smith, an extravagant image was de rigueur, whether performing under a makeshift tent or at a sophisticated urban nightclub. Smith's glittering headdresses, long strands of pearls, feathered dresses, and luxurious furs were elements of a sensuous display that affirmed working-class Black women's worth and desirability, much like the speaker of Smith's famous song "Young Woman's Blues," who boasts of being "as good as any woman."

Fur was a requisite costume of the jazz chanteuse, who was expected to project an air of glamour even as she dealt with the indignity and inconvenience of racial segregation. The histories of Black female touring jazz musicians are filled with stories of women readying themselves for performances in makeshift "dressing rooms." The jazz historian Sherrie Tucker has used the phrase "glamour as labor" to describe the efforts of female jazz instrumentalists who strived to look "fresh as a daisy" night after night despite limited access to hotels or restrooms.

Taking a public stance against Jim Crow could prove costly for such musicians, who were often subjected to police harassment. When Ella Fitzgerald challenged the segregationist seating policy of the Houston Music Hall in 1955, she and her fellow musicians Dizzy Gillespie and Illinois Jacquet were arrested on trumped-up charges of gambling. Images captured by photographers tipped off to the "sting" operation show the group at a police station, waiting to be booked and fined. Fitzgerald sits on a bench in an elegant dress and fur stole, wearing a look of profound annoyance.

Black female entertainers of later decades continued to embrace fur, injecting it with new meaning as musical expression changed. Aretha Franklin, a lover of fashion, famously used her fur coats as stage props at moments of emotional intensity. When Franklin dramatically unburdened herself of a full-length fur during her 2015 Kennedy Center tribute to Carole King, the crowd of notables in the opera house rose to its feet, as though the coat were a lever. "Watching Franklin toss her furs to the ground was a glorious sight," wrote *Washington Post* fashion critic Robin Givhan, in a posthumous appreciation of her sublime "coat drops."

For Black female musicians in the twenty-first century, fur can be particularly powerful because of the ways it has been publicly shunned. For evidence, we need look no further than Beyoncé's groundbreaking visual album *Lemonade*, the cover of which features a still photo from the video for the track "Don't Hurt Yourself." Filmed in a dank underground parking lot, the video shows the star wearing gray leggings and a crop top under a distinctive fur coat by Hood by Air, the edgy label helmed by Black designer Shayne Oliver. As she spits out the song's bitter lyrics, the fur—which hangs from a thick leather strap around her neck—sways with her as she struts and glowers at the camera.

It's an arresting image of rage ostensibly directed at the singer's philandering lover but easily extended to a nation that has long been "unfaithful" to Black women. In such a context Beyoncé's vaguely menacing, androgynous coat stylistically translates the song's warning: *Don't mess with me unless you want to get messed with*.

The pointed message of Beyoncé's fur coat—worn in an era when celebrities, working with professional stylists, understand their power as fashion arbiters—is in many ways a far cry from the integrationist message conveyed by Anderson's more decorous mink on the steps of the Lincoln Memorial. But as a fashion statement, it bears the traces of Anderson's radical challenge to the norms of her day. By standing before the massive crowd, Anderson expressed the aspirations of the nation. Wearing a coat whose ample collar gives the impression of epaulettes, Anderson steeled herself for a moment of political and social battle, using her professionalism, her voice, and her strategically diverse repertoire as her "weapon."

"What becomes a legend most?" asked the Blackglama mink advertising campaign, which, in 1970, at the height of Black Power, featured a starkly lovely portrait of the African American prima donna Leontyne Price wearing a fur coat. Anderson, then in her seventies, never got her Blackglama moment. But she was not forgotten by the Black Power generation. Writing about her in 1972, in program notes for the first festival of African American performing arts at Lincoln

Center, the producer Ellis Haizlip remembered witnessing Anderson's 1939 concert. Although in 1939 the Mall was celebrated as a symbol of American democratic values, Haizlip reminded readers that as a Black child growing up in the District of Columbia, he did not take his "ownership" of its buildings or grounds for granted. By implying that formal integration had not solved the problem of Black performing artists' "rights" to occupy prestigious stages, he insisted on the ongoing relevance of Anderson's historic concert.

While it is easy to memorialize Anderson's National Mall concert as part of a preintegrationist moment that we have happily overcome, in other words, it is more properly understood as a performance whose "vibrations" continue to resonate in the era of Black Lives Matter. Standing before the massive crowd, arrayed in a thick fur that conveyed her stature and dignity, Anderson not only sang for the day but for the future.

—Gayle Wald, *Turning the Tables*, Season 3, "Eight Women Who Invented American Popular Music," 2019 (excerpt)

I've Been Loving You Too Long

Trapped between a plea and a threat, Otis Redding's "I've Been Loving You Too Long" finds its natural habitat in the Ike & Tina Turner Revue's unhinged rendition. In a live performance, when Tina promises "I don't wanna stop now," as the script dictates, Ike interjects with a deadpan, improvised "because you're not ready to die," practically yanking any tenderness from the duet. They quickly launch into a raunchy miming of a transactional overrehearsed sex act, with Tina caressing the microphone and Ike smacking his lips like he's licking a clit. It's excessive and grotesque and turns the song's original soulful yearning into postcoital whimpering, and in 1969, it's a hit. The trance of well-decorated dysfunction, and in the case of Ike and Tina, utter malfunction, overrides its sloppiness, and we're left with forensics as music, a live confession that's part reconciliation, part renunciation, a wreck you cannot turn away from. The audience becomes invested in the suspense, part of it, anonymous enablers, forcing its performers or victims to maintain their derangements. Thus parades the cycle of spectacular eroticized violence.

The recorded version that topped the radio charts that year fascinates me for how its smooth revving is interrupted and altered by one solemn, alienated stutter Tina manages toward the end: *you-you* doubled, mirroring address, accusatory and tentative and emphatic.

Ike and Tina use this once-tender song to give one another refuge to be bitter and vindictive and pornographic aloud, to mercy fuck one another and switch roles, invisible switchblades flaring up in Ike's dire, cocaine-induced fidgeting and clenching between verses. Tina is in front, on top, Ike submissively echoing the

Tina Turner

threats we know she's a little numb to by now—we know this because her only response is to placate him by mimicking sex, pretending she doesn't hear or notice him slyly threatening her life onstage, eyes dilated, nose frozen from drugs and vengeance. Brutality so habitual it becomes soothing and familiar now has its anthem.

The camp sincerity of Ike and Tina's version of this song conceals how contrived and cyclical their rapport is becoming in private life. The subject has to become lust and the phallus. Tina has to violate herself and pretend it turns her on; otherwise, we might catch a glimpse of her mounting disgust with Ike. Shame makes her more brazen, resigned to spectacle. Victim becomes accomplice in the lie of excess; they put one another on like sad clown masks, and through this performance, reassess the swarming misery of the ballad that seemed rooted in tenderness before they mangled it and made it a caricature of their saga.

The inertia of even the most poisonous codependency has a spirit of its own and cannot be squirmed out of timidly; breaking its spell requires aggressive reimagining of the self, repossessing of the self. Ike and Tina were possessed by one another and by the spirit of their public life together, their farce. The goal is to have no experience so blatantly degrading that their version of "I've Been Loving You Too Long" arouses the same poison adrenaline they exhibit onstage together, but we've all been loving someone too long to stop now, sometimes even simply the destructive version of ourselves we bargain with and leverage to get by. When a stutter, a small, almost imperceptible break in the rhythm and change of pressure arrives like a magic talisman and we let it shrug and stumble and become a dream of a future departure from *too long*, we are Tina here, a prop in her own life always on the verge of going off script, always about to pounce into new territory and remember the self as sacred.

I've never seen a more obscene performance, mostly because you can tell that at the time each and every ridiculous or violent gesture between Ike and Tina has been normalized and codified—they thought they were fooling someone. It gets to a point where both parties lean in to it, almost viciously daring anyone to notice and do something, where both are victims of their rituals of violence and the audience can be manipulated to get as accustomed to its codes as they are.

Ike and Tina here are at the stage where it's so bad that everyone is complicit.

But Tina is waking up from her trance onstage in front of us, doubling herself—"You/you." She doesn't want to come to resent herself as much as she does her abuser, for turning everyone she loves into a helpless witness. Their display of excess is part mutual confession. How else would we find a casual death threat in the middle of a love ballad and go on gawking and swaying past it, under the spell with them?

—Harmony Holiday, Turning the Tables contributor

139

Snarl, wail, growl, shatter the glass, and bust some eardrums. If they say it's unladylike, maybe that's because it's cathartic. Let it out.

SCREAM QUEENS

The Runaways

by Margaret Flatley

72. THE RUNAWAYS
The Runaways (MERCURY, 1976)

The Runaways is the sound of a handful of untested chemicals being poured into a beaker and exploding. It's the sound of a knee-high platform boot stomping down onto the top of a guitar amp, of a gang of warriors, of defiance. It's the sound of a band too good to last—a band so sure of its chops that it *started* its record with "Cherry Bomb," the first of many hits Joan Jett would help pen in her career, and refused to back down from there. Decades of documentaries, biopics, and interviews have revealed just how much the group endured just to get into the studio and onstage, but damn if it wasn't already a chilling experience to listen to Cherie Currie wail about her "Secrets" and whisper back and forth with Jett on the album's final track, "Dead End Justice." From start to finish, *The Runaways* captures a band that tapped into the zeitgeist of its era with curiosity and passion, chugging power chords, snarls, and screams. Though it was underappreciated when it was released, it captures a moment in quintessential '70s rock.

—Andrea Swensson, Minnesota Public Radio, *Turning the Tables*,
"The 150 Greatest Albums Made by Women," 2017

143

Mallia Franklin
and the Women of
Parliament-Funkadelic

The army of Parliament-Funkadelic has sent sound shock waves to listeners, participants, and funk soldiers for more than five decades. Aside from formidable production, arranging, and musicianship, and clever lyricism, the group's key element is its signature wall of vocal power, benefiting from a blend of voices to create the blast of R&B, gospel, rock, and funk known as P-Funk. These voices included women—integral from the beginning, yet overlooked to this day.

In 1997, Parliament-Funkadelic was inducted into the Rock and Roll Hall of Fame. Out of its massive corps of contributors, sixteen members were included, like George Clinton, the genius vocalist/composer whose late-1950s doo-wop vocal group, the Parliaments, were P-Funk's original foundation. Also included was bassist Bootsy Collins, who, before becoming an integral part of the P-Funk sound and aesthetic in the 1970s, turned James Brown's funk sound upside down as an original member of the J.B.'s. And former Ohio Players member Walter "Junie" Morrison, who didn't join P-Funk until 1977, added unique direction to the group and influenced the late-1970s P-Funk sound.

Yet out of the sixteen inductees, no women were included.

This, despite the fact that Mallia Franklin and Debbie Wright sang uncredited on Parliament and Funkadelic's earliest albums going back to 1970.

This, despite Wright and Jeanette Washington being part of the original P-Funk Earth Tour, which debuted October 27, 1976, at New Orleans's Municipal

Auditorium and featured the legendary landings of the group's massive Mothership spaceship prop.

This, despite Wright and Washington also being included in publicity photos for Parliament-Funkadelic during the tour.

This, despite two women-fronted offshoot groups spun off from P-Funk, Parlet and the Brides of Funkenstein, which were signed to their own record deals.

This, despite women's voices being included on all P-Funk hits, the same hits that men's voices were inducted into the Rock Hall for.

There was a time that I, like many, took the women of P-Funk for granted. As a young college undergrad in the mid-1990s, I learned how to code HTML and built the One Nation P-Funk Page, the first interactive and graphic-based website for P-Funk fans. I corresponded with my active site users, mostly men, who ranged from new and casual fans to hardcore funkateers who could name every P-Funk member and their instruments. If someone so much as played a cowbell on a P-Funk record, the hardcore funkateer could name them. This is unless they were one of the female members. And then, they not only *could not* name, cite, identify, or include them, but *would not* make the effort to do so.

My mission to learn more and, hence, teach more about P-Funk's women artists started then. It led me to Mallia Franklin.

The first and only time I saw Franklin perform was in 1996 at a House of Blues Atlanta concert of George Clinton & the P-Funk All-Stars. She was sitting in with them as a special guest that night. Clinton introduced her, and she wailed repeatedly, powerfully, "Wait a miiiiiiiinute!" And then started rapping about being the "Queen of Funk." And then started panting rhythmically—like a dog. I immediately knew why so many of the P-Funk musicians, who I'd gotten to know because of my website, spoke so reverently of her. It was Franklin who first introduced Clinton to Bootsy Collins and Junie Morrison and others, serving as a conduit of the funk. The importance of her work as a connector—a mothership connector, if you will—cannot be overstated. But it was Franklin's artistry as a vocal conjurer that impressed Clinton enough to create a group for her, Parlet. And it was her breathtaking vocal on the final minutes of "Peek-A-Groove," the last song on Parliament's final Casablanca Records release, *Trombipulation* (1980), that Clinton and Sly Stone referred to when they called her the Queen of Funk. This made her the only P-Funk female vocalist to have an extended solo spotlight on a Parliament song released between 1974 and 1980. And the dog panting onstage in 1996? There was a reason for that, too. According to David Lee Spradley, P-Funk keyboardist and co-writer of "Atomic Dog," it was Franklin who came up with the panting for George Clinton's first solo hit, which reached No. 1 on the *Billboard* R&B Singles chart in 1983.

Franklin's fellow Parlet members, Jeanette Washington and Debbie Wright, as well as those who came after her, including Shirley Hayden, Janice Evans, and Gwen Dozier, all played a role in the P-Funk empire from 1978 to 1980. So did Lynn Mabry and Dawn Silva, who were courted by Clinton to join P-Funk while they were still singing on tour with Sly Stone in 1977. They became performing and touring members of Parliament-Funkadelic; they were featured on offshoot projects such as Eddie Hazel's *Game, Dames and Guitar Thangs* (1977); and Clinton arranged for their own recording contract, under the Brides of Funkenstein, for Atlantic Records. The Brides' debut album, *Funk or Walk* (1978), was certified gold. After Mabry departed in 1979, the Brides became a trio with the addition of vocalists Sheila Horne and Jeanette McGruder.

Jessica Cleaves, formerly with the Friends of Distinction and Earth, Wind & Fire, joined Parliament-Funkadelic shortly before Junie Morrison did. She notably provided the unforgettable operatic voice on Funkadelic's 1979 hit "(Not Just) Knee Deep," which reached No. 1 on the *Billboard* R&B Singles chart.

Women's creations and voices abounded in Parliament-Funkadelic's commercial heyday of the 1970s. And without Mallia Franklin's presence and persistence, the sonics of P-Funk would certainly be a different one, as each of the group's hits were co-written or coproduced by a member that Franklin brought to Clinton's attention. Yet women's presence and labor in P-Funk remain overlooked. Taking a cue from the Rock Hall oversight in 1997, the Recording Academy awarded Lifetime Achievement Grammy Awards to George Clinton and Parliament-Funkadelic in 2019. But none of the founding female members of the group were honored with their own trophy.

Despite these oversights, or maybe because of them, stories of the women of P-Funk are finally being told. Franklin's son Seth Neblett has written a book, *Mothership Connected: The Women of Parliament-Funkadelic*, and vocalist Dawn Silva has published her memoir, *The Funk Queen*, detailing her experiences as a member of Parliament-Funkadelic and the Brides of Funkenstein. I hope more fans will now know that women weren't just members in the line of the P-Funk army; they were generals leading the troops.

—Melissa A. Weber, *Turning the Tables* contributor

56. GERMFREE ADOLESCENTS
X-Ray Spex (EMI, 1978)

Decades before the likes of Radiohead bemoaned ecological destruction and the pitfalls of capitalism, the English punk group X-Ray Spex stormed into the world with bracing, no-bullshit anthems about the cult of cleanliness, consumerism, and exploitation on their debut album *Germfree Adolescents*. Led by the volcanic Poly Styrene, the daughter of a Somalian father and a Scottish-Irish mother, the group merged conceptual brilliance with inventive rhythms. It's hard to overstate how much *Germfree Adolescents* rattled the then-oversaturated punk scene in the late 1970s and challenged it to push past a generic formula of chugging chords, injecting the likes of saxophone-threaded hit "The Day the World

X-Ray Spex *by* Gabrielle Bell

Turned Day-Glo" and the biting "Identity" into the mainstream. From the moment it released its first single (the seething "Oh Bondage! Up Yours!") the group presented music imbued with a social consciousness, an urgent reminder of why any of us got into music in the first place: it's a damn *blast*. Clever and captivating, and sparing none in the pursuit to unmask artificiality, *Germfree Adolescents* remains one of the most searing and irresistibly danceable punk albums ever recorded.

—Paula Mejia, *Turning the Tables*,
"The 150 Greatest Albums Made by Women," 2017

44. DREAMBOAT ANNIE
Heart (MUSHROOM, 1976)

In the mid-1970s, Ann and Nancy Wilson proved that hard rock was no longer the domain of men. *Dreamboat Annie*, the debut album from the Wilson sisters and their band Heart, first found success in Canada, where they recorded the album. Later, *Dreamboat Annie*'s expansive blend of hard rock and folk crept across the border to radio stations throughout the United States. At a time when hard rock records invariably touted male perspectives, *Dreamboat Annie*—unabashedly focused on the female experience—offered a refreshing rock and roll reversal. The album's singles "Crazy on You" and "Magic Man" are bold proclamations of autonomy that center female pleasure without apology or excuse. *Dreamboat Annie* has its share of breezy '70s ballads, flutes, and orchestral arrangements; but it also features prog rock flourishes, screaming guitars, and Ann's impressive, versatile voice, replete with shrieks that would have Robert Plant shaking. Nancy's intricate acoustic guitar playing—as well as her technical prowess on electric guitar—made her an icon of hard rock guitar, especially for young women. With *Dreamboat Annie*, the sisters Wilson launched themselves into a stardom that would not be without sexist backlash. But in the process, they provided a model for a generation of unapologetic rock and roll women.

—Marissa Lorusso, NPR Music, *Turning the Tables*, "The 150 Greatest Albums Made by Women," 2017

148

74. THE RAINCOATS
The Raincoats (ROUGH TRADE, 1979)

Musicians are often asked when they first realized they could be their truest selves through art. It's as important an origin story as one's actual arrival into the world, and one that few artists have ever captured like the Raincoats. On the London band's ecstatic 1979 debut, the members of the four-piece sound as if they're playing for their lives atop a crumbling cliff, shouting joyfully into the wind, constantly reassessing their footing, and showing the simultaneous pleasure and negotiation required to survive as women and opponents of punk orthodoxy. Eight months before *The Raincoats'* release on Rough Trade, Margaret Thatcher became the UK's first female prime minister, a moment that was naively heralded as a feminist win. Although the Raincoats didn't explicitly critique the country's political climate, they represented the disempowering futility of aping men to seize power, coining a unique musical language that rebelled against the male-dominated canon and its values. *The Raincoats* is complex and "nonlinear," as noted band scholar Jenn Pelly has described it, pitting discordant emotional experiences and sounds against one another. Rather than being contradictory, the effect precisely encapsulates the messiness of being alive.

The Raincoats

149

—Laura Snapes, *Turning the Tables*,
"The 150 Greatest Albums Made by Women," 2017

CARRIE BROWNSTEIN
On the Raincoats

" It's difficult for me to pinpoint when I first heard the Raincoats' music. Most certainly, it was in Olympia, [Washington,] where all of my major and most informative musical discoveries took place (aside from my sophomore and junior years of high school). In that dreary-weathered town, lit up with bright, unceasing ideas and enthusiasm, there were so many records and shows and bands that tore into my world. The Raincoats didn't so much intrude on my world as make it shimmer. To hear the band's songs for the first time was to light a sparkler in a room, each song a tiny, magnificent, and uneven torch. The music had shape and then was shapeless, wonky edges with pure, glowing centers. I would listen and think, *How?* **"**

—NPR's *Monitor Mix* column, 2009

150

98. YEAH YEAH YEAH YEAH
Bikini Kill (KILL ROCK STARS, 1993)

In the 1990s, feminism's third wave had a soundtrack. Riot grrrl—the raucous, scathing brand of women's punk rock—decried sexism, racism, and homophobia; demanded justice for the oppressed; and celebrated solidarity among women and girls. Its personification was the rebel girl, described in a song of the same name from Olympia, Washington's Bikini Kill; she is the "queen of the neighborhood" who spurns the male gaze and embodies revolution. The song "Rebel Girl" first appeared on *Yeah Yeah Yeah Yeah*, a split album Bikini Kill did with British riot grrrl band Huggy Bear. Recorded in a DC punk house called the Embassy, it's less polished than the band's studio releases, but it celebrates its homemade veneer instead of shying away from it. Over the course of *Yeah Yeah Yeah Yeah*'s seven original songs (and those that were added in 2014's reissue), singer Kathleen Hanna takes aim at sexist oppression with terrifying force, rage, and precision. These songs gave immediate, unfiltered language to a generation of young women who were ready to shout down rapists, who knew that their struggles were interconnected, and who believed that women were stronger together. Hanna's many voices through *Yeah Yeah Yeah Yeah*—the Valley Girl–esque whine, the punk bark, the rock and roll howl—refracted the diverse needs and desires of a new movement, opening the doors for any grrrl angry enough to walk through.

—Marissa Lorusso, NPR Music, *Turning the Tables*,
"The 150 Greatest Albums Made by Women," 2017

KATHLEEN HANNA
This tension is really electrifying and satisfying

❝ The song ['Rebel Girl'] has this raw kind of emotional power. That sounds really cheesy if I'm saying it about my own song, but I'm just going to say it, because who cares. And if you take this song that's kind of raw and put this bubblegum veneer over it, it creates this tension that is, to me, really electrifying and satisfying. It's like I'm trying to scream myself out of this beautiful bubble. It needed to be produced like that because it provided a contrast to how raw the material was. ❞

—*Morning Edition* with Ann Powers,
for NPR Music's American Anthem series, 2019

50. LIVE THROUGH THIS
Hole (DGC, 1994)

Courtney Love *by* Dame Darcy

Live Through This is the first major label release and most definitive work by Courtney Love and her band Hole—released on April 12, 1994, seven days after Love's husband's suicide. Often viewed in the shadow of Kurt Cobain but built to eclipse it, the album is a mosaic of songs piecing together the band's former noise-grunge sound ("She Walks on Me") with an accessible rock melodicism ("Doll Parts"). At its heart is the turmoil of a new feminist punk revolution, images of beauty made ugly-pretty by Love's brassy vocals and distaste for expectation, tales of postpartum depression, and tender lyrics revealing a female reality deemed unacceptable in the grunge rock boy's club that Hole and Love operated outside of. *Live Through This* solidifies Love's place as one of rock music's most magnetic front people and a high-octane performer, from the raucous opener "Violet" to the sentimental and critical "Rock Star." A fellow force to be reckoned with, Bikini Kill's Kathleen Hanna famously offered the riot grrrl rallying cry "Find the biggest bitch in town and start a band with her." Courtney Love took that one step further, as though suggesting: be the bitch.

—Maria Sherman, *Turning the Tables*,
"The 150 Greatest Albums Made by Women," 2017

152

How Ella Fitzgerald's Glass-Shattering Memorex Campaign Revitalized Her Career

It's the stuff of legends: an urban legend and a jazz legend combining into a legendary advertising campaign.

In 1970, the Leo Burnett ad agency in Chicago had an imaginative idea for selling Memorex's new line of blank cassette tapes. They'd prove the old myth that an opera singer could shatter a wineglass with a high note—and then claim a Memorex cassette had such exacting sound precision that its recording of the singer could break a glass, too. Leo Burnett made a couple of TV commercials with this theme featuring tenor Enrico di Giuseppe and soprano Nancy Shade. The tagline: "Memorex Recording Tape . . . Reproduction so true it can shatter glass."

It was a good enough start, but opera was too elitist for Memorex's larger aims. After first reaching out to audiophiles—early cassette advertising was placed in magazines like *Hi Fidelity* and *Stereo Review*—the company wanted to target a broader demographic with TV commercials aired during football games on CBS. The glass-breaking cassette campaign needed a spokesperson whose musical style embodied a more casual brilliance.

Enter Ella Fitzgerald: jazz legend, gold standard for vocal excellence, and paradigm of high-fidelity sound, thanks to her influential midcentury recordings. Music historian Judith Tick, who wrote a biography of Fitzgerald, says the singer's career was a perfect fit for the campaign, as she was known at the time "not only as a legend, but as a treasure-bearer of American culture." Her immense body of work began in the 1930s; peaked in the 1940s with the bull's-eye pitch accuracy, vocal range, and sheer originality of her scat singing innovation; and then peaked again with her definitive 1950s and early 1960s songbook interpretations of Gershwin, Rodgers and Hart, Cole Porter, and others.

In a 1985 interview, Fitzgerald remembered her Memorex audition at the Algonquin Hotel in New York: "They asked me to do the ending of 'How High the Moon.' I just kept singing, 'High, high the moon,' doing the ending. And when the glass broke, they said, 'That's the one!' Then I got the job. . . . A lot of people say, 'Did you really break the glass?' We had to prove that. They had lawyers there."

So in 1972, at age fifty-five, Ella Fitzgerald became the spokesperson for Memorex cassettes. These commercials came at an important juncture both in Fitzgerald's career and in jazz. After decades as the First Lady of Song, Fitzgerald faced a time when traditional jazz was declining in popularity. But as the Memorex campaign became an institution, it fueled a career revival that helped to extend her relevance in new ways, and eventually positioned her to hand off the baton to the next generation.

In the campaign's earliest TV spots, Fitzgerald scat sings, hits a high note, and shatters a goblet. As countless sound engineers and a 2005 *MythBusters* segment have proved, breaking a glass wouldn't have been an unlikely feat for Fitzgerald, especially with her voice amplified. Most glasses resonate at a frequency around high C; with Fitzgerald's two-octave range, hitting that note would have been no problem. Just as critical to Fitzgerald's authenticity in the campaign is her unreconstructed middle-aged appearance: her wig, round body—and in some spots, cataract-correcting eyeglasses—lend warmth and conviction to her televisual style. The iconic Fitzgerald comes across as so *real* in the commercials that her mere presence authenticates the ad's claim of a Memorex cassette recording breaking a glass. "Is it live or is it Memorex?" the ads ask. What matters is that it's Fitzgerald onscreen.

In 1974, Memorex introduced a new TV spot and angle for the Fitzgerald campaign. Count Basie, Fitzgerald's old band mate, sits with his back to a recording booth, listening for the difference between Fitzgerald's live voice

Ella Fitzgerald
by Jazmin Anita

amplified through speakers and a Memorex tape recording of it. "You gotta be kidding, I can't tell!" he says, as if in on an elaborate joke. Fitzgerald or cassette recording? If jazz royalty like Count Basie can't tell and doesn't care, why should we? Consumers can only deduce that playing a Memorex tape is interchangeable with having Fitzgerald sing in their homes. Hearkening back to man versus machine fables, to John Henry against the steam-powered drill, the message in this spot is that human expression and cassette technology can come together for the win.

In the era of three-network TV, Memorex commercials aired on both CBS and NBC during football games and rock shows. Anyone who watched television at all was likely to catch a Fitzgerald Memorex spot. The "Is it live or is it Memorex?" campaign and tagline became a branding success on par with Maxwell House's "Good to the last drop" or Timex's "It takes a licking and keeps on ticking." As the campaign became an institution, Fitzgerald, pushing sixty, reveled in a Memorex-fueled career resurgence.

Fitzgerald's career revival came at a time of critical anxiety around the idea of "selling out," thanks in part to the declining commercial success of traditional jazz and the popularity of fusion bands, like Herbie Hancock's Headhunters. For some jazz purists, using the art form to hawk cassettes on TV amounted to a capital offense. One jazz critic went so far as to call Fitzgerald a "freakish cultural icon" for the ad.

Fitzgerald was indifferent to stylistic boundaries and popular anxieties. Her career dated back to the 1930s, when jazz *was* mainstream music. Fitzgerald had made onscreen appearances since 1942, when she sang her breakthrough hit "A-Tisket, A-Tasket" in the film *Ride 'Em Cowboy.* "She always wanted to reach as many people as possible," says Tick. "So for her, reaching out to a mass public was not any kind of handicap. It was what she would want to do."

For most of a decade, the Memorex commercials presented Fitzgerald as an exemplar of sound fidelity, model of authenticity, and most significantly, her own artist. Fitzgerald's peer Billie Holiday had her tragic legend overtake her art in the broader culture. In contrast, Fitzgerald's late-career Memorex ads put her inimitable style and voice right at the center of her popular reputation, helping to grow the legend of her art itself.

The commercials made Fitzgerald into a folk hero synonymous with cassette technology. Children on the street called out to Fitzgerald as "the Memorex Lady," to her delight. She'd tell of airline pilots warning her not to sing on their flights for fear of broken plane windows. The ad campaign capitalized on a folk legend about the human voice's glass-breaking force; it mythologized Fitzgerald's vocal power as timeless and inescapable. Nothing was immune. A 1987 *Jet* magazine news item mentioned the Memorex spots as it reported that firefighters had rushed to Fitzgerald's Beverly Hills home after her singing triggered a fire alarm—all while she was recovering from open-heart surgery at age sixty-nine.

Now, many technologies later and decades after Fitzgerald's 1996 death, these cassette commercials may feel like the distant past. But the question of how we relate to analog or digital voices has never left us: Memorex's marriage of cassette technology and Fitzgerald's musical presence resonates today in our relationship with AI voices like Siri and Alexa. Fitzgerald's unique talent and character in these 1970s spots point to why *her* voice in particular endures as a hallmark of style, quality, and invention. Only Ella Fitzgerald, in the living, singing flesh, could have become the Memorex Lady. She was an American original.

—Michelle Mercer, *Turning the Tables*, Season 3, "Eight Women Who Invented American Popular Music," 2019

CECILE MCLORIN SALVANT
Ella Fitzgerald's legacy: The tone of her voice hits you

In honor of Ella Fitzgerald's one-hundredth birthday, Grammy-winning jazz vocalist Cecile McLorin Salvant spoke to NPR about Fitzgerald's legacy and influence on her.

❝ When you hear the tone of her voice—which has kind of a brightness, kind of a breathiness, but it also has this really great depth, and kind of a laserlike, really clear quality to it—it hits you. I remember being seventeen and living in France and feeling really homesick and wanting to go back to Miami, and listening to Ella Fitzgerald singing 'I Didn't Know What Time It Was,' and I would listen to that all day. All day. For, like, weeks. And it felt—it created a home for me.

She was not a sex symbol, and yet she was very successful. It's a testament to both the audience and—of course, most of all—her artistry. And we're not even talking about racism. That a Black woman could be so popular across the board with both Black and white audiences—that's a beautiful thing. ❞

—*All Things Considered* with Tom Vitale, 2017

21. RID OF ME
PJ Harvey (ISLAND RECORDS, 1993)

In 1992, PJ Harvey emerged from the rural town of Yeovil, England, and into the musical world with the seething tune "Sheela-Na-Gig." While Harvey's subsequent debut album *Dry* was a radical step forward, it didn't prepare anyone for her uncompromising next album—her best—the next year, *Rid of Me*. You can hear it in the stark recording: the album was pulled together against all odds—done in isolation, while the band sparked with internal tensions, and Harvey's songwriting directly bristled against Steve Albini's abrasive production. Yet from the opening chords of *Rid of Me*'s title track—in which Harvey crooned "Tie yourself to me / No one else, no / You're not rid of me"—she made it perfectly clear not only that she was not intimidated by having all eyes on her, but also that she wasn't going anywhere. Behind the thrum of guitars on "50ft Queenie" she delivered a series of declarations that have rightful places as anthems:

I'm number one
Second to no one . . .
I'll tell you my name
F-U-C-K
Fifty foot queenie
Force ten hurricane

On *Rid of Me*, Harvey also proved that she wasn't just capable of hanging with the boys; she had surpassed them entirely. "Can you hear can you hear me now / I'm man-sized," she roars on the eponymous song, one that, among others, once caused her contemporary Courtney Love to declare: "The one rock star that makes me know I'm shit is Polly Harvey. I'm nothing next to the purity that she experiences."

—Paula Mejia, *Turning the Tables*,
"The 150 Greatest Albums Made by Women," 2017

158

122. THE SCREAM
Siouxsie and the Banshees (POLYDOR, 1978)

Siouxsie Sioux *by* Dame Darcy

The English singer-songwriter Siouxsie Sioux has stood as a fearless post-punk priestess since she released *The Scream* with her band, the Banshees, in 1978. An artist as well-known for her style as her voice, her graphic eye makeup inspired scores of Goth girls to explore the depths of black eyeliner and black hair dye. But the boldness of Siouxsie's look doesn't distract from her sound; it makes her all the more powerful and mysterious, especially when coupled with her idiosyncratic music. *The Scream* starts slow and then thrillingly takes off, propulsive and heavy, with the high notes of her voice pulling everyone to the future—echoing, calling, wailing, and yearning on the likes of "Pure." The second side of the album reveals more hard-driving punk tunes—the guitar, bass, and drum slowly hammering in a way that earned the band frequent comparisons to the Velvet Underground—but it's her voice that grounds the music and pierces your heart.

—Nina Gregory, NPR, *Turning the Tables*,
"The 150 Greatest Albums Made by Women," 2017

159

160

Diamanda Galás

111. THE LITANIES OF SATAN
Diamanda Galás (Y, 1982)

The iconoclastic pianist-vocalist Diamanda Galás grew up in a sheltered household where she wasn't allowed to listen to the radio. Her escape became music, in a way; Galás played piano from a young age and was talented enough that she started performing with the San Diego Symphonic Orchestra at age fourteen, but she was forbidden from singing [which her father considered immoral]. There is no voice like the terrifying, terrific one that Galás possesses, though, which has been said to span eight octaves. It was bound to unleash itself into the world at some point, and it did in 1982 when she released her debut album, *The Litanies of Satan*. The album is composed of two long pieces: the eponymous "The Litanies of Satan," which holds its roots in Charles Baudelaire texts, and the piercing rattle of "Wild Women with Steak-Knives (The Homicidal Love Song for Solo Scream)." The album, which clocks in at twenty-eight spine-jolting minutes of Galás's wheezing, whispering, and rhythmic wailing that can be heard into the next lifetime, is one of the most singularly influential avant-garde recordings to make its way out of hell and into our world. Artists including PJ Harvey and Zola Jesus have been shaken by *The Litanies of Satan*, thanks to Galás's stupefying vocal acrobatics—which suggest anything is possible if you dare to pick up a microphone and start screaming.

—Paula Mejia, *Turning the Tables*,
"The 150 Greatest Albums Made by Women," 2017

In many ways, skill is
at the core of this book.
Women in music are
too often erroneously
celebrated for being
instead of doing,
springing from the
imagined half shell
fully formed instead of
(like the wizards here)
getting bloody fingers
from honing their
jaw-dropping virtuosity.

SHREDDERS

St. Vincent

St. Vincent Is the 21st Century's Guitar Vanguard

For more than ten years, since the release of 2007's *Marry Me*, Annie Clark has inhabited her musical persona with a ferocious curiosity, a keen hunger for the unheard. She has said that she picked up the guitar because of her love for grunge bands like Nirvana, Pearl Jam, and Soundgarden, all acts that forged newly abject masculinities at the dawn of the '90s, in contrast to the polished bombast of '80s hair metal. Though it was gospel guitarist Sister Rosetta Tharpe who pioneered many of rock music's electric guitar techniques, the instrument inevitably became phallicized, bound up with the masculinity of popular rock musicians through the second half of the twentieth century. It's a loud machine, ripe with power, and any woman who picks it up must negotiate its baggage in her own way. Most artists who have undermined the electric guitar's chauvinistic appeal so far have been men: Mick Ronson, playing in sequined pants while David Bowie simulated a blow job on his guitar; Kurt Cobain, who would rather slough off blasé solos than aim for masculinist virtuosity. But of course, these subversions succeeded because the subverters, to begin with, were men. They arrived insulated from any doubt that the instrument was for them.

To repurpose the guitar to her own expression, a woman must usually start from a place of advanced skill, though she need not end there. She needs to prove herself worthy of the instrument, and so she must play it better than the majority of men, for whom worthiness is an untested given. It is awe-inducing to watch Clark's hands dance fluidly across her instrument, navigating dense, complicated riffs. She has a rare skill, and yet the skill is not the point; it is the means. With it, she has undercut the stubborn assumption that rock music is an arena for men to express their power. She has crept onto that stage and interrogated that very power: by playing fast solos through thick, strange distortion; by contorting her voice into a disarming shriek; by shredding her guitar against the ultimate rockist taboo: a prerecorded backing track.

On any St. Vincent album, even the early ones, the traditional relationship between voice and accompaniment destabilizes. It feels wrong even to call her instrumentation "accompaniment," as if it were playing a supporting role. Rather than build foundations with her guitars and her electronics, then top them with her singing, she mimics her instruments with her voice, or vice versa; it often sounds as though she is dueting with the guitar.

The guitar, for Clark, is not an appendage, not a phallus, not an extension of the body. It is its own body with its own voice. By thinking of her guitar as a peer and not a tool, Clark frees her own voice to take on new textures and movements. Because the guitar does not always sound like a guitar, it disorients the listener, who expects St. Vincent's instruments to play their typical roles: bass in back, treble in front, voice somewhere in between. By loosening the structure of her music, Clark frees her instrument from its historical status as a masculinity amplifier, an assertion of gendered power. She doesn't use it to embellish her songs; she uses it to build worlds. Forget the glass ceiling. Inside a St. Vincent song, you don't even know where the floor is.

—Sasha Geffen, *Turning the Tables*, Season 2,
"25 Most Influential Women+ Musicians of the 21st Century," 2018 (excerpt)

BONNIE RAITT:
I have a musical idea

WNXP's Jewly Hight talked to guitar icon Bonnie Raitt not about her slide technique, but about her decades in the driver's seat of her band.

Jewly Hight: You recently received the Icon award from *Billboard*. They reeled off numerous career accomplishments, but I was so glad to hear that one thing they included was your longtime band-leading, because to see and hear you moving with such comfortable authority through these supposedly masculine domains was huge. What did it take? And what kind of satisfaction has it offered you to work your way to owning those spaces and those roles and making them your own?

Bonnie Raitt: Well, sometimes being the youngest or the only female in the room telling other experienced players who've been in bands for years, when they don't quite know what you're talking about if you're not a school musician and you can't just reel off the chords and time signatures—you just have to sing it live for them or say, Can you move the register? So the fact that I'm not a trained musician traditionally has held me back a little bit in my ability to communicate what I want, including with my longtime band. So a lot of times I'll have to play something on someone else's record, or show them physically what I'm talking about. Because you know, there's an art to carving out a sound that you want to have, you have to give people the leeway and the respect to play the way they feel it. And then you just have to use a great deal of diplomacy and sensitivity so that you're not pushing the "mom button" of ordering people around when you're not the best musician in the room. So I don't want to ever be in that position.

That said, I have a musical idea. And I have a compass that I'm trying to get to this place, and I have to just surround myself with musicians that are willing to be flexible and understand that I come with that set of skills where I eventually am going to end up with something that's really original and new. But to get there, sometimes this is a circuitous route. And it's not always successful. . . . So it's a lot of risk of not being liked to be a musical director. But it makes an added layer of complication when you're a female as well. . . . I had to earn their respect. And I

167

think they ultimately know that the proof is in the pudding when you look back at the work, the music that I've done, those arrangements and picking the songs, has really been me all along.

—Interview by Jewly Hight, WNXP,
All Songs Considered, 2022

Sheila E.

SHEILA E.: A plant being watered every day

NPR: There must be a lot of young women now who play drums and percussion that saw you when they were little girls. Have you heard from them?

Sheila E.: Yes. They come to me and say that, you know if it wasn't for you, I would not be playing right now. And there are older women that are older than me that come up to me and say, I always wanted to play, but, you know, in school they didn't have it or it wasn't accepted or my parents didn't, you know, didn't want me to do it or whatever. And I said, it is never too late to play. I grabbed [this woman's] hand. She was eighty-something years old. I pulled her onstage and I had her sit down and play congas with the band. We played live and she had never experienced anything like that before. She'll never forget it. It makes you happy, you know; it's like a plant being watered every day; and for me, it's like if I don't get my food, my water, my nourishment musically some kind of way or creatively, I feel like I'm gonna die.

—*All Things Considered* with Arun Rath, 2014

126. A SONG FOR YOU
The Carpenters (A&M RECORDS, 1972)

The late Karen Carpenter's singular voice—a no-frills contralto—shone whenever she stepped onstage, but nowhere more brightly than on the Carpenters' *A Song for You*. While "Top of the World" was the 1972 album's biggest hit, its first single, "Hurting Each Other," was a power ballad turned loving, angsty, and dramatic. Besides displaying her mastery of the lower vocal range on the album, Karen Carpenter also showed off her talents on the drums here. On *A Song for You*, you get a sampling of her chops—among others, as she also played electric bass—on instrumental tracks like "Flat Baroque." In the years following her death, many prominent musicians would point to her complementary skills as a singing drummer as a key influence, one that still rings true today.

—Tanya Ballard Brown, NPR, *Turning the Tables*,
"The 150 Greatest Albums Made by Women," 2017

TORI AMOS:
The piano and I are cohorts

Tori Amos: I don't feel guilty when I'm at the piano. There's no guilt. So I have a whole 'nother world that's going on that's very real to me. I do understand when I'm back in my hotel room that this world that I'm creating at the piano, whether I'm writing things about people that I've just met or run into—when I run into them again, say, I don't know, at dinner, I'm not really having certain relationships with them that I'm having at the piano, that I'm creating. But at the piano, all this is existing, and she and I are totally cohorts. We know exactly what we're creating, and this world is very real to us. It's very real. But nobody else acknowledges it except when I'm onstage because that's like fantasyland for everybody. But it's just the opposite to me. Real life is really when I'm playing, and then when I'm off, I'm just waiting to do the next gig.

NPR: Could it be any other instrument than the piano?

Tori Amos: No. . . .

NPR: Why?

Tori Amos: The thing about this instrument is it's orchestral, really. It's very much a warm, living, breathing woman to me. It's very female. She's my best friend. I sit and talk to her, curl up around her sometimes. It's a real being to me.

—All Things Considered with Noah Adams, 1994

Suzanne Ciani

The Cyborg
Inventions
of Suzanne Ciani

When electronic composer Suzanne Ciani began making and performing music with synthesizers in the 1970s, very few people in the music industry knew what to make of her. Granted, she wasn't sure what to make of the music industry either. She had gone to graduate school to get her master's degree in composition and found herself staring down a traditional career in music gnarled in logistical—but also gendered—limitations. "The reality of being a composer is a challenging one because a lot of composers would die without ever hearing [their] music," Ciani told NPR's *All Things Considered* in 2012. "And if you were a woman and you were a composer you had even less of a chance of ever hearing your music."

That was until a chance visit to the studio of Don Buchla, the pioneering electronic instrument designer, would splinter Ciani's conceptions of not just what a career in music could look like, but what music *could be*—how she could unspool notes of hidden beauty from an intimidating, tangled piece of machinery like a modular synth, how she could create mini-universes of futuristic sound at her fingertips.

"I think there was some kind of subconscious attraction to this machine that would give me my independence, that would allow me to be in complete control of my composition and to not depend on some outside political system to give me the right to hear my music," she told NPR.

Thoroughly attached to working with the Buchla 200 synth, which she discovered while working for Don's studio, Ciani harbored dreams of becoming a recording artist. But she met resistance regarding her chosen equipment from nearly every corner of the industry. Record executives asked why she, a woman, didn't sing, or play something more suitable, like a guitar; avant-garde artists like Steve Reich memorably commented that synths like hers should be banished "to the moon." Ironically, she found more support in the world of advertising, where she was enlisted to soundtrack commercials and oddball sound effects.

What's singular about Ciani's approach to electronic music is not simply that she was an early pioneer in the field, but the ways in which she managed to make something as alien as modular synthesis accessible to wide audiences without completely taming its wild, otherworldly qualities. She brought electronic music into the homes of Middle America, demonstrating her synthesizers on television alongside David Letterman, sound-tracking pinball machines and composing film scores (as the first woman to do so solo). And yet her recorded music, which spans gloomy experiments in quadraphonic sound to soft, New Age classics like *Seven Waves*, is confoundingly mesmerizing even today, when "computer music" is the norm, not some freaky outlier.

What Ciani did and continues to do is chart unknown territory with a playfulness and an ear for expansion in all directions, even in the face of naysayers. She proved that commercial music could be experimental, and that a computer could replicate the sonic wonder of a wave crashing to shore. Devoid of a world that would fully support her creative independence, with each far-reaching sound she culled from her synthesizer, she managed to build one for herself.

—Hazel Cills, NPR Music

172

5. SUPA DUPA FLY
Missy Elliott (THE GOLDMIND/ELEKTRA, 1997)

This album dismantled the hip-hop boy's club. For the first time in history a woman rapped, sang, wrote, and produced every song on a major rap release. Within the first sounds that we hear, Missy Elliott invites you to become engulfed with the undeniable Virginia-based funk, a region that's equally Southern and Eastern, through aquatic synth sounds paired with earthy drum patterns. The result? A vibe that's both familiar and futuristic. Without selling overly sexualized imagery and without imitating hypermasculine gangster rap, Elliott awards us with pure originality. She didn't just change the scope on how we interpreted sexy and gangster: the genres bent to her liking.

Missy Elliott

The sound shifted to jazz with her vocal improvisations and scatting on "The Rain (Supa Dupa Fly)," over an Ann Peebles sample. It became the blues on "Beep Me 911," a somber song about uncertainty and urgency. And her esteemed comrades Busta Rhymes, Timbaland, Lil' Kim, Aaliyah, Da Brat, and Ginuwine complemented and fit comfortably within the theme of the perfect album. Elliott presciently knew her music was groundbreaking and reminded us throughout the record with her boisterous lyrics. Today, *Supa Dupa Fly* remains one of the best hip-hop records of all time, and its level of innovation and musicianship remains unparalleled.

—Stasia Irons, KEXP, *Turning the Tables*,
"The 150 Greatest Albums Made by Women," 2017

86. JOURNEY IN SATCHIDANANDA
Alice Coltrane (GRP/IMPULSE!, 1971)

Alice Coltrane

Alice Coltrane made some of the deepest, most luminous, and spiritual music of any musician, jazz or otherwise. She died in 2007, and it is strange that she is still continually compared to the accomplishments of her husband, John Coltrane, who died in 1967, or thought of as being in John Coltrane's long shadow. Alice Coltrane was her own artist. Alice McLeod was an accomplished pianist before she met John—she was a respected player in Detroit's diverse and thriving music scenes, and awesome 1960s footage of her furious performances can be found on YouTube. She soon mastered many other instruments, most famously the harp, which underpinned so many of her greatest records. *Journey in Satchidananda* was named for Alice's guru, the charismatic Swami Satchidananda, who was a great source of support and solace for her after her husband's untimely death at age forty; Alice later became a guru of her own, adopting the name Swamini Turiyasangitananda and establishing her own ashram in California. *Journey in Satchidananda* is a transporting experience combining oud, tamboura, bass, harp, drums, bells, tambourine, and piano. There's a cast of all-star jazz players on the record—Pharoah Sanders, Charlie Haden, and Rashied Ali among them—but the true star is Alice and her cosmic harp.

—Geeta Dayal, *Turning the Tables*,
"The 150 Greatest Albums Made by Women," 2017

ALICE COLTRANE
All those keys

Alice Coltrane talked about the release of her first album in twenty-five years, *Translinear Light*, and recalled her husband John Coltrane's impact on her style.

❝ He said, 'You have all those keys.' He said, 'Why don't you play all of them as completely as you can?' So that's why you always hear that sound. You will hear it forever, as long as I live. ❞

—*Morning Edition* with Ashley Kahn, 2004

90. FUNNY GIRL
Broadway Cast Album, Barbra Streisand
(CAPITOL RECORDS, 1964)

Any number of doors—the blues, gospel, R&B, country, rap, rock and roll, even opera—can lead to pop music. Barbra Streisand entered via Broadway. While ambivalent about a pop career in the early 1960s, Streisand nevertheless sang at New York City nightclubs before landing her first Broadway theater role. Her second job, as the 1920s comedy star Fanny Brice in the musical *Funny Girl*, changed popular culture, launching Streisand to superstardom as both a vocalist and actor. "She threw her head back, sang her heart out, and knocked New York on its ear," JoAnne Stang wrote of Streisand in her 1964 *New York Times* review. The original cast album is neither Streisand's first, nor most successful, but it captured a rare cultural moment in which one performer emerges bigger than the medium itself, outshining an entire Broadway cast with an unmistakable voice and a most extraordinary musical ear.

—Gwen Thompkins, WWNO, *Turning the Tables*, "The 150 Greatest Albums Made by Women," 2017

BARBRA STREISAND
I couldn't get any jobs

" I always wanted to be an actress, a classical actress, actually, but I couldn't get any jobs. I mean, I made rounds for a couple of days and it was so discouraging. And so I decided to enter a talent contest as a singer. And I got the job. And because I couldn't get jobs as an actress, I approached my singing as an actress and gave myself acting exercises or parts to play. **"**

—*Weekend Edition*, 2010

51. SASSY SWINGS AGAIN
Sarah Vaughan (MERCURY, 1967)

Hearing Sarah Vaughan's 1967 recording *Sassy Swings Again* is like taking a master class in the juxtaposition of vocal acuity and fluidity. Here, she teaches women how to run a band with the sheer grace and unassuming power of her voice. On this album, she also effortlessly takes on horn solos and goes toe-to-toe with the likes of Freddie Hubbard on trumpet and Kai Winding on trombone. Manny Albam and Thad Jones arranged the instrumentation like a mosaic around Vaughan's vocals, putting the spotlight on her signature sound while ushering her seamlessly through each measure. The perfectly complementary relationship between the orchestra and Vaughan's vocalese makes this classic recording required listening for jazz disciples and fanatics alike.

—Keanna Faircloth, NPR, *Turning the Tables*,
"The 150 Greatest Albums Made by Women," 2017

Meg White Is the 21st Century's Loudest Introvert

Meg White
by Nicole Rifkin

Comedy lore has it that when Bud Abbott and Lou Costello first started performing together, Abbott was paid 60 percent to Costello's 40 percent. Abbott was the straight man, Costello the kooky comic, and their salary ratios were in keeping with burlesque tradition that put a premium on the straight man's skill.

In one of the most famous comedy bits of all time, "Who's on First?," it's Abbott's persistence and composure that make Costello's increasing frustration and hysteria funny. No matter how frenetic Costello gets losing his proverbial baseballs, Abbott keeps time. Before finding Abbott, Costello had worked with a number of partners. But it was Abbott who made all the difference in anchoring a scene; according to Costello, "A good straight man is hard to find."

Jack and Meg White weren't a comedy duo. But they also kinda were. And Meg was always the straight man. Listen to "Girl, You Have No Faith in Medicine" as Jack builds toward total vocal and guitar hysteria, challenging Meg's drums in a race to the cliff's edge. Jack's tiptoes are hanging off as he wails, "Give me a sugar pill and watch me just rattle down the street." Meg doesn't give in; instead, she hits a simple *boom crack* and then *ts ts ts ts ts ts*—laughing her high-hat head off watching him rattle. Hear Meg's insistent thwack in the face of absolute frustration followed by the four-beat desperation of bashing her metaphorical head against the wall on "The Hardest Button to Button." Hear Jack wail the title lyric of "I Just Don't Know What to Do with Myself" and feel Meg's wry smile as she lets him suffer all alone for just a hair too uncomfortably long before barreling back in. The timing of their dynamic, and the balance between bonkers and basic, is what made the White Stripes stand out among the garage-rock bands that would usher in the twenty-first century. It allowed Jack and Meg to mash the simplicity of the blues with the spirit of punk to create theater.

Meg White started drumming because of Jack. It was 1997, a year after they got married and Jack Gillis took her last name. At the time, Jack was trying on a lot of different musical outfits. He played guitar and sang lead on songs for Two-Star Tabernacle, played bass with the Hentchmen, drummed in cowpunk band Goober & the Peas, and played on the first album by garage-rock band the Go. But one night, Jack asked Meg to play a simple beat for something he was working on, and shortly after, they started a band that would change rock history. I hate to feed into the sexist trope that a woman's worth is framed by a man's story, or that a woman's primary purpose is to fill a void for a man. But this is not a trope or an assumption. This is the real origin story of the White Stripes, and to ignore it would be to miss an opportunity to credit Meg for the amount of work she did in forming the backbone of twenty-first-century rock.

When they burst on the scene, the White Stripes were called "the greatest band since the Sex Pistols" and "the future of rock and roll." *New York* magazine credits the band's 2001 album *White Blood Cells* with helping the early-aughts rock revival go national and "blissfully ending nu-metal and boy-band chart domination." The momentum the White Stripes created, along with other rock revival bands like the Strokes and Black Rebel Motorcycle Club, proved to the industry that back-to-basics could be bankable. Yeah Yeah Yeahs played its first public show opening for the White Stripes in 2000, and the second wave of postpunk revival bands like the Killers, the Shins, the National, the Libertines, and Arctic Monkeys certainly reaped the benefits of plugging into a scene while the amps were already on. The White Stripes' "Seven Nation Army" would go on to become one of the most instantly recognizable sporting chants in arenas around the world, and the band's success has allowed Jack White the clout to continue running his label, Third Man Records. Meg herself has also inspired Ray LaMontagne to write a flattering ode in her name, and apparently Dave Grohl's daughter has a favorite drummer, and it's not her dad.

Jack has said that "the whole point of the White Stripes," since the band's beginning, was "the liberation of limiting yourself." Meg's simple style of drumming was the absolute embodiment of that goal and, paradoxically, the primary source of criticism lobbed against her as a musician during the band's ascent to fame. Meg's role in the band was often framed by critics (professional and civilian alike) as an audition rather than an essence due to her lack of training or elaborate technique. Just Google "Jack White Defends Meg's Drumming" or search for Meg White on Reddit. To question whether someone has earned the right to a seat at the table (or the kit, as it were) in a band that she has been half of since its inception, to play the songs that she originated, is ludicrous. But the question *is* significant, and even helpful, if it helps us understand the way many people see women in bands as accessories rather than authors. In the same 2005 *Rolling Stone* feature where Jack explains to journalist David Fricke how the foundation of the White Stripes is finding creativity through imposing limitations, Fricke later asks, "Are there times when Meg's style of drumming is too limiting—that you can't take a song as far as you'd like to go?" Jack responds: "No. I never thought, 'God, I wish Neil Peart was in this band.' It's kind of funny: When people critique hip hop, they're scared to open up, for fear of being called racist. But they're not scared to open up on female musicians, out of pure sexism."

Meg is at the center of another paradox. Her bashing, smashing, and booming made her one of the loudest musicians of this century. And yet she's often remembered as, and in some cases criticized for being, a quiet person. She was certainly more reserved than Jack in public, and rarely spoke in interviews. History is full of examples of women who do not speak because men will not let them, and so it's understandable that many people's default assumption was that Meg was silenced by Jack. In the 2009 concert film *Under Great White Northern Lights*, which chronicles the duo's last tour together, Jack begs Meg to clear things up. "What would you say to people who say, 'Jack won't ever let Meg talk'?" he asks. Meg simply replies, "I would say that you have nothing to do with it." As someone who interviews musicians for a living, I do believe that hearing what artists have to say about their art can help illuminate it in a different way or help me hear things differently than before. It's a delight when that does happen. But the most humbling lesson I have learned by digging into Meg's story is that an artist who has already given so much of herself through her work does not owe anybody any conversation about it. Through that lens maybe Meg wasn't quiet, but instead radical in the defiant template she set for how to be a famous person who makes no apologies for letting the work speak for itself.

In September 2007, months after releasing the radically creative album *Icky Thump*, the White Stripes made an announcement that marked the beginning of the end. They were canceling their entire upcoming fall US tour. An official statement from the duo read, "Meg White is suffering from acute anxiety and is unable to travel at this time." Cue any Meg naysayers to come out of the woodwork and complain that not only was she not worthy of being in the band in the first place, but that she was responsible for its demise. But what music history ought really to remember here is that this was an artist who, at the very height of fame, had the courage to be upfront about taking care of her own mental health, whether or not it was disappointing to fans. At a time when even fewer artists were publicly broaching the subject of mental health than they are now, Meg shared her reality with bravery, clarity, and no drama. By allowing that statement into the world, Meg said a lot about something that is hard for people to talk about.

By all accounts, including his own, Jack White was the more outwardly emotionally demonstrative member of the White Stripes—the big personality foil to Meg's straight man. See the end of any given live performance: Jack's hair is drenched in sweat and he looks like he might crumple into a catharsis puddle;

Meg, whose job was arguably the more athletic of the two, is bone dry and still exuding the same composed air as she did an hour earlier. But do not make the mistake of confusing Meg's outward persona of nonchalance for a lack of tremendous musical emotion. On the drums, Meg White smashed out carnal, visceral, raw, sometimes funny, and always urgent stories that told of the human experience. Maybe *that's* the thumping feeling that penetrates our pores and anchors our attention when we listen to the White Stripes. Maybe that's why we ever cared about the band in the first place.

—Talia Schlanger, *Turning the Tables*, Season 2,
"25 Most Influential Women+ Musicians of the 21st Century," 2018

 ## 42. ESPERANZA SPALDING, "I KNOW YOU KNOW"

Prince once said he thought he could play bass until he met Esperanza Spalding. That's not hard to believe once you've heard the deeply funky opening bars of "I Know You Know," which heralded Spalding's career as a shape-shifting, jazz-rooted virtuoso who can dip fluidly in and out of pop, R&B, and rock without sacrificing her music's complexity. On this track, Spalding's buoyant vocals came to the forefront for the first time, reassuring a wary romantic partner that she's there to stay. She might as well have been addressing the music world at large.

—Rachel Horn, *Turning the Tables*, Season 2,
"The 200 Greatest Songs by 21st-Century Women+," 2018

181

Maybelle Carter:
Mother, Matriarch,
and Mentor

Maybelle Carter apparently made a mean chicken gizzard soup, which called for chicken livers, necks, and backs, besides the gizzards. Her daughter June Carter Cash published that recipe, along with a host of others, in *Mother Maybelle's Cookbook: A Kitchen Visit with America's First Family of Country Song* in 1989, a little more than a decade after her mother's passing. Only those who'd had the privilege of being guests in Maybelle's home had witnessed what she could do with soup pots and frying pans in the name of painstaking hospitality. Even so, the notion of being able to purchase the recipes for her home-cooked meals fit with how the public knew her—as the musical matron who put her Gibson L-5 archtop guitar, autoharp, and long memory to use holding her rightful place in professional communities she helped inspire.

There was really no precedent for Maybelle Carter, not at the beginning nor by the end of her five-decade career. In the late 1920s and '30s, when she was starting out, people who hadn't seen her perform live had only heard her on Carter Family records and radio broadcasts and scarcely believed it could be a young woman supplying the trio's primary accompaniment on guitar. Late in her performing tenure, throughout the '60s into the '70s, she was both a grandmotherly figure, demure in her high-collared dresses and graying bob, and an instrumentalist sharing her technique and repertoire, and the spotlight, with mostly male, star musicians a generation or two her junior.

Society tends to treat woman of a certain age like they're irrelevant, even invisible, their ways antiquated and their powers, skills, and accomplishments long forgotten. Even in the realm of country and folk music, each defined in relation to its own idea of preserving noble cultural lineage, Carter's enduring presence was striking. She was still out there working, in an industry vastly changed from the one she started in, still taking unpretentious pride in her abilities, when she finally came to be recognized as a foundational figure, an originator.

In her bucolic southwest Virginia youth, she got her hands on a mail-order guitar and proceeded to absorb and apply musical ideas from an array of sources, beginning with her mother's banjo picking. Maybelle would spend much of her life on the opposite end of that exchange, making herself an approachable source to her literal and figurative progeny.

First, though, she focused on her own development. The guitar playing approach she devised combined the brisk, swinging rhythms of strummed chords and terse, melodic lead licks, and she was serious about its execution. In *Will You Miss Me When I'm Gone?: The Carter Family & Their Legacy in American Music*, authors Mark Zwonitzer and Charles Hirshberg describe how much it irked Maybelle when record man Ralph Peer wouldn't allow her a do-over in the studio to fix a mistake or elected to release a flawed take anyhow for the sake of "authenticity." Decades on in a promotional interview, she sounded both pleased and amused by folkloric appraisals of her playing. "When I started playing the guitar," she recalled, "I didn't have nobody to play with me, so that's how I developed this style of pickin', and the rhythm, too. They call it the 'Carter scratch' now," she goes on, starting to chuckle, "some of 'em do."

In her late teens, Maybelle had been drafted into the singing duo of her older cousin Sara and Sara's song-collecting spouse A.P., who happened to be big brother to Maybelle's husband Ezra. After Maybelle and Ezra started their own family, Maybelle encouraged the musical aptitude she saw in her daughters Anita and Helen and helped their less tunefully advanced younger sister June find a performing role by purchasing her an autoharp. When the original Carter trio of Sara, A.P., and Maybelle permanently parted ways in 1943, following the long disintegration of Sara and A.P.'s marriage, Maybelle and her brood carried on, billed as the Carter Sisters and Mother Maybelle. She was thirty-four years old at the time, and the "mother" prefix would be attached to her name forever after.

Eventually, Maybelle's daughters dispersed on separate professional paths. Their success genuinely pleased her, though the tapering off of the sisters-and-mother act, along with country music's increasing reliance on electrified sounds, left her resigned to supplementing her musical income with overnight nursing shifts. But she would increasingly find herself looked to as a matriarch by male stars, all of them at least a generation younger than her and almost all from outside her family circle. Their interactions, whether folksy or formal, began to bring more serious attention to her musicianship and vast knowledge of songs from a bygone era.

Earl Scruggs, easily the best-known bluegrass instrumentalist on the planet by the early '60s, made it known that he considered Maybelle a guitar hero when he and his duo partner Lester Flatt made an album of Carter Family favorites. On it, Scruggs attempted to emulate Maybelle's distinctive parts. Zwonitzer and Hirshberg noted that that was easier said than done, even when Maybelle, who was mostly playing autoharp on the sessions, offered the use of the archtop she'd used on the original recordings. "He had trouble reproducing Maybelle's unique tones and nuances," they wrote, "no matter how perfectly he copied her notes." During one of her televised appearances with Flatt and Scruggs, the announcer instructed the audience, "Pay attention to the real high notes that Earl's picking. He said Mama Maybelle taught him these chords."

Johnny Cash, who'd become a son-in-law to Maybelle upon marrying June, faithfully championed her skill and the Carter Family's historic contributions to commercial country music, which couldn't have hurt the case for their 1970 induction in the Country Music Hall of Fame, belated as it was, coming nine years after their contemporary Jimmie Rodgers went in as part of the inaugural class. Cash gave her an affectionately ceremonious introduction on an episode of his television show when she was in her sixties: "Whether country music is played in New York City, as we are tonight, in an American rural crossroads town, or in a foreign land, this next lady is loved and respected, and you can't really measure her influence in our business, so important she's been," intoned the imposing, black-clad host. "She's been recording now for forty-six years, and I hope her new record with a young singer named Johnny Cash doesn't hurt her career too much."

His droll self-deprecation drew a grin from her. She gave a slight nod toward the audience to acknowledge its applause and, still smiling, kicked off her spry, signature guitar figure from the Carter standard "Wildwood Flower," leading Cash's band into a song descended from it, "Pick the Wildwood Flower." Eventually Cash strode over to his mother-in-law, leaned over her shoulder, and watched her fingers move. He urged her to demonstrate her licks once more, pointed his microphone at her guitar, and played up his own ineptitude by comparison. "I see the way you do it," he said, "but I can't ever get it going, mama."

His stage patter brought to life a mother figure's paradoxical truth: just because she passes her knowledge along doesn't mean you'll ever be able to replicate her unique touch.

At the beginning of the '70s, the long-haired, California country-rockers in the Nitty Gritty Dirt Band invited Maybelle, by then in her sixties, along with Scruggs and a slew of other musical elders, to be venerated guests on what became the sprawling, generation-bridging landmark of an album *Will the Circle Be Unbroken*. Maybelle's granddaughter Carlene Carter was then in her teens, and the members of the Dirt Band were only about a decade older. In a 2018 interview with NPR, she described how easily her grandmother once more slipped into a matriarchal role at the request of a group of studious, enthusiastic young musicians. Carlene laughed heartily recalling the conversation: "She was like, 'Well, I guess I'll go down there with those Dirt Boys. They seem real nice.' It was just so cute."

After the album took off, the Dirt Band decided to bring a third incarnation of the Carter Family, featuring Maybelle and various configurations of her daughters and grandchildren, on tour. They knew that there could be no substitute for the presence of a musical mentor who taught everyone what they needed to know to move the picking tradition forward.

Carlene shared the stage with her grandmother those nights. "I think she always amazed people when they actually heard her play live, because she was such a perfectionist about it," she observed with a mixture of affection and admiration. "And as simple as everything might seem, it's not that simple. You ask any guitar player if you try to mimic it. They'll always put way more notes in than they need to and they'll miss the nuances of the smaller things."

—Jewly Hight, WNXP, *Turning the Tables*, Season 3, "Eight Women Who Invented American Popular Music," 2019

148. THE MOSAIC PROJECT
Terri Lyne Carrington (CONCORD JAZZ, 2011)

Some will say jazz, in a word, is improvisation. An equally appropriate word might be transformation: each player comes to the gig with her arsenal of licks and voicings, but when the tune starts, it's all about reacting to and being inspired by one another, giving each other space to create and shaping the simultaneous offerings into a transmuted whole. Fittingly, "Transformation," a cover of the Nona Hendryx track sung by Hendryx herself, set the tone for drummer Terri Lyne Carrington's formidable convention of female musicians. Nestled confidently between jazz and R&B, her album *The Mosaic Project* was at turns brainy, sassy, soulful, and revolutionary—rather like the women it celebrated. Carrington's project, which spawned a sequel album in 2015, remains a necessary intervention in a musical community whose presumed leading lights still allege that women don't care for solos. (Tell that to Ingrid Jensen or Esperanza Spalding or the late Geri Allen, or any of the other women who played fine solos on this record.) It sounded like a communal metamorphosis, a circle of women passing inspiration—as rapper Shea Rose declared in "Sisters on the Rise"—"From a sister to another to another funky sister."

—Rachel Horn, NPR Music, *Turning the Tables*,
"The 150 Greatest Albums Made by Women," 2017

186

Terri Lyne Carrington: How Do You Learn Jazz?

Terri Lyne Carrington is a Grammy-winning drummer, composer, educator, and bandleader.

———————

It's really interesting how we can replicate these systems of oppression that have affected us. Even with myself, I've had to start to train myself to try to listen differently, because everything that I've heard in jazz, greatness has been defined by men. And it's very difficult to think, "What is another sound possibility coming from another body, a different body?" It's difficult to embrace that if you've been listening one way for forty or fifty years.

How do you learn jazz? You learn by listening to the records, you learn by teachers, and you learn by experience, jam sessions, or touring. And if you look at those three areas, the people who have dominated those areas have been men. So the great sound of jazz has been defined by male players who have had all of the opportunities to develop their craft. They have had the fortune of feeling the right to be there. People have invested in them, whether it's a record label or agents and people investing time or even wives and family investing by letting this person just go off and study, or be off in a room practicing and being looked at as a budding genius.

So we support this, and women just don't get the same support in general, which is why I'm so grateful for my parents—because even though my dad wanted a boy to carry on a jazz tradition in our family, once I showed an interest and showed an aptitude, he treated me as he would've treated a son who would've been carrying on this tradition in our family. But women don't see anybody who looks like them. It's hard to find women role models, peers, colleagues, and so you'd have to just be okay with being in a male-dominated environment. And I was actually okay with that. It didn't bother me.

But I can see now, it's funny because once I did start touring with more women, some tours I did with lead vocalists and background singers, I gravitated to hanging out with the women because it was different from what I was used to. And then what's really interesting is when I did Mosaic Project where I was the bandleader, and we were mostly surrounded by other women, I felt there was a bit of a balance issue. I felt like that just being around all women, that didn't feel natural to me either. And I do feel like bands and institutions and all of these places should be diverse places, and I think it's more interesting and the result is going to have more potential.

—Terri Lyne Carrington, as told to
Alison Fensterstock, 2022

ROBERTA FLACK:
Find your light

———

NPR: You could have had a classical career, but the opportunities for Blacks and classical music not being perhaps what they are today, I wonder if you ever regretted that—given the fact that classical music is not susceptible to those ups and downs that pop music is?

Roberta Flack: Oh, but it is as a matter of fact, probably in the most intense way you can imagine. Dedication is the key word, dedication and devotion because you may study voice for years and never get a chance to find—as my voice teacher said to me years ago—that light. He used to say to me, Roberta, find your light, where's your light, pretend you're underneath it, find the light. . . . [At] the time that I was a real student of music, meaning a student at Howard University and anticipating that I would go on and be a concert pianist, which is certainly my first goal—that was it. But then I discovered that I wasn't going to be able to do that. It was a wonderful thing for me to have the opportunity to move into other areas that would give me a springboard to do something. The idea in my mind was always to do something musical—it was not necessarily if I can't be a concert pianist, I'm going to quit. I mean, after you practice all those years and all those hours, you must find a light of some kind.

—Roberta Flack with Bob Edwards,
Morning Edition, 1989

Roberta Flack

Roberta Flack's Career Demands a New Way of Thinking About the Word "Genius"

Roberta Flack has always held two souls within her body. From her childhood days onward, she was herself, the daughter of a draftsman and a church choir organist who learned to play music at her mother's knee. This Roberta strove to understand both Chopin and Methodist hymnody and was precocious enough to gain admission to Howard University at age fifteen. She was a shy, awkward, diligent girl with her nose always in a book and fingers tired from practicing piano scales.

Even then, in her deepest being, she was also alter ego Rubina Flake, renowned concert *artiste*, effortlessly dazzling Carnegie Hall crowds with her performances. Rubina helped Roberta endure the indignities faced by gifted Black children in the South, as when she'd sing "Carry Me Back to Old Virginny" for contest judges in hotels where she wasn't allowed to stay the night. Her alter ego helped her feel glamorous and capable when others told her she was imperfect. Rubina had no need to respect others' restrictions. She was a diva, surrounded by bouquets of backstage flowers and the approval of an elite who didn't describe her as having "a chipmunk smile and a nut-brown face."

Flack graduated from Howard with dreams of becoming an opera singer. Discouragement from a vocal coach led her to reconsider and turn toward music education as a career and popular music as an avocation. She taught in rural North

Carolina and at several Washington, DC–area schools, eventually establishing herself as a nightclub performer on the side. Her repertoire and her warmth as a performer made her a sensation at Capitol Hill's Mr. Henry's, where she played up the classical elements in folk revival ballads and Motown hits, explaining how she did so as she went along—"It's based on an interesting baroque form called the *passacaglia*," she'd tell the crowd, offering a song, maybe, by Leonard Cohen. It was this unexpected blend of elements, not only in repertoire, but playing out within each song, that drew other musicians like the soul jazz pioneer Les McCann to Flack. After a night at Mr. Henry's he decided he needed to hook her up with his producer, Joel Dorn. Dorn soon signed Flack to Atlantic Records, and in 1969 they made *First Take*, the debut effort in a recording career that would bring her eighteen *Billboard*-charting songs, four Grammy awards and thirteen nominations, and, in 2020, a lifetime achievement award.

She is best known for majestic ballads like 1973's "Killing Me Softly with His Song," which laid the groundwork for the neo-soul sounds of R&B in the twenty-first century. But real heads, as the perennially hip Flack might say herself, continually find their way to her albums, which are funky, sexy, and political, blending jazz and Latin and rock and, always, classical elements in ways that defy the "adult contemporary" label often attached to her work. She's so often been ahead of the curve in her fifty years of recording, bringing the Brazilian arranger and composer Eumir Deodato out of the jazz world into her sessions in the 1970s, helping R&B stalwart and future Disney balladeer Peabo Bryson break through to the mainstream in the early '80s, connecting with new wave reggae star Maxi Priest for a Top 10 hit in the 1990s, "Set the Night to Music." Long before "post-genre" was a cliché on a million pop aspirants' lips, Flack showed how to build a legacy based on a quiet belief in limitlessness. Starting with *First Take*, she established her own parameters and then continually transcended them.

Though she does occasionally co-write her material, Flack came to fame as an interpreter as bold and discerning as her role models Nina Simone and Frank Sinatra. Like them, she had no fear of putting a Broadway ballad like "The Impossible Dream" next to a Bee Gees song on her setlists. Her inventiveness and panache placed Flack beside Aretha Franklin, Judy Collins, and Joan Baez as prime revisionists of the American songbook at the turn of the 1970s. She made room in the repertoire for the new generation of singer-songwriters emerging from the folk revival, like Cohen and Laura Nyro, and for civil rights movement–inspired Black composers like Eugene McDaniels, who authored many of her most powerful and political songs. Later she would work with McDaniels and others to invent a new style of R&B that built musical all-inclusiveness into its circulatory system—the marketing term applied to it was "quiet storm"—and which, after too many years of critical underestimation, would reveal itself as a prime element in twenty-first-century pop.

Flack is primed for the kind of critical and popular renaissance that brought Nina Simone back into the forefront of the musical conversation not long ago, and unlike that lost genius, she is still with us to enjoy it during her lifetime. As the only solo artist to win the Grammy for Record of the Year two years in a row—in 1973 for "The First Time Ever I Saw Your Face" and in 1974 for "Killing Me Softly with His Song"— she should have been granted, at the very least, a spotlight tribute during this year's televised ceremony, especially since host Alicia Keys owes Flack a considerable (and, by her, acknowledged) artistic debt. Instead, there was merely one quick shot of Flack smiling beatifically in the audience. Perhaps that cutaway did capture something: the failure of popular music's official institutions to fully track Flack's importance. She is beloved, yet underestimated, a treasure too rarely held up to the light.

One reason for this, unavoidably, is racism. The influence of this firebrand who had openly defied others' definitions of "soul" has been downplayed within the emerging histories of both rock *and* soul. (One obvious slight: though she has been eligible since 1994, as of 2023 she's never even been nominated to the Rock and Roll Hall of Fame.) The values her music conveys—virtuosity's attention to detail, the warm sensuality and tender eroticism shared by longtime friends and lovers, revelations reached slowly and thoughtfully instead of in a clattering crash—didn't coalesce within a rock and roll–defined hierarchy that puts rebels and gritty individualists at the top. Within Black communities and among artists of color, Flack's music has always remained a central guiding force. But to fully acknowledge Roberta Flack's importance is to rethink the presumptions that have haunted popular music for as long as she herself has been making music. Really listening to her seems like a good place to start.

It was classical music that first taught Flack that anything could be incorporated into her art. The compositions she loved struck her as open fields where any idea or feeling could circulate. For the young Roberta, music-making became the space where she could show that strength, not through florid emotional exertion but in the care she put into each note she sang, each phrase she explored on the piano. "I think everything you do as a Black person in this country represents a struggle for survival," she told *Essence* editor Susan L. Taylor in 1989, going on to explain that her power came in knowing "*I have intelligence* that no one can *ever* take away from me."

Psychologists popularized the term "emotional intelligence" twenty years after Flack made her first landmark albums, but its meanings resonate throughout her entire catalog. She could infuse a simple lyric like the one Ewan MacColl wrote for "The First Time Ever I Saw Your Face" with so many shades that, as MacColl later remarked, "an hors d'oeuvre became the main course." A light-spirited, wandering tune hastily written because the folk singer's future wife Peggy Seeger needed a "very short, modern love song" for a radio program, "First Time" in Flack's hands became virtually infinite. She found a slow rondo within it, building up its tension in waves, turning it into a firsthand account of desire that builds in a nonlinear way that evokes a woman's erotic responses. It's not surprising that, after lovers, new mothers are those likely to find the intensity of Flack's rendition relatable, as they enter into a relationship that redefines the basic rhythms of their bodies and their lives.

The wide scope of Flack's appeal, and her fearlessness about traveling beyond artistic borders, helped make her a major figure in 1970s popular culture. Her biography dazzles with surprising details. She sang at Jackie Robinson's funeral in 1972. She was the sole guest on a live broadcast of Bill Cosby's hugely influential television show in April 1970, and in 1971, she performed at the Soul to Soul Festival in Accra, Ghana, alongside Wilson Pickett and Ike and Tina Turner. She became one of the first Black investors in the radio station WBLS in 1974, and the first Black person to buy an apartment in the famous Dakota apartment building on Manhattan's Upper West Side, in the mid-1970s. In the 1980s she toured with Miles Davis; in 2001, not long after he left the White House, she accompanied Bill Clinton to a Harlem AIDS fund-raiser. In the 1970s, as much as Joni Mitchell embodied the complexities of women's liberation for white women, and Patti Smith stood for an emergent punk androgyny, Flack represented the sophistication of Black women in an era when mores were rapidly changing, and she remained an influential presence in many different cultural spheres.

Across the decades, Flack turned what is often misinterpreted as her "mood music" into a unique musical form that integrated elements across musical genres with unparalleled grace and receptiveness. As Flack developed her approach, she brought Rubina Flake with her, using the pseudonym when she took over from Dorn as producer of her fifth solo album, 1975's *Feel Like Makin' Love*. Flack had, in fact, played an increasingly central role in producing each of the five albums they did together, but only after Dorn exited the scene did she take credit. Flack has collaborated with producers including Arif Mardin and her protégé, the jazz bassist Marcus Miller, but since the late 1970s has retained primary control in the studio.

In his definitive essay on her legacy, the critic Jason King extolled Flack's mastery of "vibe": the outward expression of the feeling and spirit that motivate the creative process, first within one person and then in collaboration with others, a musical experience that, as King writes, "produced certain scales of social possibility around intimacy and communion." Flack created a musical language that made the ineffable palpable. This language is erotic, but not narrowly sexual. It is political, as when she takes on Black-power protest songs like McDaniels's "Compared to What," but never strident. It's masterful without devolving into posturing. And it's hugely influential across the spectrum of pop music.

As King discusses, Flack's vibing centrally shaped quiet storm, that R&B style that would sustain her career after her initial success in the early 1970s. Though the 1975 ballad by Smokey Robinson gave that elegant format its name, Flack's blueprint, set down on her first three albums, preceded that effort, and with *Feel Like Makin' Love* she would make a whole world of it. Flack continued to shape the subgenre with her 1980s duets with Peabo Bryson and generate classics, like 1994's *Roberta*, for its playlists into the 1990s. By then, Erykah Badu, D'Angelo, and others were referencing her intensity and cool to develop the style dubbed neo-soul. Hip-hop trio the Fugees put her legacy front and center in their 1996 reinvention of "Killing Me Softly," which itself won a Grammy and established Lauryn Hill as a new generational voice. Later, Solange would present her own spin on the introversion at the heart of Flack's music. Working with these artists and in their own solo efforts, essential producers like J Dilla, Flying Lotus, and Raphael Saadiq borrowed from Flack's sense of dynamics— that way of revealing the complex strata of what seems like sonic air.

Her music was always centered in her experience as a Black woman who grew up in the South, crossing lines but also connecting her expanding universe back to her personal experience and her community. One way Flack maintained this link was through gospel music—not the shouting Pentecostalism most rock and roll fans associated with that world, but the "long line hymnody" cultivated within Methodist congregations. Those indelible early hits, "The First Time Ever I Saw Your Face" and "Killing Me Softly with His Song," both invoke that style of sacred singing, one of the oldest forms of African American sacred self-expression, in which leaders would spin out phrases like wool becoming thread, so that responders could absorb the words and find their own ways into the melodies. "You know me, I like to slow everything down," Flack told an audience in 1971. It was this sense of time upended, rooted in Black sacred music, that gave Flack's signature songs such power. King names this effect as an expression of "silent frenzy," the form of spiritual rapture that, in African diaspora religions, results in almost ghostly stillness instead of the frenetic "falling out" that characterizes popular cultural depictions of gospelized joy.

Roberta Flack always returned to Blackness as the wellspring of her creative life. The community she's cultivated, from her early days being mentored by McCann to her later years guiding fresh talent like the brother-sister duo Jerry and Katreese Barnes, stands at the center of contemporary R&B's history, a kind of Jedi force charting its path. But Flack has also felt entitled to travel widely, claiming songs from everywhere. Hers is the freedom of the interpreter, who finds herself anew in many writers' voices instead of being entrapped, as many singer-songwriters can be, in autobiography.

Many who love her consider Flack's music a comfort—an oasis, as she called it in one album title. Yet the qualities that make her a constant companion in her fans' lives, and within the evolution of R&B and pop itself, are dynamic: her artistic mobility, her creative intelligence, her ambition. As a child, she projected these gifts onto her dream self, Rubina Flake. They've become her signature as, over fifty years, she's made each song she touches a means for telling her own story. "Every single song I've recorded expressed something deep and personal to me," she said in summing up her career. "Each was my singular focus whether in the studio or on the stage."

—Ann Powers, *Turning the Tables*, 2020 (excerpt)

195

Embrace the multitudes you contain. Shed your skin, and see what wriggles out. It's all you; these are some of the artists whose examples sign your permission slip.

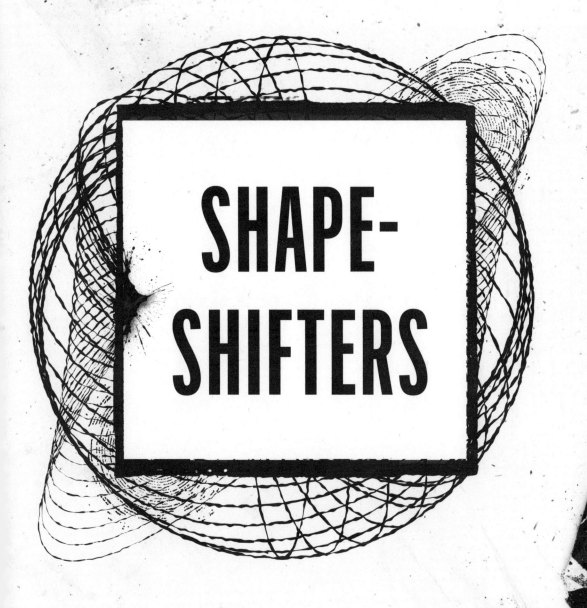

SHAPE-SHIFTERS

Joni Mitchell

JONI MITCHELL:
They usually shoot the innovator

Promoting her fifteenth album, *Turbulent Indigo*, Joni Mitchell talked to NPR's Liane Hansen about form, media, personae, inspiration, and truth.

Joni Mitchell: I think the danger is confusing the art with the artist. The songs are really designed, and some are autobiographical and some are portraits. Even if they're sung in the first person, frequently, they're portraits. So, a lot is written from identification, much of it historically.

And then again, too, in this particular art form, even a portrait, you can put someone else's eyes in it. You know, it's like with Gertrude Stein, Picasso's portrait of Gertrude Stein, he put his own eyes in it. She said, "It doesn't look like me," and he said, "It will." But I think the point of the songs—I object to a certain degree that the public is more fascinated by the artist than the art form itself, and I think that the people who get the most out of my music see themselves in it.

In "The Last Time I Saw Richard," one of the characters in that song says to the character that I play, you know, like, all romantics, you know, get that way, "cynical and drunk and boring someone in some dark cafe. You laugh. Look at your eyes, they're full of moons," right? So that character assumes that it's true, and frequently I'm called a cynic and usually by people who can't look at the truth. And there may be a tone when I'm delivering something that resembles cynicism, but a lot of times the things I'm saying when I'm called a cynic are factual.

I'm reading a book on Van Gogh right now, and much of his discourse is taking place also at the brink of a change of a millennium, and I wouldn't call anything he's saying cynicism, but it's more truth than most people can bite off. Basically, I relate to his frustration. In the world of painters, innovation and originality has always been a criteria, whereas in the world of pop music, copycat-ism is rewarded. They usually shoot the innovator. And it takes about two or three generations of copycats, and by the time they like it you've got a real watered down kind of insipid thing going on. I kind of cut my ear off many a night over that. [*laughter*]

NPR: You are, I think, as well-known for your visual art and the fact that you paint as you are for being a musician, and I wanted to know, do you approach a song like a painting?

Joni Mitchell: I was always an artist. I was always the school artist and I had a kind of precocious ability to render. And I was putting up drawings for a parent-teacher day in the sixth grade when one of the two great seventh-grade teachers came up to me and said, "You like to paint?" And I said, "Yes." He said to me, "If you can paint with a brush, you can paint with words." Now that is a tremendous gift to give a young child. When I met Georgia O'Keeffe, she was in her nineties, and she said to me, "Well, I would have liked to have been a musician, too, but you can't do both." And I said, "Oh yes you can." And she leaned in on her elbows and said, "Really? You know, I would have liked to have played the violin." I said, you know, "Well, take it up, Georgia," you know? I mean, you know, start today.

—*Weekend Edition* with Liane Hansen, 1995

200

Janelle Monáe
Is the 21st Century's
Time Traveler

Janelle Monáe is many people in alternate timelines at once. She's an archivist of right now, interpreter of back then, dreamer of one day. She imagines Black people into the future in the midst of past and present threats of erasure. The full scope of her work illuminates how the past, present, and future might exist simultaneously. Who we were, who we are, and who we'd like to be swirl and layer until timelines merge.

She's Cindi Mayweather, an android on the run from an oppressive government dressed in black and white. She's Jane, a human who holds on to her memories even as powers-that-be aim to systematically erase them. She's a singer and actress; a queer, Black woman who grew up in Kansas City, Kansas, with working-class parents; an Atlanta transplant who sold her CDs and sang on Atlanta University Center library steps before signing with Bad Boy in 2008.

These characters allow Monáe to sometimes speak in symbol and shadow. Timelines blur, then sharpen, and visions of the future collide with present realities. "Left the city, my mama she said, 'Don't come back home / These kids round' killin' each other, they lost they minds, they gone,'" she sings in *Metropolis*'s "Sincerely, Jane." Even when Monáe sings in character, the sense of something immediately true to her own life bobs into and outside of these voices.

The idea of envisioning a reality uncoupled from the structures that tie us to a threatening present is the power and affirmation of imagining Black futures. Ytasha Womack, author of *Afrofuturism: The World of Black Sci-Fi and Fantasy*

Janelle Monáe
by Jazmin Anita

Culture, describes Afrofuturism as "an intersection of black cultures as well as imagination, technology, mysticism, and liberation."

Musically, Monáe's vision of the future drew closer with *The Electric Lady* (2013). By the time she released *Dirty Computer* in 2018, Monáe had shifted to an image of reality that felt familiar. In the album and its visual counterpart, there's color and joy that spans timelines. The project's rollout came with an announcement tied to Monáe's most contemporary character, herself, publicly sharing her queerness for the first time. This is digital archiving: building records of now and preserving histories to analyze, celebrate, and reinterpret in the future.

In light of the current and continued marginalization and silencing of Black, brown, and queer communities, Monáe's work reminds us that it's not just collective memory that informs our future. When we document the ways we intimately and publicly exist in these moments in time, we build that future, too.

And Monáe shows us that we don't need to be tied to one vision of the future. We can create worlds that help us process current hierarchies and others that try to break out of those structures. Through this imagination, our vision of what's to come sharpens and adapts.

Monáe's time travel reminds us that while the present may be unsafe, the intimacies of right now are worth savoring. How we may love, and with whom we may find love, brings us light and longing in absurd and hateful circumstances. It inspires action. It not only anchors us in the present moment while considering the whole past, but it propels us into a new vision of the future—perhaps one that will be extricated from systems that oppress us; that is free, queer, Black, and only as far away as we can see on the horizon.

—Sydnee Monday, *Turning the Tables*, Season 2, "25 Most Influential Women+ Musicians of the 21st Century," 2018 (excerpt)

32. POST
Björk (ELEKTRA, 1995)

From the moment you hear the electronic explosion and driving drum beat of "Army of Me" that opens Björk's 1995 album *Post*, you can tell that the Icelandic singer is not messing around. The album, the follow-up to her much-beloved 1993 *Debut*, is even more emotive and electronically influenced and is reflective of a move from her small island homeland to London. Björk coproduced the album with a variety of collaborators, but her singular vision is unmistakable here. This is the album that secured in every fan's mind who Björk was as an artist—not one to repeat herself, and one so far removed from the alternative rock that was popular at the time that she inhabited an entirely separate universe. Björk's playful and dark sides are writ large here; she draws on '50s big band jazz ("It's Oh So Quiet") and a futuristic combo of melodic bleeps, strings, and a heavily effected beat ("Hyperballad"). At the time, critics loved the album for its originality and freewheeling embrace of a variety of sounds. And for the most innovative artists making music today, particularly those who enjoy a carefree sense of melody (like David Longstreth of Dirty Projectors), Björk is still a refreshing role model.

—Kimberly Junod, *World Café*, *Turning the Tables*, "The 150 Greatest Albums Made by Women," 2017

80. BIG SCIENCE
Laurie Anderson (WARNER BROS., 1982)

Laurie Anderson never intended to become a pop star. After an initially tiny pressing of "O Superman" found its way to BBC DJ John Peel's ears and later became an unexpected UK hit, Warner Bros. beseeched her to make an album. She assented, turning the "politics" section of her six-hour performance piece *United States I–IV* into her 1982 debut *Big Science*, and in doing so, wielded a mass medium as a critique against itself. Aware of her novelty value, she used her uncanny delivery to highlight humankind's frighteningly banal secession to the postindustrial age, lulling audiences into the placid state that she sought to critique. *Big Science* is simultaneously silly and prescient and takes a refreshingly wry attitude to technology's perils compared with today's often obvious commentary on the subject. Anderson's playful use of machine-speak subverts the industry's reliance on women's voices as a shortcut to maternal comfort while also progressing the trailblazing synthesizer work of pioneers like Delia Derbyshire and Suzanne Ciani. Despite Anderson's clear aversion to dehumanization at the hands of technology, *Big Science* is thrilling because it isn't a case of clashing binaries arguing for or against. "I don't want to nail things down," she told *Sounds* in 1986. "I want them to either breathe or explode."

—Laura Snapes, *Turning the Tables*,
"The 150 Greatest Albums Made by Women," 2017

LAURIE ANDERSON
A talking violin

❝ I got a real cheap violin, like a fifteen-dollar violin, and I took the back off and put a little speaker inside and ran it to a cassette deck. So the violin is playing totally by itself, you just hold it in place. And then you can play duets with it live, simultaneously with strings. It was a talking violin. Then the second violin that I made was via phonograph. It had a battery-operated turntable built into the violin itself so that you could play records on it. A little on-off switch and then the needle, it's usually on the end of the arm, was in the middle of the bow. It sounded like barking seals. Both of those were real low-quality sound instruments. And I love low-quality sound. I love the way sound comes over car radios, you know, at fifty miles an hour. I like it because you can hear the air and you can hear static and you can hear all kinds of things that you don't normally hear. When you speak to someone who's sitting next to you, you get a sense that the sound is traveling, it's come a long way to get to you. 🙮

—NPR's *Voices in the Wind* with Nancy Fushan, 1978

28. NINA SIMONE SINGS THE BLUES
Nina Simone (RCA VICTOR, 1967)

The High Priestess of Soul, Nina Simone, was thirty-four years old in 1967. She'd been making music her whole life—she was trained as a classical pianist—and, at twenty-one, started singing in clubs. For the next decade, she bounced around, recording jazz and blues standards and steadily earning a reputation as a remarkable performer. People loved watching and hearing Simone perform, though critics weren't quite sure what to do with her. Was she a blues singer? A jazz pianist and performer? And what about those original songs—how did *they* fit in? When Simone made the move to RCA in 1967, those questions started to become less important, and the focus now found itself on her voice—that voice! Slip-sliding between sultry sensuality ("In the Dark"), heart-wrenching reminiscences ("My Man's Gone Now"), and biting social commentary ("Backlash Blues," a song she co-wrote with Langston Hughes), Nina Simone proved, with *Sings the Blues*, that hers was a voice capable of anything. It made people fall in and out of love, it made them pay attention to the past, and it forced them to become aware of the social inequalities all around them.

—Elena See, *Folk Alley*, Minnesota Public Radio, *Turning the Tables*, "The 150 Greatest Albums Made by Women," 2017

136. YOKO ONO/PLASTIC ONO BAND
Yoko Ono/Plastic Ono Band (APPLE RECORDS, 1970)

Yoko Ono *by* Dame Darcy

Has there ever been a female artist so overshadowed by her proximity to male greatness as Yoko Ono? A truly cutting-edge figure across multiple disciplines, Ono is nonetheless more often spited for daring to influence her collaborator-turned-husband John Lennon than lauded for her pioneering works of music and performance art. The 1970 twin releases from Ono and Lennon, with their newly formed Plastic Ono Band, epitomize this. Whereas *John Lennon/ Plastic Ono Band* was critically acclaimed as an intimate, honest rock and roll album, few audiences knew what to do with *Yoko Ono/Plastic Ono Band*. Jarring, experimental, and stunning, Ono's album sounds like a head-on collision between her avant-garde art and Lennon's rock and roll (with touches of free jazz by way of an Ornette Coleman quartet on "AOS"). Yoko's voice is a powerful instrument, and it's honed to near perfection on this album; it ricochets with prepunk raw aggression and incorporates *hetai*, a vocal style from Japanese kabuki theater. At the time of its release, critical reception to *Yoko Ono/Plastic Ono Band* was paternalistic at best and outright disdainful at worst; however, bands like the B-52's, Sonic Youth, Public Image Ltd, the Slits, and many others bear strong signs of Ono's influence. Wide swaths of avant-garde rock, postpunk, sound art, and experimental electronic music simply wouldn't exist without the fearless curiosity of *Yoko Ono/Plastic Ono Band*.

—Marissa Lorusso, NPR Music, *Turning the Tables*, "The 150 Greatest Albums Made by Women," 2017

206

36. NIGHTCLUBBING
Grace Jones (ISLAND RECORDS, 1981)

On her fifth album, model, actress, and scenester Grace Jones hit a winning and lasting formula. Tethered by the ace rhythm section of Sly Dunbar and Robbie Shakespeare, keyboardist Wally Badarou, drummer Uziah "Sticky" Thompson, and guitarists Mikey Chung and Barry Reynolds—together known as the Compass Point All Stars—*Nightclubbing* is a new wave, postdisco blend with a visceral thread of reggae throughout. This newly found sound proved to be the perfect foundation for Jones's vocals, with the reggae bounce serving as a foil to her staccato snarl. She's every bit as imposing, angular, and intimidating in her music as she is on her iconic album cover and in her music videos. Every line sounds like a command, and the

Grace Jones *by* Asiah Fulmore

listener has no choice but to do what they are told. Use her—okay. Pull up to the bumper—no problem. Don't mess around with the demolition man—wouldn't dream of it! And yet, underneath the surface of those cheekbones and shoulder pads is a sly wink and a devil-may-care smile. Looking like a beautiful chain-smoking Amazonian android, Jones serves up cool funk that up until that very moment had always been served piping hot.

—Jill Sternheimer, Lincoln Center, *Turning the Tables*,
"The 150 Greatest Albums Made by Women," 2017

207

15. NICKI MINAJ, "SUPER BASS"

Nicki Lewinsky. Nicki the Boss. Nicki the Ninja. The Harajuku Barbie. The Female Weezy. Roman Zolanski. Chun-Li. Onika Maraj, best known to the masses as Nicki Minaj, has been one of rap's greatest chameleons. She has redefined what a successful female rapper is capable of. And although she's fully established herself in the canon of hip-hop crossover stars, it's almost funny to recall that it was fewer than ten years ago that she was busting down music industry expectations.

Coming off the success of her debut album, *Pink Friday*, no one expected a deep cut mixing pop, EDM, and rap to eclipse the initial release. But the bonus track became a sleeper hit as well as Nicki's sonic catapult to international stardom. "Super Bass" was co-written with Ester Dean, Roahn Hylton, and Kane Beatz (the song's producer) to sugarcoat Nicki's signature raunch just enough to appeal to the radio and beyond. The message is playful enough that it can be censored down to a PG level, and the hook makes use of catchy, cute onomatopoeia so virtually anyone, regardless of age or native language, can sing along. But as much as "Super Bass" gives a wink to the pop world, Nicki didn't sacrifice her punch lines and similes in the process. Rhyming double and triple time—often in the same verse—she proved candy-coated hip hop can still deliver rap prowess.

—Sidney Madden, *Turning the Tables*, Season 2,
"The 200 Greatest Songs by 21st-Century Women+," 2018

Rihanna:
Crown Yourself

Rihanna's music has soundtracked most of this century, and that kind of ubiquity is easily taken for granted, like air. She released a full-length studio album every single year between 2005 and 2012, save for a one-year break in 2008. Of the sixty-one Rihanna songs on the *Billboard* Hot 100, fourteen of them were No. 1 hits, and thirty-one of them were Top 10 hits. No album has landed as many No. 1 songs on *Billboard*'s Dance Club Songs chart as *ANTI*, the album Rihanna released in 2016 after an unprecedented (for her) hiatus.

For most of my life, there has been a Rihanna single—or multiple Rihanna singles, or multiple songs defined by a Rihanna hook—playing prominently on Top 40 radio. Rihanna shaped the texture and taste of the air by consistently doing what pop, at its very best, is supposed to do: taking disparate genres—rock, EDM, dancehall, trap, and even dubstep—and turning them into something that makes sense to us, to everyone. If she's not seen as taking musical risks, it's only because so many of them paid off. It's still worth asking, however, how we as an audience can adequately love Rihanna the person.

When Rihanna received the Video Vanguard Award at the 2016 MTV VMAs, Drake introduced her. "She succeeds by doing something that no one in this music industry does, which is being herself," Drake said. "We love the music, which can change styles from album to album; we love the videos, which change their artistic vision from year to year; but most of all, we love the woman, who hasn't changed since day one."

Rihanna was gracious in her acceptance speech. She spoke about how her success is never just about her—it's about Barbados, her family, her fans, and "women, Black women." She also went on to thank the directors who went along with her "crazy ideas"—her subtle way of asserting what Drake did not: that she is pop music's vanguard, and that the work itself is where her prowess lies.

It matters that Rihanna comes across as genuine, that her sense of self appears unshaken by celebrity, that she feels accessible to her fans. But this is not a persona that occurs without effort. Rihanna has been performing what it means to be in the thick of things—not above them, not outside looking in, not past them—for her whole career. That takes emotional and intellectual work, especially when you consider—as scholar Esther L. Jones does in her essay "'What's My Name?': Reading Rihanna's Autobiographical Acts"—that the public-private distinction Rihanna had spent years cultivating was shattered in 2009, when Rihanna's then-boyfriend Chris Brown physically assaulted her just ahead of the Grammys and the photo evidence spread across the internet.

To really love Rihanna, one must respect that what we so often find lovable about her—her so-called relatability, the way she's able to deemphasize the significant social and artistic distance between herself and her fans—is also her work.

"We Found Love," released two and a half years after Chris Brown attacked Rihanna, is classic dance pop with an edge. It's meant to sound like joy, but the lyrics are vague enough to account for a whole range of human feeling. In the video, Rihanna chooses darkness. It's about two people who are not good for each other. There are fights that look unhealthy. There are plenty of drugs. It starts with an opening monologue about a relationship gone wrong. "When it's over, and it's gone," the English actress Agyness Deyn reads, "you almost wish that you could have all that bad stuff back so that you could have the good."

On the album *Unapologetic*, which came out as rumors of Rihanna and Chris Brown's romantic reunion swirled (they were later confirmed), critic Jessica Hopper wrote for *Pitchfork*: "She's quite a distance from the tidy narrative we'd like, the one where she's learned from her pain and is back to doing diva triumph club stomp in the shadow of Beyoncé. *Unapologetic* rubs our faces in the inconvenient, messy truth of Rihanna's life which, even if it were done well, would be hard to celebrate as a success."

But *Unapologetic* was also home to "Pour It Up," the song and video in which Rihanna plays both the dancer and the client in a strip club. It's a meditation on financial independence and an assertion of control. Rihanna's realness is not just about her carefree Instagram posts, or her habit of taking wine to-go. Her realness is popular art that cuts to the hard questions. She stretched the boundaries of genre, of course, but she also demanded that her vast audience grapple with the complexity of her inner life—both when it was empowering *and* when it was difficult. The worry that often accompanies this kind of bravery is that it won't be legible to your audience—or that you'll be misunderstood.

My favorite Rihanna moment is the line in "Bitch Better Have My Money" where she sings, "Turn up to Rihanna while the whole club fuckin' wasted." It's an acknowledgment that she has the privilege of living in the sonic landscape she created herself—that she is a collector of herself. That line is delivered in the archetypical "Rihanna voice," which is, as Jayson Greene argued for *Pitchfork*, the most influential vocal of the past decade in pop. Apparently, she wears a chain with the word "Savage" on her neck, or at least she did for a 2018 *Vogue* interview. "Savage is really about taking complete ownership of how you feel and the choices you make," she says. "Basically making sure everybody knows the ball is in your court."

The question I asked was about whether Rihanna's audience has ever adequately loved her—whether we've given her the kind of love that respects both what she's created and all the labor that went into creating it. But the answer Rihanna gives, through *ANTI*, is that Rihanna probably doesn't care about the question to begin with.

In a promotional video for *ANTI*, Rihanna is given a crown from a child who we can only assume is that same child on the album cover, a young Rihanna. The moment is a lesson: you can wait—wait for *ANTI* to get the Grammy it deserved, wait for the world to give the genius of your work its due—or you can crown yourself.

—Jenny Gathright, *Turning the Tables*, Season 2,
"25 Most Influential Women+ Musicians of the 21st Century," 2018 (excerpt)

BILLIE EILISH
You have to try things out

66 That's the thing about everything in life, you have to try certain things out to figure out what you want. You can't just be born and be completely original. You don't know enough to do that. So, when you're younger, you try out different personalities because you don't know which one is you, to be honest. Obviously, that's what you need to do to grow and to get where you need to be. You should always be able to have that moment of figuring out who you are by using a bunch of different things that you've heard already. And then, instead of still doing that for your whole career—which I think *some* people do—you have to take that and digest it and then come out with something that's everything combined and it's your own thing. 99

—*All Things Considered* with Michel Martin, 2019

212

 1. M.I.A., "PAPER PLANES"

This runaway hit was hardly Maya Arulpragasam's first song about the dual consciousness and dissonance of being a refugee seeking to make sense in a hostile foreign culture, but it proved the most salient. Its immortal chorus, a gloriously acerbic flip on Wreckx-n-Effect's "Rump Shaker," posited that nothing's more thuggish than Western capitalist expansion, and her languorous vocal operated as both narrator and indicter, as she sang, heavy-lidded and purposely pitchy, about her own survivalist swagger. Written around the time she said the US was giving her visa issues in 2006 but stamped with a yearslong shelf life, ironically "Paper Planes" proffered her biggest platform yet: a spot on the 2009 Grammys where, nine months pregnant, she performed with Jay-Z and T.I., proving that the immigrant hustle never ceases. It brought her music to the very mass American audience she was critiquing, a central tension within M.I.A.'s oeuvre that has kept her music so vital. She understood that colonization was the antagonist, capitalism was the vessel, and that she could subvert them both to get her point across. "Paper Planes" made M.I.A. famous, but more significantly, it solidified her as a biting analyst willing to use her pop stardom to expose the flaws in the very system of pop stardom itself—an uncomfortable outsider and iconoclast whose incongruities are as fascinating as her brilliant music.

—Julianne Escobedo Shepherd, *Turning the Tables*,
Season 2, "The 200 Greatest Songs by 21st-Century
Women+," 2018

KATE BUSH
A continual experiment

66 I think I've always played with my voice. Because I've never really thought of myself as a singer. And it's, it's always, in many ways, a continual experiment for me to see what kind of voice suits the song that you're working on. It's quite often trying to create a bit of a character through the voice to help tell the story. 55

—*All Things Considered*
with Lynn Neary, 1990

Kate Bush *by* Maggie Thrash

How Kate Bush's *The Dreaming* Made My Monsters My Own

There are so many ways that women are made into monsters. As girls, they bleed too soon, or grow too fat, or remain too boyish. They have the wrong color skin in a country that has turned lies about race into law. Becoming pregnant, they cannot contain themselves, losing the baby, or losing their firm bodies after the birth. Failing to become pregnant, they find themselves marked as barren, bony, half. Women may be called monstrous simply for keeping to themselves, unkempt and unbeautiful, especially as they age. Or for the opposite—claiming space with too large a footprint. Women are identified as monsters for being, speaking, changing, being alive. Some are punished openly for these violations. Most carry the judgment within.

Occasionally, a woman—usually an artist—will make it her mission to speak as the monster others fear her to be. Living through abnormality, she sees something else in it. Potential to claim the ugliness, to refine it like blood turning into energy inside her body, until it lends strength. Shape-shifting can become shame-shifting. The voice of the monster says, I am here, motherfuckers, I feel with every fiber of my being, I am wholly myself and have the right to be alive.

Throughout Kate Bush's fourth album *The Dreaming*, the voice of a twenty-two-year-old woman speaks the pain and explores the potential of monstrous transformation. "With my ego in my gut, / my babbling mouth would wash it up,"

Bush sings in the drum-struck "Leave It Open." Her mouth issues moans and screams, sounds less and more than human; she keeps it shut. Then she leaves it open: "Harm is in us, but power to arm," the backing vocalists, her consorts and twins, chant. She will wrestle with unnamed forces within and without. By the end of the song she has found her statement of purpose, rendered in a complex layer of manipulated lines and backward tracks. "We let the weirdness in," she sings.

Released in 1982, after Bush had achieved stardom in her native England but before she solidified her status as a founder of singer-songwriterly art rock, *The Dreaming* is generally viewed as transitional, an assemblage of daring but almost unlistenable experiments. After its release Bush enthused to reporters that she'd achieved all she'd wanted to do. "All this energy, my frustrations, my fears, my wish to succeed, all that went into the record," she said in 1986. *The Dreaming* is Bush's *One Thousand and One Nights*, casting Bush as both teller and subject. Half the songs bring alive characters that require her to make huge identity leaps: she is a man riding a dented van through the Australian Outback, another in mortal combat, a thief who might be man or woman, a woman turning into a beast. The others recount her own frustrated quest for spiritual and artistic insight, a struggle that surpasses the lessons of her Catholic girlhood and leaves her gasping for both more grace and fewer visions.

Working with new musical tools, notably the Fairlight synthesizer, that allowed her to stretch and rend her vocals, distort guitars and drums, and interweave fragments of supposedly nonmusical sounds—samples, in the same moment hip-hop pioneers were doing so in America—Bush created a collection of immersive accounts of psychic death and rebirth. A self-aware storyteller, she makes sure to touch on myriad sites of such transformations: conquest, crime and hauntings, mystical altered states, visions of and beyond the grave. Building dense, simultaneously lush and jarring arrangements to enliven these scenes, Bush uses her voice, the emissary of her body, to become the monsters her stories need.

Me, a Monster

Recently, blessed with a free day and a YouTube instructional video, I pried open the dented lock of a trunk containing relics of my adolescence. Under stacks of

215

unsorted photographs and the issue of *Rolling Stone* with John and Yoko naked on the cover, I found the cheap clothbound journals I kept to help me become a "real" writer. "Why does beauty sleep with sorrow?" I wrote in my journal in an uneven hand. "I am failing in my life." I was eighteen.

That diary was dated 1981, the year before *The Dreaming* came out. A year earlier I'd stumbled on Bush's first album, 1978's *The Kick Inside*, at a church rummage sale. The cover told me I needed it. My high school punk rock models of female independence were tough, but they had never really stood alone. Chrissie Hynde and Debbie Harry always had the boys in their bands behind them, leaning against their assuring masculinity as if it were an alley wall. Exene Cervenka was married to John Doe, her co-lead vocalist in my favorite band, X. Even the Go-Go's had each other, their glam-gang image mirroring the strategic friendships that helped daring girls move with self-assurance through rock's male-dominated scenes. But Kate—she was a solitary. On *The Kick Inside*'s American album cover she curls in the corner of what looks like an attic room, gazing out beneath her bangs with eyebrows raised. In fact, she's in a box, placed there by photographer Gered Mankowitz. Yet she remains defiant. My mind is so big, the picture says, no one else can fit into this space.

I was that kind of unmanageably dreamy girl myself. The internal life Bush's early albums evoked in stories of imaginary lovers and spiritual raptures felt like my own, shut off from easy expression, frighteningly intense. Some songs, like "Room for the Life," reassured me in language that recalled the bell-bottomed lecturers in my Women Studies 101 class, a hotbed of powerful sisterhood where students were encouraged to celebrate their genitalia and march against male violence. Others, though, stretched past gendered rhetoric. Bush was a lion, a spy, a bat, a kite. I'd lock into her photographed gaze while listening to her soprano bouncing untethered across an atmosphere of unchecked anxieties and ambitions. "I got no limbs, I'm like a feather on the wind," she sings in "Kite," an account of possibly chemically induced euphoria. "I'm not sure I want to be up here at all." I related to that chaos.

The lush arrangements male producers encouraged her to accept on her first albums still couldn't contain Bush's disruptive singing. Critics called her vocals "irritatingly yelpy," "schoolgirl-siren," "braying like a donkey." The mix of decidedly uncool, not coincidentally womanly elements—her plummy middle-class diction and swooning melodies, sometimes enhanced by saxophone—and unfettered vocal and lyrical experimenting threw off many rock fans, though it enraptured me. My Kate fandom grew in a kind of spiritual terrarium, solitary and humid. "I am Athena—I am Diana—I am my own answer," I wrote in that 1981 diary, quoting the title of a Kate song in the same paragraph. "There's 'Room for the Life' in my womb and in my *soul*. I am a mysterious and beautiful creature, glorying in the independent realisation [British spelling was my thing, then] of my essence." That radical feminist literature from my Women Studies 101 class was definitely getting to me, and Kate's music filled my anima-centric dreams.

Yet the florid positivity in my journal is matched throughout with self-admonition and dismissal. "I MUST DO SERIOUS WRITING!! Otherwise I have no excuse for existing in my present state." Or: "It hurts to hate oneself. I must work on stopping." Or: "I ate pizza tonight, and feel like throwing myself off a bridge because of it." I wanted to be a kite, like Kate, but I felt like a gorgon. The struggle to become sometimes hurt so much. Only when I heard *The Dreaming* did I hear music that captured that feeling in sound.

The Howl

I can still remember lowering the needle onto the vinyl in the junk-furnished living room of the rented house I shared with my Goth-leaning housemates, lying on the floor right beneath the turntable, turning up the volume until the speakers shook. The drums on *The Dreaming* announced it as something new. I knew next to nothing about African music at eighteen, but I could recognize syncopation, which brought the noise to Stravinsky's *Rite of Spring* (my verging-on-ex boyfriend, a classical cellist, had turned me on to that) and the artist who ruled the speakers at arty kids' parties that year—Prince. "Sat in Your Lap," *The Dreaming*'s first track, hit with a huge bass drum intermingled with something else. What was it? My ears tried to grab the song's moving parts. Kate screaming: "I must admit, just when I think I'm king, / I just begin!" Bang, bang!

This was the sound of a soul who believes in its own boundlessness but can't make the feeling stick. Swagger laced with rage. She'd composed "Sat in Your Lap," her first wholly self-produced track, after coming home from a Stevie Wonder show at Wembley Stadium. Wonder's late-1970s sound, freewheeling and prickly with synths and funky beat, gave her a new direction. She'd recently acquired several synths of her own, including one of only a few Fairlights in England. The Fairlight, which Wonder had used throughout his experimental album *Stevie Wonder's Journey Through "The Secret Life of Plants,"* was known as an orchestra in a box, and it could also loop and remix short "nonmusical" effects. Bush recognized it as a portal. She could risk sounding really strange and unpretty now. Playing the album through, I felt almost dazed. Images from favorite movies entered my head. "There Goes a Tenner," about a caper gone wrong, made me think of Mickey Mouse in Disney's *Fantasia*; the battle epic "Pull Out the Pin" hit dank and dark, like *Apocalypse Now*. I didn't know it, but Bush had used a sample of helicopter blades beating in it.

And then there were those songs about Bush's own struggles, so like my own. At their heart was a clanging rage, partly stemming from Bush's impatience with being objectified as either a nut case or a sex symbol. I sank my whole monstrous-to-me body into *The Dreaming* and imagined myself shape-shifting as Kate could. What made it seem possible was the struggle I could hear in every track. She was teaching herself how to be a new kind of musician; I needed to be a new kind of me. The fight inside me pitted my longing to become shameless—to own that punk attitude the prettier, thinner girls around me seemed to effortlessly adopt—and the shame I felt inside. Shame about being too fat, too loud, not the kind of girl the rock boys I wanted, wanted back. Shame because I slept with those guys anyway and then they turned away from me. Shame because my mother thought I was still a virgin. Shame when I spoke too much in class and the male professors raised their eyebrows. Shame when I didn't speak up, standing in the kitchen at punk parties dominated by playful fistfights between the boys while the girls slinked off to smoke menthols on the porch.

The Dreaming is all about shame, and crisis, and feeling trapped, and speaking—howling!—anyway. The characters Bush wrote across its soundscapes, including herself, make bad decisions or inevitable but deeply damaging ones; they cry out in anguish. Its wild, cacophonous sound resulted from Bush's new sense of freedom in possession of the Fairlight and other synthesizers, but also from the difficulty she had mastering them, the frustration that she built into each mix even after she'd found ways to break through. "Suddenly my feet are feet of mud," Bush moans in the chorus of "Suspended in Gaffa," the more pensive and playful but equally heart-stricken counterpart to "Sat in Your Lap." "Gaffa" is her word for the sticky tape that's everywhere on a soundstage; she's imagining herself entangled, unable to move toward the mastery she craves. Stuck was how I felt more often than not in the years when I listened to it every day—stuck and ugly, trying to shape-shift but ending up half-formed. "I detest myself for not having the class to rise above it all," I wrote in my diary. "I don't know why I'm crying," Kate sang.

Still Dreaming

The limitations of *The Dreaming* have become clearer to me as I've tried to face my own mistakes as a thinker and a person. Many of its songs qualify, in some ways, as exotica—a white artist's attempt to access the "other" within by borrowing decontextualized material from unfamiliar sources. The soldier's story in "Pull Out the Pin" was inspired by a documentary she saw about the sacrifices of the Viet Cong. The album's title track is a white working-class laborer's account of Australian industry's destruction of the Outback, but as Daphne Carr points out in her 2019 *Pitchfork* reassessment of the album, the song fetishizes aboriginal people in words and grunts. Bush intended to express empathy for the oppressed in these songs, but her attempts to critique colonialism fall short. The insularity of *The Dreaming* feeds its alpha energy, but limits it possibilities. What would the album be if Bush had engaged the living counterparts of even a few of the characters she so ardently invoked?

I also now know that Bush's refusal to fully pursue stardom in America was, for me, a boon—for one thing, with only limited access to the interviews she gave in the British press, I didn't have to face her scorn for the feminist cultural work I consider her music's best complement. It's all there for web searchers with the stomach for it: her slurs against "butch lesbians" with "hairy legs and big muscles," her suggestion that feminist dialogues pander to women, her stalwart identification with men. "When I'm at the piano writing a song, I like to think I'm a man," she told a *Melody Maker* reporter in 1978. "What it is, basically, is that all the songwriters I admire and listen to are male."

Most punk and new wave women who hit the mainstream in the 1980s made announcements like these. It's easy to forget how marginalized feminism was then, how excoriated across media and within most institutions, including academia and the art world and, most of all, in music. The lesbian world of women's music remained strategically separatist and is forever underestimated; the rock underground where explicitly feminist bands like the Raincoats operated was small and, as Jenn Pelly has written, seemingly unprecedented. (In most cities in England and America, there was one band like that, doing gender politics in relative isolation.) Much more frequently, the women now embraced as proto-liberationists—Patti Smith, Joan Jett, Chrissie Hynde, Debbie Harry—refused the F-word and identified with men, if not as male.

Monsters are lonely creatures. Embodiments of shame and the struggle against it, in most stories they face exile, if not annihilation. One poignant aspect of *The Dreaming* is the way Bush's characters so often cry out for connection even as they are falling, the grip loosened, away from the objects of their desire. Houdini's wife is panicked by his death and possessed by the hope that his ghost will speak to her. The smuggler's lover in "Night of the Swallow," fearing he'll perish on his next run, betrays him. The hermitlike homebody of "Get Out of My House" fends off the demon at her door only by becoming a beast. And Kate herself, stalking the muse that is both her truest self and a spirit that always feels foreign, decides, in the end, to embrace the harm within herself. "This is the first time I actually enjoy hearing my voice," Bush told an interviewer upon the release of *The Dreaming*. This roar was weird, but it was hers. And it was my monster, myself.

—Ann Powers, "*Turning the Tables*: Records That Changed Our Lives," 2021

Volta,
or Gal Costa's
Eternal Return

My mother was the one who showed me the clip: grainy, brief, black-and-white. The woman who would sing was barefoot and her dress shimmered darkly like a river in moonlight. There were flowers in her cloud of hair. She hiked her knees up on the stool, strips of sequins dripped between her thighs, her toes were tense. The guitar cried a little in the cradle of her hips. I traced the precise articulation of her top lip—the dip—and from somewhere inside where none of us could see, a voice bubbled up, which made her mouth move, but barely, and the sound was more sublime than what our eyes had seen. "*Volta, volta*"—sang Gal Costa—and we did— we came back—we played the clip again.

In Portuguese, *volta* means "return"—a common romantic refrain—but my ear picked up, instead, the term that critics use for the lyric poem's crucial turn. The *volta* marks the moment, especially in sonnets, when the mind or heart must change, calling into question all that's gone before. The road forks, or doubles back, or disappears, making way for risk, the possibility of transformation. Gal's voice produced a *volta* in me, as it did for the Brazilian musician Caetano Veloso the first time he heard her sing, "a surprise so deep and large that I still live inside it." She sang like that for fifty years, without pause, so that "the silver rain of her voice covered the country," saturating even the most brutal periods of Brazilian history with subversive sweetness. She was, many say, Brazil's greatest interpreter. But her interpretations did not explain anything—not Brazil, not bossa nova, not Tropicália, not freedom, not desire. Not even herself. The best interpreters don't explain, they explode.

Who was Gal and where did she come from? Maria da Graça Costa Penna Burgos was born in Salvador de Bahia, the Black Brazilian origin of capoeira, candomblé, and samba. It was 1945. Her mother played her music in the womb, hoping the child might someday sing. Gal never met her father, who kept a second family. "Were you poor?" asked the magazines. "We were never rich." In photographs, her mother looks white; Gal seems to have more blackness in her face and hair. She never studied voice or dance and barely finished middle school. She learned to sing by singing, to move by moving, to play by ear. "The desire was everything," she told Canal Brazil. At fourteen she heard João Gilberto's "Desafinado" on the radio, and those *antimusical* melodic intervals mapped her wayward road. She was so shy, and sang so soft—when she performed she wouldn't lift her gaze. But the voice itself was born for bossa nova: pure yearning, perfect pitch.

"Bossa nova overwhelmed us," wrote Caetano in his memoir. He was speaking for his friends in the Bahian scene: his sister, the singer Maria Bethânia; his schoolmates at the state university in Salvador; the polymath musician Gilberto Gil; and the irreverent composer Tom Zé. The subtlety of bossa nova's melodies matched the complexity of samba's rhythms, but the new arrangements were minimal and intimate, scaled to the living room or corner bar rather than the street parade. Somehow, in pioneering the new style, João Gilberto had figured out how to honor "the popular musical traditions of Brazil" while "establishing a position from which to innovate." Gal, Caetano wrote, listened to him "more and better than anyone else," keying into his sophisticated relationship to the Brazilian musical legacy. She drew strength from her new friends, making her debut at concerts they put on together. They sang bossa nova, of course, as well as samba classics from the thirties, and the new songs the boys were writing.

Brazil's military coup came in 1964. They were finding their voices together just as the regime closed in with its fist of silence: "One swallow does not make a summer," Gilberto said, "we needed a tribe"—and that's how they emerged, as an experimental, androgynous, multiracial collective with their fingerprints all over each other's projects. In 1967, Gal released her first record, a repertoire of bossa nova duets with Caetano. Gilberto wrote a few of the songs. *Domingo* was so smooth you might be tempted to mistake *saudade* for nostalgia. But Caetano was clear in the liner notes: their *saudade* was a longing for the future, not the past. In the record's breakout hit, "Coração Vagabundo," Gal expresses *saudade* as a kind of wanderlust: "my vagabond heart / wants to keep the world in me." She never left bossa nova behind—she kept that world in her—but almost as soon as she let those songs loose from her lips, she had to find new ones.

In 1968, the regime cracked down harder. Act AI–5 shuttered congress and outlawed political opposition. Still, the counterculture's tide kept rising. Many young people who opposed the dictatorship grew frustrated with bossa nova's apolitical introspection and cool middle-class elegance. One response, dubbed *música popular brasiliera*, was emphatically nationalist: regional roots music with a critical edge, acoustic, like the music of their contemporaries in the Greenwich Village scene. Then there was the Jovem Guarda, kids who went electric and mimicked the rockers of the British Invasion.

The Bahian group didn't know where they fit. The party line of *música popular brasiliera* was that rock was imperial poison, but Gal and her friends loved James Brown, Jimi Hendrix, the Beatles, Janis Joplin. And wasn't bossa nova born from jazz as much as samba? Didn't they have a right to steal, not just get stolen from? True, Brazil's regional folk music was more sophisticated than the *yeah-yeah-yeah*s of mop top imitators, but there was an insurgent internationalism in the cities of the Global South, there were hot dogs and Afros and TV and undercover cops and margarine and gasoline and T-shirts that said *baby*. The boys dreamed of "a great transformative synthesis," a "universal sound," and this ambition coalesced, briefly and brightly, under the banner of Tropicália, an aesthetic alliance with poets, filmmakers, and the band Os Mutantes in São Paolo.

Gal took longer to claim her platform. But by 1969, the drive to express herself differently became "so strong and violent that it couldn't have come under pressure from anyone." The collective crisis demanded a personal reply. Her first solo record, *Gal Costa*, opens with distorted electric guitars wailing in and out of range, announcing the cosmic love song she'll inscribe on a flying saucer for her carnival queen. I'm never sure, on "Não Identificado," whether the unidentified object of her lyricism is another woman, or the woman she herself is straining to become, somewhere beyond the reaches of terrestrial taxonomy. "I can no longer find beauty in things that are conventional," she confessed. "Sometimes people don't know it, but my scream is very musical."

Gal and Gilberto shared what she called "a certain complicity." She had liberated herself, and there was no going back: "That thing of being bold, I'm like that, too." If the feminine pronouns of "Não Identificado" had seemed ambiguous, almost accidental, she grew increasingly brazen in her erotic autonomy, sharing a passionate kiss onstage with Maria Bethânia, and frequenting the piers at Ipanema where hippies, artists, and queer people sought refuge behind "Gal's Dunes"—as if her presence had the power to consecrate the whole insurgent scene.

Later that year, Caetano and Gilberto Gil were arrested for fomenting dissent. They spent months in jail, then under house arrest, before they were exiled to London. Gal was the only Tropicálist left in Brazil to pick up the pieces of the broken movement, to devise subtler forms of freedom within an ever more repressive regime. Maybe she'd been left alone because the government underestimated her influence as a woman—or as an interpreter, rather than an author, of the new culture. But her friends still sent songs home for her to sing; they remained, as Gilberto promised, "a permanent mirror for one another."

Gal released my favorite album, *Índia*, in 1973. The cover framed her hips in a red bikini, a grass skirt slung low across her waist and thighs. There was no retouching, no artificial smoothness erasing the folds of her intimate topography. Naturally, the image was censored, so clerks sold the album wrapped in blue plastic. The title track was adapted from the Guaraní poet Manuel Ortiz Guerrero, whose people straddled the border between Paraguay and Brazil. It wouldn't be the first or last time that Gal Costa exploited her own racial ambiguity to explore contested terrain. But what startled her listeners more, at the time, was the sapphic yearning in her rendition: "Índia, Tupi, you smell like a flower. Let my lips kiss yours." Was she invoking a more intimate relationship with her own indigenous inheritance, the Índia she seemed to embody on the album cover?

Índia highlights Gal's tremendous fluency across forms. On the Portuguese folk song "Milho Verde," she builds up the buoyant refrain only to break it down into percussive syllables, following the Afro-Brazilian rhythms undergirding the melody into a dense jungle of sound: now she's the flute, now she's the birds, the frogs, the wind in the canopy. She closes the album with a classic, but here the lyrics of "Desafinado" seem to defend her ongoing experiment even as she delivers a flawless bossa nova: "If you insist on classifying my antimusical behavior, I must contend, it's very natural." "Time passes and we change, thank God," she told an interviewer. "I like changes."

Gal would go on to render almost every song in the national repertoire—well-worn classics, deep cuts, contemporary experiments—a durational performance that raises fundamental questions about the nature of the new. If the terms are given, is it possible to *interpret* your way elsewhere? Through inflection, arrangement, strategic pauses and tricks of tone? Many of Gal's covers became standards, but her practice was less about *deciding* the true meaning of her musical inheritance than about animating the plentitude of possible meanings available to the individual voice. She was, first and foremost, a live performer, so even her own word was never final: she always found a new note to strike inside the same song as she moved from stage to stage.

Sometimes she couldn't be sure if she was changing the music, or the music was changing her. Gal was from Salvador but had little contact with candomblé before she began to perform "Oração de Mãe Menininha," Dorival Caymmi's prayer for his own spiritual godmother, a daughter of Oxum. Caymmi had produced Gal's first album, *Domingo*. Back then, the beads she wore onstage were ornamental. But when Mãe Menininha do Gantois heard her sing that prayer, she could feel some deeper reverence running through Gal's voice and summoned her home. Soon, she was initiated as a daughter of Obalauaye, orixa of contagion and cure, and Oya-Iansa, she who turns and changes. It seems right, to me, that Gal should follow the spirits most associated with movement, as well as those who wear a mask. Obalauye's face, the story goes, is so beautiful it would blind us to see it plain; Oya's mask protects her privacy as she guides lost spirits through difficult transitions.

Gal has given us so much—public protest, queer kisses, bare-breasted hymns to her homeland—that it startles us to sense, now and then, the dark side of her moon. How she flatly refused to "come out" and turned her back on those—even former lovers—who tried to identify her sexuality in contemporary terms. Her voice itself retains a certain mystery: I think her versatility, longevity, and ubiquity have made it hard to name the luminous singularity of her tone, the strange force animating each note. In "Força Estranha"—another song Caetano wrote for her—we find the story of her singing, but we also find the story of our listening: "I put my feet in the river, and I never stepped back out." For Gal, the river is us, her audience. For us, the river is her voice—too elemental to bear description.

I've been speaking to my mother as I write this essay, swapping songs, anecdotes, and speculations. Back in the 1970s, when she first discovered the Brazilian counterculture, all she had were liner notes, and the Portuguese dictionary she bought to decipher the lyrics whose poetry shimmered just beyond the threshold of her understanding. It would be years before she saw any of her Brazilian muses in motion, at a screening in Puerto Rico: not Gal, but another queer icon, Simone, laid out on a round bed in the middle of the stage. My mother was the same age as these women, and they all collaborate, in my mind, to transmit the passionate cosmopolitanism that defined my young life before I'd ever left the country. Their sensuality, in particular, seemed to transcend, without avoiding, every mass-produced cliché about Latin American women. How marvelous to learn that a style so recognizable to me, so close to home, could open portals to other languages, other times, other worlds.

Recently, my mother sent me another clip I hadn't seen before: Gal Costa and Djavan in 1982, performing "Acaí" as an acoustic duet. She'd recorded his song alone for her album *Fantasia*—electric guitar, glittering synthesizers. But here, they slow down, passing the verses back and forth between them like sunbeams through crystal. As in her performance of "Volta," Gal's got her knees hiked up on the stool, and she flutters them open and closed in her white dress—heedless, free, as natural as a butterfly. Without the orchestration, I notice how the lyrics seem, finally, to describe the tone she gives them: "A gust of wind . . . pure desire . . . mystic mermaid clan." I can feel my pulse accelerate as I pass the Portuguese through my own translation. Her voice, yes, is *acaí*—tart, juicy, Amazonian—"a beetle's hum, a magnet" for our dreaming. Every voice is plural if you listen long enough. "Gal or Gau was always her name, more than Maria da Graça," Caetano wrote, but "there were and are thousands of Gaus in Bahia: it is the term of endearment used for all the Marias da Graças out there." Now, when we pronounce it—even those of us far from Brazil, stumbling over the simplest syllables—the tenderness we feel for Gal Costa can travel back to that communal source. Gal, gal, never and always another Gal.

—Carina del Valle Schorske,
Turning the Tables contributor

Gal Costa

Troubadours, bards, killer MCs, chroniclers, and fantasists bear witness, spin tales, share secrets, and write history.

STORYTELLERS

Carole King

10. TAPESTRY
Carole King (ODE, 1971)

With *Tapestry*, Carole King cemented her place as one of the key architects of twentieth-century popular music. Here, she fully claims the spotlight, not only as a top-notch composer, but as a deeply soulful lyricist and singer. Critics considered the album her crowning achievement, and record sales of more than twenty-five million confirmed that the public agreed. From "I Feel the Earth Move" to "You've Got a Friend," the track list is a veritable master class in pop standards, with King, one of America's most dependable hit-makers, flexing in a new genre. With her unadorned piano wrapped in plainspoken lyrics about the pulls of kinship and self-actualization, it's no wonder the record stands the test of time not only as a bedrock in the singer-songwriter genre, but also as the soundtrack of suburban feminism of the early 1970s. King's evolution as both an artist and a woman is perhaps most evident in the grown-up version of "Will You Love Me Tomorrow?" that appears on *Tapestry*. The first major writing credit for the then-teenage King and lyricist husband Gerry Goffin, which hit No. 1 for the Shirelles in 1961, is transformed from a girl's yearning question into the bittersweet doubts of a woman wise enough to know that even true love doesn't always last "till the night meets the morning sun."

—Jill Sternheimer, Lincoln Center, *Turning the Tables*, "The 150 Greatest Albums Made by Women," 2017

CAROLE KING
My song taken to the *n*th power

66 I think in some ways, it's harder to write for me. When I'm writing for somebody else, I mentally adopt the persona of that person. Or of my lyricist, as in the case when I write with Gerry Goffin and we do it together, you kind of put yourself in the headset that you think the other person is in. They may not even be, but it's your perception of them. So it's sort of another dynamic that you can write towards. Whereas when I'm writing for myself, there isn't that extra thing. I'm just sort of writing as it comes out. And in some ways, it's good; in other ways, it's more difficult.

One of the great moments of my life as a songwriter was the first time that I heard Aretha Franklin's version of 'Natural Woman,' which was, in many ways, not like the demo at all. It was amazing, because this was the ultimate singer in the world to me. And she was singing my song, and she's taken what I did with it and did what I never dreamed could be done with it. . . . It was, it was my song taken to the *n*th power. 99

—*Fresh Air* with Terry Gross, 1989

49. PIRATES
Rickie Lee Jones (WARNER BROS., 1981)

Her startling debut album and "Chuck E's in Love" made Rickie Lee Jones a fast-rising star, but her follow-up album, which came two years later, proved to be her masterwork. On *Pirates*, Jones refined the sonic stew of jazz, pop, and R&B that earned her the Best New Artist Grammy Award, adding lyrical finesse in the form of high-culture nods and colorful street smarts that fly by so fast you nearly miss them. (Take *that*, Springsteen.) Add to that a breakup with Tom Waits and a

232

move to New York to bring hard-earned life experience to the forefront—the opening piano notes of "We Belong Together" signal the beautiful, melodic drama about to unfold: "I say this was no game of chicken / You were aiming at your best friend." Characters shine in pictures so vivid it's remarkable they were squeezed into song structure: "Eddie's got one crazy eye / That turns him into a cartoon / When a pretty girl comes by," she sings. The rare mix of swagger and fragility on *Pirates* makes it clear how underrated Rickie Lee Jones has been, and how much we still need her now.

—Rita Houston, WFUV, *Turning the Tables*,
"The 150 Greatest Albums Made by Women," 2017

RICKIE LEE JONES:
A singer is the one who interprets the song

Rickie Lee Jones is a vivid crafter of musical fictions—but also a playful interpreter of jazz and rock and roll standards. In 2012, she spoke to NPR about the pleasure of interpretation, specifically the Rolling Stones' "Sympathy for the Devil," which appeared on her album *The Devil You Know*.

NPR: You've made a point of not only doing your own music over the years, but also reinterpreting other people's songs.

Rickie Lee Jones: Well, it's because when I started out there was this kind of glamour associated with singer-songwriterdom that wasn't being given to *just* singers. And so I think partially, I want to remind people that a singer is the one who interprets the song. And once you do that, it's yours. It doesn't really—to me, it doesn't make it more mine because I wrote it. You know what I mean? ["Sympathy for the Devil"] is kind of an evocation, you know, and I do it by myself. It's a powerful, frightening, fun romp through the upper echelon of hell. And every time I do it so far—it's like acting, you know, some other thing you can embody, or wear the skin of another thing and tell another kind of story than your own. I like it.

—*Weekend Edition* with Scott Simon, 2012

LAURA NYRO
Art is an affirmation of your life

❝ I see a connection between all the arts, a song, a poem, a sculpture. Like sometimes I'll see in the city, if I'm walking, a big colored mobile or sculpture, and if I really connect with it, it's a wonderful thing, because it just uplifts your spirit. So I think that the best of art, it does that—it's an affirmation of your life in your spirit. It's just real. ❞

—*Weekend Edition* with Scott Simon, 1989

234

Mia X,
Good Girl Gone Bad

There was a tremendous output of Black women's writing from the 1970s to 1990s that consciously centered Black women's experiences from enslavement to the post–civil rights movement as essential to understanding the way power works in our nation. Now canonical texts, these works include Ntozake Shange's choreopoem *for colored girls who have considered suicide / when the rainbow is enuf* (1976); Alice Walker's novel *The Color Purple* (1982); Angela Y. Davis's book of essays *Women, Race, and Class* and Barbara Smith's incisive Black queer women's anthology *Home Girls* (1983); Kimberlé Crenshaw's essays on intersectionality and jurisprudence (1989, 1991); Patricia Hill Collins's academic monograph *Black Feminist Thought* (1990); Beverly Guy-Sheftall's anthology of Black women's writing from the 1830s to the 1990s, *Words of Fire* (1995); and Mia X's debut album, *Good Girl Gone Bad* (1995).

Within the first few bars of the first track, "Ghetto Sarah Lee," the Seventh Ward's Mia X, the first woman emcee of Master P's burgeoning No Limit Records label in New Orleans, distinguished herself as the indisputable "Mama of Southern Gangsta Rap," a title that only she can hold. Her dizzying versatility across New Orleans bounce to West Coast–influenced gangsta beats and the blend thereof are second only to her narrative dexterity and clarity about who she is as a Black woman oppressed by racism, patriarchy, and capitalism in the shadow of the Clinton Administration's crime bill. She is every woman—a woman struggling through the challenges of single motherhood, holding it down in a community choked by mass incarceration, managing heartbreak, mourning the loss of a dear friend to domestic violence, and moreover a woman seeking and declaring herself worthy of life and pleasure. It's these multitudes that beget the righteous Rapsody, the baby mothering BbyMutha, the sensuality-centering Trina, and the gangsta Megan Thee Stallion. Mia X *cooks* on this album, a method of survival forged by improvising nourishing recipes from whatever she had on hand and in her ancestral lineage to feed herself, her family, and Southern hip hop. We are still lucky to sit at Mama's table.

—Zandria F. Robinson, NPR Music's *The South Got Something to Say: A Celebration of Southern Rap*, 2020

7. HORSES
Patti Smith (ARISTA, 1975)

The very nature of Patti Smith's debut album, *Horses*, rails against what many other "best of" albums are celebrated for—broad appeal, sonically pleasing aesthetics, and hits. *Horses* is confrontational, defiant, and completely unafraid of the ugly. And so was its author, who in 1975, for arguably the first time in music, set the lyrical stage for academia and animalism to writhe together; for the sophisticated and heady virtues of capital-P Poetry to crash into the visceral, bodily base of rock and roll. Any beauty on *Horses* feels like a byproduct of story—from Smith's breathless bleating to wailing and warbling against collaborator Lenny Kaye's characteristically jagged guitar to her historic presentation on the album's cover. As photographed by Robert Mapplethorpe, Smith's unapologetic androgyny predates a time when that was an en vogue or even available option for women, and represents a seminal moment in the reversal of the female gaze. Smith is looking at you, and could care less what you think about looking at her. That was radical for a woman in 1975. It is still radical today. There are legions of artists who cite Patti Smith's *Horses* as an earth-shattering influence, from Courtney Love to R.E.M.'s Michael Stipe to Garbage's Shirley Manson to the Smiths' Johnny Marr—

but they don't necessarily reflect Smith's influence in terms of sound so much as attitude. It was her unfiltered, fearless singularity that galvanized believers in the Church of Smith not to become more like her but to become more like themselves. And for that, we owe Smith everything.

—Talia Schlanger, *World Café*, *Turning the Tables*, "The 150 Greatest Albums Made by Women," 2017

GILLIAN WELCH
Getting through the next day

66 For some reason, the mountain or Appalachian blues idiom tends to confuse some people. Our stuff is like very forward-looking. Really, if anything, it's largely about getting through the next day and getting through the trouble at hand, which is not really anything to do with nostalgia. 99

—*All Things Considered* with Steve Inskeep, 2003

Let Me See the Mark: Gillian Welch

"One More Dollar," *Revival*, 1996

A long time ago I left my home
For a job in the fruit trees.

Peach trees had grown there once, and apples. Given water, they thrived in the volcanic soil of Central Oregon's high desert. But after Portland General Electric built the dam in 1964, the rains came with a duration and fury nobody expected. The lake rose and covered the orchards four hundred feet deep.

I learned about all of that in the summer of 2001. I was there as a seasonal park ranger, giving campfire talks and leading kayak floats. Osprey dove, catching salmon, and woolly mullein raised tall spikes from the canyon's rocky walls. I was twenty-five and far from home; everything was new to me. Juniper and sage, serviceberry and bitterbrush.

I listened to Gillian Welch a lot that summer. Here was a woman who sang about love, sure, but also about work, figuring out who you were, and a clean getaway car—I had one myself, smooth and fast, a Crown Vic I'd driven there from Texas. I listened to *Revival* in the kitchenette of the singlewide where I lived, fixing macaroni and cheese from a box and writing letters to the folks back home. No landline, no cell service. The only way to reach me was by calling the campground pay phone at a prearranged time. When it rang, I'd answer.

It's tough to find real friend chemistry. With Gillian Welch's albums, I feel that click. *Soul Journey* (2003) is more pop-adjacent, *The Harrow and the Harvest* (2011) carries Great Recession energy, *Time (The Revelator)* (2001) I come back to again and again, but I'll always love her debut. The vinegar tang of those close harmonies kept company with me across the country. "When I reach those hills, boys, I'll never roam." I missed home so much when I lived at the Cove Palisades, and singing along to this song helped. Where I'd end up, I didn't know.

"I Dream a Highway," *Time (The Revelator)*, 2001

Most of Welch's songs feel like old folk songs, though she and partner David Rawlings wrote them. From the traditional "John the Revelator" ("Who's that writin'? / John the Revelator") she built *Time (The Revelator)*. From the story of John Henry she took the line "Lord let me die with a hammer in my hand."

Said Ecclesiastes, "There is no new thing under the sun." Maybe. Gillian Welch sings of Elvis and the Dust Bowl, the *Titanic* and Abraham Lincoln. Greil Marcus points out that Bob Dylan is at his best in the folk mode, writing songs that feel older than they are.

"Write your own time," says a character in *I'm Not There*, Todd Haynes's 2007 movie about Dylan. *Live your own time*. What happens when you turn a folk sensibility toward the current moment?

Which brings me to "I Dream a Highway," a song almost fifteen minutes long, hypnotic and slow, incantatory. To listen is to enter a waking dream. Each of the song's eleven verses ends with "I dream a highway back to you," an embedded reprise of the chorus. It's a song that takes its own good time.

And feels as though it could go on forever. Most songs signal where they're headed, through a note or a lyric or both, and once you get there, you feel it. You can relax. Not so with "I Dream a Highway," which reads more like knots in a line, or a string of beads passed between fingers. It's capacious enough for the mythic— "Drank whiskey with my water, sugar with my tea"—and for the fits and starts of lived life.

But as many years as I've been listening to it, there's a passage I never heard until the first summer of the pandemic:

239

Step into the light, poor Lazarus
Don't lie alone behind the window shade
Let me see the mark death made

Let me see the mark death made. I'm standing alone in my kitchen, and that line stops me cold. My own face has gone strange to me.

I think how life writes itself across our bodies; I think of what we inherit and bequeath. The song is roomy enough to allow space even for coming back from the dead, like Lazarus, like the strain of flu that swept the world in 1918–1919. Essie Jenkins sang of it in her "1919 Influenza Blues." Flu epidemics returned in 1929, 1946, 1957, 1968, and most recently, in 2009, the so-called swine flu. No new thing under the sun. Sometime in 2020, Dr. Anthony Fauci said that normal would come back eventually. Maybe this, now, is normal.

"Dark Turn of Mind," *The Harrow and the Harvest*, 2011

This summer, after twenty-one years away, I went back to the Oregon desert. There sat the singlewide where I used to live; at the ranger station, a young woman took my camping fee. "Ever been here before?" she asked. "Yeah, but it's been a while," I said.

I've forgotten plenty of things about that season—which wildflowers grew along the Tam-a-lau Trail; the hang of backing the park's old Dodge pickup and boat trailer into its narrow spot. But when I hear "Dark Turn of Mind," I remember exactly how it felt to be there, then, to be me.

They've built more cell phone towers in Central Oregon, and the pay phone is gone. I showed my daughter the cement pad where it used to stand, told my husband about the porcupine who napped high in the big cottonwood tree that grew nearby. No sign of him, but feathers and whitewash marked the grass. Vultures, ten or twelve of them. They settled and flapped, feet clamped to the boughs.

One thing I love most about Welch's voice is its weary quality; I don't think she'd lie to me. "Some girls are bright as the morning," she sings. "And some girls are blessed with a dark turn of mind." Here's to the serious girls who had to find

where they fit, who know if you're lucky, you'll meet someone who understands. The vultures shifted their weight, hissed. You can make your obsession into something other people can use. If they need it, they'll find it.

From a water expert I learned that water carries specific isotopic signatures. So if you've lived in a place any length of time, its particular water marks your bones. I think about that as I listen to Gillian Welch, again, on a rainy Thursday. "One more dollar, boys, I'm going home."

Good advice; I took it. I carry her songs scrawled on my bones, like I carry the mark of that summer. Far below the skin of the lake, peach orchards still stand, their seeds buried in dark mud. I drank that water every day.

—Joni Tevis, *Turning the Tables* contributor

83. ODE TO BILLIE JOE
Bobbie Gentry
(CAPITOL RECORDS, 1967)

After a fifteen-week reign that lasted through the Summer of Love and well into the fall of 1967, the album that bumped the psychedelic three-ring English circus *Sgt. Pepper's Lonely Hearts Club Band* off the top of the charts was debut singer-songwriter Bobbie Gentry's dispatch from the sweatiest, swampiest bottom of America. *Ode to Billie Joe* is a richly atmospheric production, juxtaposing the sounds of the deepest American South— raw, funky blues guitar, sprightly fiddles, rattlesnake percussion—into a gorgeous slice of country soul. The title track, of course, became one of American music's most compelling riddles, the splash off the

Bobbie Gentry *by Jess Rotter*

Tallahatchie Bridge heard 'round the world forever. The power of "Ode to Billie Joe," a Southern Gothic mystery about the loneliness, distance, and ultimately, tragedy lurking beneath a pleasant family scene, is so enduring that it almost distracts from the extraordinary storytelling craft of the album as a whole. All of the songs are complex and abstract, full of bright details—a checkered feed-sack dress, two postcards from California—and few of them tell you the whole story. Dramatized by cinematic string arrangements, *Ode to Billie Joe* is a compendium of intriguing, evocative scraps of poetry that always hint at something more lingering just outside the frame, in the dark.

—Alison Fensterstock, *Turning the Tables*,
"The 150 Greatest Albums Made by Women," 2017

Silly Sisters:
Acid and Honey

In the late '80s I had the extraordinary good fortune to spend a year abroad at the University of St. Andrews in Scotland. My mother said two things to me—one, that perhaps I might meet a nice boy with a castle and fall in love, and two, that no doubt this year would be the happiest of my life. One of these things she meant as a joke, but the other she did not.

My housing at St. Andrews was a grouping of no-nonsense modernist cubes. Students left milk and perishables outside on the sills of their windows, and you often saw ravens flying off with a cheese sandwich or a donut. The David Russell Apartments were a mile and half out from my classes and the town center, however, and buses were few and far between. But the walk was very beautiful, with endless green fields on either side, long hillsides covered in tall, golden-crowned rape (I was fascinated and horrified to learn the name). I had my Walkman and plenty of cassettes and various painstakingly compiled mixtapes (Suzanne Vega, Indigo Girls, 10,000 Maniacs, Amy Grant, *Jesus Christ Superstar*, to give you a sense of my taste at the time). I was often alone but rarely lonely. Music was good company.

Left to my own devices and with so much free time, I made frequent trips to St. Andrews's small public library and read my way through various new-to-me British writers like Emma Tennant and Simon Raven; you could also borrow cassette tapes. And this is how I first listened to the two albums that Maddy Prior and June Tabor made as Silly Sisters. No doubt some part of me was more open to the idea of listening to folk music now that I was in Scotland, where so much of the past was still visible, where side streets were cobbled, not paved, where you could see iron railings broken off at their bases to be melted down for the war effort and never replaced, where you could sneak out onto the ruined ramparts of a castle built in 1200 and drink beer with friends, dangling your feet over the sea.

Silly Sisters's first, eponymous album had come out in 1976. The image on the cover features a photograph of Prior and Tabor, narrow-waisted in flower-printed dresses. They both have longish brown hair, which floats off their shoulders and around their faces. Tabor wears a heavy torque, and Prior a coiling armband. They've been dancing, or jumping, and there is something solemnly ecstatic about their faces, as if they are two priestesses caught out on the town. They look like two sphinxes Gustave Moreau might have painted. The second album, *No More to the Dance*, was quite recent, from 1988. I listened with a kind of astonished, delighted attention, as part of me was being shaken awake. It had not occurred to me that people still sang ballads, that there was music which felt like fairy tales or something in a fantasy novel. I knew about the connection between folk tales and folk music, that Tam Lin was a story and also a ballad, but I hadn't realized there were contemporary artists who were making this material their own. I knew the stories of some of the songs, but I'd never heard them sung.

Silly Sister was my introduction to the concept of contemporary folk music. Maddy Prior, of course, had been a founding member of Steeleye Span at the forefront of the UK folk revival. The strangest thing I know about her is that she inspired two characters in Chris Claremont's *Uncanny X-Men*, which seems fair enough! Her alto has the quality of a strange metal. It still cuts through my brain like a sharp wire through cheese. June Tabor, a self-taught musician who trained her voice by listening to the songs of Anne Briggs, has a sinuous, sturdy, tensile alto you can imagine belonging to a dragon or a haunted well. I'm always aware of how she is organizing silence as well as sound. It makes me want to hold my breath. The instrumentation on both albums is fairly stripped down, and often Prior and Tabor sing unaccompanied, harmonizing, or taking turns. Listening to music through headphones is the closest I've ever gotten, personally, to a ghostly encounter, that voice that seduces or mutters in your ear, that raises the hair on the back of your neck, and the kind of harmonies that Prior and Tabor achieve are particularly haunting, as if they are making you into a ghost and their music has become three-dimensional.

When I think of their voices, I often think of silver and a ripe greenness, perhaps in part because of the landscape in which I first heard them, where the sea and sky so often seemed composed of electric, changeable metal, where the town itself was made up of weathered gray stone, where the fields stayed green even through the winter. There's tremendous kinetic power to Prior and Tabor's harmonies, trading off warmth and coolness, acid and honey, a kind of light and darkness that suited my walks that year between town and David Russell Apartments, which as autumn became winter, were mostly made in darkness. By December, the sun went down in the early afternoon and did not bother to rise again until near 9 a.m. Sleeping in, I often missed it altogether. And then as summer came on, it began to seem as if the sun hardly left the sky at all. All year long, the sky was astonishing, in all seasons—sometimes low and heavy as if a pewter plate were hanging over the day; sometimes a wide, flat blue, so thin it seemed you could scratch it away with a fingernail. As the year went on, I began to run every day, with my headphones on, from David Russell through the town and down to the ruins of the medieval cathedral and the North Sea, or the remains of St. Andrews Castle, where, during a torch-lit night performance of *Macbeth*, the actress playing Lady Macbeth had fallen on the flagstones, knocked out her two front teeth, and then gotten right back up and continued her lines, lisping, blood all down her chin.

I would listen to the first song on *Silly Sisters*, "Doffin' Mistress," and then rewind and listen again. It's about mill workers, and nothing much happens in it, only a small act of defiance, but my god does it feel as if the people it describes are still alive. "The Grey Funnel Line" was written in the late '50s by Cyril Tawney. Prior and Tabor's version is a cappella through the first verse, a kind of aching hymn to life in the Royal Navy, and the desire to return to shore. I've kept this song on various playlists almost all of my writing life, no doubt in part because when I listen to it, it still recalls to me the North Sea and the silvery light that rises off it. "Geordie," a bouncing ballad about a maiden rescuing her lover, has remained a favorite, and Tabor and Prior sound sly and extraordinarily pleased with themselves on "The Game of Cards"—a song about a sexual encounter between a card sharp and an older woman—in a way that invites the listener to enjoy the battle of the sexes. There's a ferocious lament by a sexually unsatisfied wife, "My Husband's Got No Courage in Him," that ends in a murderous shout drenched in a kind of bitterness you can taste. The lives of women make up much of the material of their songs—fine ladies, the undowried daughters of poor folk, abandoned lovers, and weavers. "The Barring of the Door" on *No More to the Dance* is about a petty wager between a husband and a wife that I've listened to more times than I can count, until finally it made itself into part of the skeleton of the novel I spent seven years writing.

I've made a life for myself as a writer engaging with some very old story forms—ghost stories, fairy tales, gothics, romances, pulp fantasy, and science fiction, but when I was first writing, these weren't much in vogue. They weren't considered serious fiction. The landscape looks quite different now. I can see this in the revival of folk music, that there is a kind of cycle, that dormant forms can return to liveliness or freshness, that individual voices or points of view transform familiar material.

No doubt I disappointed my mother by returning home again from St. Andrews without having managed to become engaged to a man with a Scottish castle. But a few years later, working at a bookstore in Boston, I met a fellow bookseller, an expatriate Scot who'd been at St. Andrews the same time as I was, though we'd never met each other. We had, in fact, been in the same spaces many times (at concerts, at student dances, and so on), but neither of us had ever noticed the other. And now we are married. There's something balladlike about this, something of that cycle, or the cassette tape that I used to pop out and turn over and then turn over again, the music the same, but me never in the same place in that same moment, the familiar song accompanying me as I kept on moving—how he and I missed each other the first time around, on every possible occasion, and then managed to find each other after all.

—Kelly Link, *Turning the Tables* contributor

LUCINDA WILLIAMS:
Songs like little short stories

Lucinda Williams: Talking about my influences, I always like to mention Flannery O'Connor and Eudora Welty, because I read a lot of that when I was a teenager. It's sort of a Southern gothic feel, that dark, twisted side of life. I guess it's what I'm kind of trying to do in my songs, kind of like little short stories.

NPR: I was going to ask you about "Sweet Old World." It's one of two songs on this album [*Sweet Old World*, 1992] where you're addressing yourself to someone who's committed suicide.

Lucinda Williams: Yeah, it's strange. I don't really consider it a taboo subject. It seems to bother some people though. It's been brought up several times. I did a concert in Central Park, and this woman reviewed it and said something like "Lucinda Williams cast a depressing pall over the whole audience, you know, because of the content of her material," which is completely ridiculous. It wasn't like that at all. I mean, I do blues songs, I have a sense of humor. And I don't like to dwell on the unrequited love theme over and over again.

NPR: Why is that? It's a great subject.

Lucinda Williams: Yeah, it is a great subject and it's the easiest thing to write about, but there are other things to write about, and I just think that's more interesting. And also because I like to write from my own experience, and you can't stay in a chaotic situation for the rest of your life in order to be able to write. I mean, at some point, you hope to be somewhat content in your life personally but still have things to write about.

—*Morning Edition* with Renee Montagne, 1992

QUEEN LATIFAH
You can talk about so many things

" For me, hip hop has been the catalyst for everything, a form of expression, a way for me to kind of get my feelings out and, you know, release whatever is going on inside. Initially, it was poems and songs, and then it kind of became the spoken word through hip hop. And, you know, it's just the energy that comes with the music, you know, being able to kind of get up and, you know, you could brag and boast at the same time. You can talk about political issues. You can talk about things going on in the world. You can talk about your pride as a woman and so many different things. "

—*News & Notes* with Farai Chideya, 2007

Queen Latifah

248

13. LANA DEL REY, "VIDEO GAMES"

When Lana Del Rey released what would eventually become her breakthrough single, old-guard rock critics weren't quite certain how to receive her. Like so many starlets before, she'd journeyed west to reinvent herself—a new name, a new sound, a different, more glamorous look. Because her aesthetic was so plainly cultivated, she became an unlikely lightning rod for whatever authenticity panic was then seizing the culture. For a while, the extra-musical narratives about Del Rey—that she was too passive, too vapid, too scripted—subsumed any talk about "Video Games" itself. Yet the song is rich and transfixing, a devotional in the old-fashioned sense: Del Rey is pledging undying allegiance to the man she loves, regardless of whether or not he appreciates or even returns her feelings (one gets the sense, hearing the deep longing in her voice, that he doesn't). It's one of the most immediate and evocative depictions of doomed love I can think of—the sound of being young and sad and in the grips of senseless passion.

—Amanda Petrusich, *Turning the Tables*, Season 2,
"The 200 Greatest Songs by 21st-Century Women+," 2018

98. SOPHIE, "LEMONADE"

In her early work, SOPHIE shirked the expectation that women (especially trans women) use lyrics as a vehicle for self-exposition. Like her breakthrough single "Bipp," "Lemonade" told its story primarily through texture: the ASMR pop of synthesized bubbles; the wobble of detuned bass; the high, serrated whine of a treble patch; the laminated edge of a pitch-shifted voice. "I'll get that thirsty feeling / And I want lemonade," goes the quasi-surrealist chorus, refusing to make logical sense but reeling with the thrill of pop abandon.

—Sasha Geffen, *Turning the Tables*, Season 2,
"The 200 Greatest Songs by 21st-Century Women+," 2018

31. EXILE IN GUYVILLE
Liz Phair (CAPITOL/EMI/MATADOR, 1993)

Liz Phair's eighteen-song double-LP *Exile in Guyville* is her first and best album. Thick with tomboy swagger, it's a wrecked confessional detailing the insanity of dating and screwing in your twenties. It's also an ingenious, track-by-track response to the Rolling Stones' oppressively masculine *Exile on Main Street*. In her unsparing songs, the twenty-five-year-old Oberlin graduate broke through Chicago's indie scene with some of the most self-assured and explicit feminist rock to date, with lyrics like "I want to fuck you like a dog / I'll take you home and make you like it." Phair wasn't afraid of anything, and in many ways, this album is one big middle finger to the dudes of her personal Guyville. In addition to humor and confidence, she navigates vulnerability and heavy emotion across tracks, especially in less-celebrated songs like "Shatter" and "Strange Loop," which hold up just as well as hits like "Fuck and Run." The entirety of this album is timeless: *Guyville* resonates as much for those maneuvering messy relationships today as it did in the early '90s.

—Alyssa Edes, NPR, *Turning the Tables*,
"The 150 Greatest Albums Made by Women," 2017

LIZ PHAIR:
Where Men Are Men and Women Are Learning

Liz Phair: Well now it's [the word "Guyville"] a media sound bite. It's nothing more; it's very sad. But anyway, these things come and go. It was a state of mind and/or neighborhood that I was living in. Guyville, because it was definitely their sensibilities that held the aesthetic, you know what I mean? It was sort of guy things—comic books with really disfigured, screwed-up people in them, this sort of like constant love of social aberration. You know what I mean? This kind of guy mentality, you know, where men are men and women are learning. In Oberlin there was a Guyville. In New York there's a Guyville. In San Francisco there's a Guyville. I didn't happen to live in it there.

NPR: What did you figure out you wanted to do about Guyville from your perspective?

Liz Phair: Get out.

—*All Things Considered* with Noah Adams, 1993

24. COAL MINER'S DAUGHTER
Loretta Lynn (DECCA, 1970)

If Loretta Lynn is one of the queens of country music, *Coal Miner's Daughter* is the jewel in her honky-tonk crown. By 1971, Lynn was already a well-established Nashville songwriter, had sung her way onto the *Grand Ole Opry*, and had a reputation for her boundary-pushing, feminist songs about infidelity and domestic abuse. While the album doesn't betray those roots, its most beloved song is a sentimental autobiography; furthermore, *Coal Miner's Daughter* tells the story of Lynn's childhood in Butcher Hollow, Kentucky. She grew up with eight siblings, a mother who worked hard to care for them, and a father who worked in the Van Lear coal mines, an experience that's immortalized in the album's title track:

Well I was born a coal miner's daughter
In a cabin, on a hill in Butcher Holler
We were poor but we had love

It became her best-known song, the title of her autobiography, and a 1980 Oscar-award-winning movie about her life. But sadly, her father never lived to hear the album, or any of Lynn's recordings. He died of black lung disease in 1959.

—Lauren Migaki, NPR, *Turning the Tables*,
"The 150 Greatest Albums Made by Women," 2017

Loretta Lynn

LORETTA LYNN
But this is my story of my life

❝ My husband says, 'Go ahead and put that ["Coal Miner's Daughter"] on an album,' and I had eight more verses to it. So I started putting the song down. And Owen Bradley come out and said, 'Loretta, you're gonna have to take some of them verses off of that song.' I guess it was six minutes long. And I said, 'But this is my story of my life.' And he said, 'I can't help it. There ain't nobody gonna listen to the story of your life for no eight more verses.' So I had to take eight verses off, but I had six left. **❞**

—*Weekend Edition* with Liane Hansen, 2000

The Countermelodies
That Changed Us:
A Lifetime of Loving
Indigo Girls

Are you an Emily or an Amy? Few mainstream fans of the Indigo Girls would even consider that question, but for the lesbians over age forty who love them, it's an elemental personality test. The duo, which releases their fifteenth studio album *Look Long* tomorrow [May 22, 2020], has been together for thirty-five years. Early publicity materials established an enduring impression of the contrast between them—like this bio, written three years before their self-titled 1989 album: "Amy's songs are gutsy, powerful and upbeat. Emily's are lyrical, jazzy and more ballad-like."

Like a lot of baby butches in the '90s, I wanted to be like Amy: an aloof yet accessible alpha butch whose salt-of-the-earth zeal, both political and emotional, broke a lot of guitar strings, and presumably a lot of hearts. But in my own heart, the one I wear on my sleeve, I knew that I was at core an Emily: a formally skilled sentimentalist with a deft touch for finely wrought love songs, a sensualist with a penchant for the good things in life like food and literature. Though the "Emily and Amy dialectic" might initially present itself as neatly divided, all the gradients and the inevitable syntheses between the two are what ultimately matter. Thinking about what it means to be part Emily and part Amy, and how those identities or stances both merge and diverge, gave many women a way to understand themselves along the lines of what the radical feminist poet Adrienne Rich called "the lesbian continuum."

What the Indigo Girls' story—as longtime collaborators and friends who practice a healthy and gregarious exogamy with other romantic partners, musicians, producers, and political comrades—models for us is an enduring, communitarian project of world-building. In other words, the Indigo Girls have, with music as their conduit, accomplished the very best of what both queer theory and queer politics always aspired to achieve. A deeper dive into the Emily/Amy dialectic—the heart of what makes the Indigo Girls' music so compelling with its wide swerves between gentle, lovelorn balladry and the anguished yawps of activist souls struggling to be born (at least in their earliest records)—gives us insight into what female friendship, what lesbian friendship in particular, can offer to our divided worlds.

Ray and Saliers, or Amy and Emily (as their true fans refer to them with a loving ease and familiarity), have been making music together since they were young teens in Decatur, Georgia. The two met in elementary school but didn't start harmonizing until the dawn of the Reagan era in 1981, when they were both in the choir at Shamrock High School. Their young hearts swelled with music, while their eager sentimentality was stoked by Literature with a capital "L." Indeed, their catalog is replete with songs alluding to literary personages like Virginia Woolf ("Virginia Woolf") and the poet Frank Stanford ("Three Hits"). "When We Were Writers," from *Look Long*, looks back with a mix of fondness and maybe even a little mortification at some of their youthful pretensions as would-be scribes. For what it's worth, Emily majored in English at Tulane (a time that served as the inspiration for "When We Were Writers"), before transferring to Emory and narrowly escaping English graduate school once the Indigo Girls' career began to pick up steam in the mid-1980s. Amy majored in religion at Vanderbilt and Emory, which explains something about the devotional fervor in her compositions.

The musical partnership forged between Emily and Amy flickered with the platonic passion of teen girlhood, musical fellowship, and a younger girl's admiration for a slightly older one (Emily was a year ahead of Amy in school). The two spent all their time together picking apart chords, crafting countermelodies, and learning to cover their favorite songs by artists like Jackson Browne, Carole King, and James Taylor. Both admit that Emily, who comes from a musical family, was more adept at plucking out the intricacies of Joni Mitchell songs; her grandfather was a professional big band musician, after all, and her father was an aspiring jazz pianist before the life of a theologian called him. As Emily describes it, the guitar began to feel like a physical extension of her truest self: "Playing the guitar captured me fully from the moment I took my first lesson at the YMCA in the third grade."

Meanwhile Amy, the younger, was fueled by a sense of urgency and ardency that surpassed her nascent skill level when the two first met. She knew with absolute certainty that she wanted nothing more than to express the increasing confusion and tumult within her soul by making music with her best friend Emily: "As soon as I felt the way our voices sounded together, I was inconsolable, except by the music we would make." The acuteness of this need endures nearly forty years later, through our current global crises.

This give and take, this fundamental trust between them, and among the people in their musical orbit and their fans, is fitting given the formal signature of their songwriting as a duo: the countermelody.

Countermelody is a foundational form in the Indigo Girls' musical arrangements, as "Reunion" (composed by Amy) and "The Wood Song" (composed by Emily), both from 1994's *Swamp Ophelia*, most clearly illustrate, though nearly all of their compositions to this day feature it in some way or other. The basest definition for a countermelody is that it's a subordinate or secondary melody played alongside, or in counterpoint with, a primary melody. A countermelody played by itself can be beautiful all on its own, yet it becomes something infinitely more special, and more gratifying, when you hear it interact with the main line. Sometimes an untrained ear can drift to a well-crafted countermelody and hear it as the main one. In my mind, no songwriting style models humility more, nor captures the Indigo Girls' ethos better, than this generous interplay with subordination, this mutual willingness to take the countermelody in one circumstance, with the trust and knowledge that you'll get your turn taking the lead in another.

To *know* if you are an Emily or an Amy is akin to declaring a strong preference for Wordsworth or Coleridge, as much as for Lennon or McCartney. The question I asked at the beginning of this piece is less about who we find more erotically appealing, or "cute," on the level of preference, but a much weightier character assessment calibrated to our aesthetic sensibilities. It offers an impression of where we might situate ourselves on a spectrum between the sentimental and the prophetic; between realist musings on tenderness and blunt irruptions of passion. It is also the declaration of a political style and approach, from the reformist to the revolutionary, from electoral change to grassroots transformation.

Early on in their careers, and in ways that persist as quick and ready points of contrast to this day, each of the Indigo Girls' compositions branched off into stark musical styles depending on who wrote which song. (An easy way to tell, with a couple of rare exceptions, is that each of them sings lead on the songs they write.) Over the course of the past several decades, to be an Emily has often meant indulging one's belletristic sensibilities and (no matter how young one is) undertaking a long, melancholy look upon those Wordsworthian "hedgerows, hardly hedgerows," imagining we might "Soon Be to Nothing." To be an Amy has meant being visited upon by visions that come in dreamlike fragments, only in the folksier form of a "Chickenman" instead of Coleridge's mystical Kubla Khan. After listening to their body of work across the decades, these assessments no longer hold true given the maturation of each of their writing styles, even if they remain nostalgically resonant to those of us who've bothered to stick around for the whole journey. But as Amy reminds us about the Indigo Girls: "The difference between us is what helped to define us, and it helped us create our sound."

To a mainstream listening public, these important differences across all registers, from the stylistic to the political, must constantly reassert themselves against the tired misconceptions of what "lesbianism"—the putative framework, for better and worse, of the Indigo Girls' identity and their presumed audience— signifies. To be lesbians *together* implies an unbounded confluence, a compulsive "urge to merge" between two distinct entities. As Emily herself has sung in "Power of Two," a wedding standard for all genders and configurations of lovers, "the closer I'm bound in love to you, the closer I am to free."

Despite the kindheartedness and, let's admit it, the codependency of sentiments like this, lesbianism also infers a certain sternness, a stubborn imperviousness to evolving that seems to fuel only the crankiest forms of separatism. The Indigo Girls' screen cameos as a plaid-wearing bar band in 1995's *Boys on the Side*, and more recently as themselves singing "Hammer and a Nail" at a Michigan-style women's festival on season two of *Transparent* (2015), strike just the right note of herstory and earnestness that overburdens this idea of lesbianism. As Amy once wrote, "I feel like our earnestness served us well, if not always artistically. It helped us have the energy and convictions to persevere."

Thirty-five years into a career that has made each of them rethink the wisdom of using "girls" in their band name, that earnestness and perseverance is the Indigo Girls' true musical and spiritual legacy. Even though mainstream chart success has never been a major feature of the band's résumé, their music and they have endured. Their peak success during the mainstreaming of gay pride during the Clinton era can be read as a happy set of historical confluences. The '90s was a decade that began unplugged, and felt more amenable to guitar-slinging female singer-songwriters like Amy and Emily. "The trend gods were shining upon women with acoustic guitars: Suzanne Vega, Tracy Chapman, Melissa Etheridge, Shawn Colvin, Mary Chapin Carpenter and so on," Emily reflects now.

In the annals of American popular music, it's possible the Indigo Girls will be reduced to a historical moment that can't contain them. Throughout the '90s, the Indigo Girls captured the swell of yet another feminist wave that swept up within it a handful of harmless gays and chic lesbians who just wanted to get married like everybody else. Yet the Indigo Girls were never really *that* kind of creative class, cosmopolitan gay, the kind audiences became habituated to through sitcoms like *Will & Grace*. They were never so flashy, and to paraphrase their own lyrics, they were never that "cool." They simply did the work and learned how to work well with others.

As they've come full circle—from recording themselves on cassettes in Amy's basement to broadcasting themselves on Facebook Live from their manager's modest office with a water-stained ceiling—both Indigo Girls, each cornering sixty, are deeply self-reflective about the echelon they occupy as artists. In my separate conversations with each of them, both used the word "echelon" to strongly imply they didn't quite belong to an upper one. It didn't read as false modesty but instead as a clear-eyed, contented assessment of their enduring role in American popular music. Both downplayed any notion of their legacy and continued to express a kind of wonderment and surprise at the major achievements they've logged, as well as at the expansiveness of the audiences they've reached.

True to their collective sensibilities, they see themselves as part of a groundswell of music from a Georgia that is in every fiber of their being, and that radiates outward to a larger interconnected world of like-minded musicians, artists, and activists, many of whom they've given a platform to and many of whom are female, queer, trans, of color. Of course, the two would probably say they merely *shared* these platforms with artists whom they happen to admire, not the other way around. "We just have more fun playing with other people, because we're fans of a lot of other musicians," Amy admits. This genuine, multidirectional admiration applies not only to the many famous people they've worked with, including their idol Joni Mitchell, but also to each and every musician they've ever played with on tour, in the studio, or in a bar. Emily and Amy remember everyone and hold them close to their hearts.

What is abundantly clear throughout their many decades of collaboration is that Amy and Emily have, most crucially, remained fans of each other. Even in the affectless environs of a two-dimensional Zoom, one can spy the twinkle in each of their eyes when they look back on what they've accomplished, and what they're still continuing to do not only for themselves, but for the fellowship of artists, activists, and "good people" they accrued throughout their years putting in the work on the road.

For some of us, especially those of us who've spent a lifetime in queer worlds, our longest relationships aren't always with our lovers or our spouses. They're with our communities, with our best friends, often geographically scattered, receding in and out of our lives through many twists, turns, and transformations of self and the world. So many of us found one another through the Indigo Girls. So many of us rediscovered each other again, when, in our current crisis of pandemic isolation, the Indigo Girls played their first Facebook Live set on March 19, 2020. Over sixty thousand people tuned into that live broadcast, which also coincided with the early chaos of the COVID-19 shelter-in-place orders.

By the time they concluded with encores of "Closer to Fine" and "Galileo"—two of their biggest "sing-along songs," as they call them—many of us were in tears, both real and emoji, because we felt a momentary reprieve from our anxious vigils for symptoms. The physical distance imposed by state decrees felt broached, if ever so briefly. Emily and Amy spun together the threads of our remote intimacy, as they so often have, with the countermelodies we committed to our queer hearts. Our bodies somatically remembered, even as we sang along to our screens, that we used to sling our arms around each other, wantonly fluid-bonding through our botched harmonies. And in the end they sparked the hope, as they so often have, that we might someday all gather to sing together again.

—Karen Tongson, *Turning the Tables: Deep Listening*, 2020 (excerpt)

Melissa Etheridge argues for turning emotional intensity up past eleven; Mary J. Blige, bard of heartbreak and resilience, talks about how the music that made so many others feel heard helped her get through it all, too. Sometimes the song is playing just for you, and you're not alone.

EMPATHS

MARY J. BLIGE
I understand what you're going through

❝ When you say 'no more drama,' you realize who your worst enemy is—you realize it's you, you realize that only you can fix these things. But that's a lot of work. You got to take your fists and bust through it, and it hurts really bad. But at the end of the day, I made a lot of progress. I'm actually able to see my issues and say, Okay, I'm prideful here, okay, I gotta fix that. I'm stubborn. Okay, I gotta fix that. And even though I'm able to say it, it's easier said than done.

It's like this, I can't live for you. I'm writing songs because I understand what you're going through because I've been through it, and I can make twenty more really depressed albums. But I choose to do something different because my depression and my pain—people have no idea how much it hurts trying to fix yourself. You listen to people saying 'Mary needs a hug, everybody.' And then now that I got my hug, they're saying I wish you didn't get the hug. It's like, what do you really want? You know, what I've learned to do is really look at the bigger picture and the bigger picture is not all about me. It's about some little girl that's watching me right now. ❞

—*All Things Considered* with Debbie Elliott, 2006

101. TOUCH
Eurythmics (RCA, 1983)

In 1983, Eurythmics—the formerly romantic creative duo of Annie Lennox and Dave Stewart—finally had a hit, one that would prove to be the biggest of their career: "Sweet Dreams (Are Made of This)." The soulful synthpop masterpiece was plagued by romantic longing—sonic storytelling far removed from the robotic isolation that punctuated many new wave songs at the time. The same year, the prolific pop savants released *Touch*, another commercial success confirming their idiosyncratic greatness. Who knew that sad, strange,

Annie Lennox
by Margaret Flatley

and human could also be popular? Melancholy, as delivered by vocalist Lennox, is what made them great. Her rich contralto teeters a line of theatrics and overdramatics that creates a cohesion to *Touch* that would otherwise go unrealized. In "Right by Your Side," she levitates in love, only to tear herself down with a cringe-worthy moment of clarity: "When depression starts to win / I need to be right by your side." Even steel pans and joyous synthesizers can't distract from harsh reality—and there is a particular loneliness to this album, particularly on "Who's That Girl?," which allows narrative longing and minimal production to cut to the core. Sadness never sounded so cool.

—Maria Sherman, *Turning the Tables*,
"The 150 Greatest Albums Made by Women," 2017

MELISSA ETHERIDGE
Our civilization lacks intensity

" I hold a lot of weight in honesty and truth, and I don't think there's any reason to hold back on that. And if I ever find myself thinking, oh, I can't say that, that's just, that's too direct, or that's too harsh, then that's when I absolutely say I must say that. It's very important to me. I think our civilization as a whole lacks intensity. I think we, our Western society, sort of grows up with *we're all just supposed to behave*, and don't be too angry, don't be too sad, don't be too happy, just, just be right there in the middle and don't bother anybody. I absolutely think that it's healthy to feel those extremes, that that's the only way one can be balanced.

Love is desperate to me, love is very important, love is that other half of your life. I spent my twenties trying to figure it out, coming to the conclusion I have to love myself before I can really have relationships with someone else. But those things are desperate, they're life and death in my heart and in my soul, that's the way it feels. **"**

—*All Things Considered* with Jacki Lyden, 1994

 ## 129. JOANNA NEWSOM, "SAPOKANIKAN"

Because Joanna Newsom is such a singular composer and arranger, it's easy to get lost in the dizzying craftsmanship of her records—all the oddball harmonic shifts and unexpected turns of phrase. But each of her songs has a heavy emotional center, too. "Sapokanikan," like much of her fourth LP, *Divers*, is about death, and the way it grounds and gives real stakes to human relationships. It's a strange and beautiful tribute to the risks we take to love each other.

—Amanda Petrusich, *Turning the Tables*, Season 2,
"The 200 Greatest Songs by 21st-Century Women+," 2018

Shocking Omissions: Irma Thomas, "Wish Someone Would Care"

New Orleans soul singer Irma Thomas cut stone classic after classic in the early 1960s on the legendary Minit Records, Allen Toussaint's first home base as a producer. The singles she recorded there, ballads like "Ruler of My Heart" and sassy stompers like "Hittin' on Nothing," are still her most well-loved songs; maybe that's because the aching love songs and dance floor fillers had toughness and emotional depth that belied her years.

Her contract with Minit, inked at age nineteen, had led to a fruitful partnership with Toussaint, who wrote, arranged, or produced her run of sides that remain catnip to soul collectors and record nerds, not to mention part of the core soundtrack of New Orleans. ("Irma's voice stayed in my head all the time," Toussaint told me during a 2007 interview. "And it still does.") In 1963, not long after Toussaint left for the army, Minit was sold to its distributor, and they flew Thomas out to Los Angeles to record 1964's *Wish Someone Would Care*, her first long-player.

The centerpiece is the title track, Thomas's first composition of her own that she had ever recorded. It's a song about a yearning that's deeper than romance or physical want—a purely existential desire for the relief of being seen. At the time she recorded it, Thomas was twenty-two, the mother of little kids and in the middle of her second divorce. She was angry and tired, and she wished someone would care. The slow-burning track was as devastating as a hurricane, and it scooted up to No. 2 on the R&B chart and No. 17 on the Hot 100—still her highest-charting hit to date.

Now seventy-six, the woman who's been working overtime since adolescence shows little sign of slowing down: if anything, after her first Grammy win in 2006, her star has taken on even more sparkle. But to get to the essence of Irma Thomas, there's no better key than "Wish Someone Would Care"—a song that, with its agony and honesty, draws heart's blood.

—Alison Fensterstock, *Turning the Tables*, Season 1,
"Shocking Omissions," 2017 (excerpt)

129. BROKEN ENGLISH
Marianne Faithfull (ISLAND, 1979)

Marianne Faithfull
by Jess Rotter

Eager to escape the pigeonhole of being Mick Jagger's beautiful girlfriend, Marianne Faithfull dropped out of her life of privilege and wound up a heroin addict on the London streets. In 1979, she resurfaced with her seventh studio album, the new wave–inflected *Broken English*. Her sweet and lovely lilt had disappeared, replaced by a gravelly snarl that was the permanent aftermath of an untreated case of bronchitis. It turns out that this was the voice she needed to unleash her innate powers; she spat sonic bombs in the title track, summoned her dark tribe in "Witches' Song," and eviscerated a cheating lover in "Why'd Ya Do It." But it's in "The Ballad of Lucy Jordan" that her masterful reading of a lyric really shines. Here Faithfull invoked the Shel Silverstein story of a suburban housewife who, realizing "she'd never ride through Paris in a sports car with the warm wind in her hair," slowly becomes untethered, ending up on the roof before being taken away to a mental institution. Performed with chilling empathy, Faithfull showed that even a woman who has ridden in that sports car and stood at dizzyingly glamorous heights can still end up on that proverbial roof—the singer and the song intertwined.

—Jill Sternheimer, Lincoln Center, *Turning the Tables*, "The 150 Greatest Albums Made by Women," 2017

MARIANNE FAITHFULL:
Very angry indeed

NPR: On the album *Broken English* there are some songs that I would say had a very angry sound. Is that right? Were you angry?

Marianne Faithfull: Yeah. Yeah, I was very, very angry indeed. And it was a great thing for me to express that. I think I would have gone insane if I hadn't done that. And you know, I can still tap into that anger when I want to. It's not that you just do it once and that's it, you're cured of it and you never feel anger again. It's not.

—*All Things Considered* with Lynn Neary, 1987

268

ALICIA KEYS
It's like a declaration, it's a passion

Alicia Keys speaks about the smash debut of her No. 1 album *Girl on Fire*:

❝ It feels so good to sing in this really high space because it's almost like I'm screaming at the top of my lungs when I say 'This girl is on fire.' It's like a declaration, it's a passion. It's like this is me. And so when I was recording it, it felt perfect. I didn't have any feelings like it was too high or not. I just felt like it was that breaking spot in my voice that feels like the emotion that I wanted it to feel like. ❞

—*Weekend Edition* with Rachel Martin, 2012

70. BELLA DONNA
Stevie Nicks (MODERN, 1981)

On September 3, 1981, Stevie Nicks graced the cover of *Rolling Stone* magazine, flanked only by the same pet cockatoo that accompanied her on the cover of her newly released solo debut, *Bella Donna*. In the subheader, *Rolling Stone* dubbed Nicks the "Reigning Queen of Rock & Roll"—a title cemented two days later when *Bella Donna* hit No. 1 on the *Billboard* 200 chart. It was a seminal turning point in Nicks's career, transforming her from one of three songwriters in Fleetwood Mac into a bona fide icon. Here was the ethereal gypsy woman pulling back the shroud and emerging stronger than ever. Her voice unfurled, backed by a propulsive guitar riff on "Edge of Seventeen," one of the album's four Top 40 singles and arguably her most recognizable song. (Destiny's Child even sampled the riff in their 2001 hit "Bootylicious," with Nicks making a cameo appearance in the music video.) With "Stop Draggin' My Heart Around" (featuring Tom Petty and the Heartbreakers) and "Leather and Lace" (featuring the Eagles' Don Henley) peaking at No. 3 and No. 6, respectively, Nicks not only proved that she could hold court with some of the biggest male names in rock, but that she was a pioneer in her own right. Throughout the years, Nicks's voice has been a gateway to a world of depth, and her words a vehicle for nostalgia. As she sings midway through *Bella Donna*, "the feelings remain" long after these songs end. But when it comes to Stevie Nicks, the glitter never fades.

—Desiré Moses, WNRN, *Turning the Tables*,
"The 150 Greatest Albums Made by Women," 2017

124. NO SECRETS
Carly Simon (ELEKTRA, 1972)

In 2013, Taylor Swift asked a sold-out stadium crowd in Foxborough, Massachusetts: "Before I bring out my special guest, I have this question that I've always, always had. Who is the song 'You're So Vain' by Carly Simon written about?" Then, Simon joined Swift onstage to perform the former's hit, which they did with the joyful abandon of preteens singing into hair-dryer microphones while dancing around their bedrooms. That one of the biggest pop stars in the world today would be fixated on a who's-dating-who tabloid story from 1972, and that tens of thousands of her young female fans would sing along to every word of a tune that came out forty years prior, makes no sense. Except that it does when you consider Carly Simon as one of the most influential artists of her generation, and one who essentially templated the breakup song that's since become ubiquitous. "You're So Vain" alone is not what makes Simon's breakthrough 1972 album *No Secrets* significant, but it does point to Simon's gift for getting at universal and eternal truths through personal confessions—a gift that's exemplified in simple and profound lyrics like, "Often I wish that I never knew some of those secrets of yours." Simon's deft storytelling, coupled with her stunningly precise vocal performance, made this album feel automatically nostalgic upon its release and absolutely timeless today.

—Talia Schlanger, *World Cafe*, *Turning the Tables*, "The 150 Greatest Albums Made by Women," 2017

270

CARLY SIMON
A reporter of emotions

❝ I think the line that is carried through from 'That's the Way I've Always Heard It Should Be' to now is my voice. And it's my internal voice as well. It's the thoughts that go on in my head. It's what I'm preoccupied by. It's what I think about. I've always been a reporter of emotions.

People assume that my songs are even more personal than they are. It's true that they start off from a place where there's a strong identification, where there may be an autobiographical element. But then, I certainly use my imagination and create some kind of fiction at some point along the way in my songs. They're not as literal as people imagined them to be. ❞

—*Morning Edition* with Andy Lyman, 1985

CASSANDRA WILSON
Something raw that's already there

❝ The song often will touch you in a way that makes you remember a very specific incident, or a very specific moment, or a very specific feeling. It almost happens instantaneously. When you listen to the song, it kind of pulls you in because it taps an emotion, something that's kind of raw that's already there. **❞**

—*News & Notes* with Ed Gordon, 2006

125. TIDAL
Fiona Apple (WORK GROUP/CLEAN SLATE/COLUMBIA, 1996)

Fiona Apple unfurled her debut album with a roll of thunder, in the form of "Sleep to Dream." Over the course of *Tidal*'s ten songs, the clouds may part, but the threat of a storm is always on the horizon. Just nineteen years old when *Tidal* was released, Apple put a voice to the crushing swirl of emotions familiar to so many teenagers, a heady combination of disdain and uncertainty, barely contained rage, and rebellious independence. As it turned out, her songwriting sprang from a past checkered with trauma and deep pain, which she plumbed to write songs right at the edge of—or just past—what many listeners were comfortable with. What's remarkable about this album, especially twenty years later, is its maturity. It doesn't read like a sullen teenager's diary. Instead, it's a declaration, a willful confession, and a mission statement from a woman wrestling power back from her demons and trying to own all the parts of herself that make her human.

—Sarah Handel, NPR, *Turning the Tables*, "The 150 Greatest Albums Made by Women," 2017

Meeting Tracy Chapman in the Spaces Between

Watching Tracy Chapman, and listening to her 1988 self-titled debut album, helped me say what I hadn't yet said out loud.

For a brief while after the release of the album, Tracy Chapman occupied my dreams—and perhaps everyone else's. She was everywhere in pop: at age twenty-four, plucked from a coffee house near her college campus for her sincerity and stage presence and chops, and offered a contract by Elektra Records, Chapman became a star, albeit a reluctant, or at least a quiet, one. *Tracy Chapman* captured the attention of the world with these eleven songs of struggle, resilience, and survival, without cleavage, without choreography, without bling.

I remember watching Tracy Chapman perform "Fast Car" on a live broadcast from London's Wembley Stadium for Nelson Mandela's seventieth birthday in June 1988. Legend has it that Chapman had been called onstage to perform her songs after Stevie Wonder ran into a glitch with his technology. Chapman, armed with only her voice, an acoustic guitar, and a microphone, was the woman for the job. But it was a daunting one.

The day is windy, the audience well-meaning but restless and huge. For the first lines, her voice is a tad off key, a little shaky, but then she gains momentum as the story takes over: her narrator yearning for a better life, for speed and freedom and escape from drudgery and exploitation. Through voice and gesture and the power of her eyes, Chapman transports us, letting us feel vicariously the narrator's cycles of yearning and disappointment.

Watching from my undergraduate dorm room, I felt Chapman's presence like a miracle. I remembered a feeling that I hadn't had since I first watched Spike Lee's *She's Gotta Have It* with my all-white group of friends in Kansas a few years before—that the ancestors were sending me a gift: the chance to see and hear myself onscreen, to help me get through the hard times ahead.

In cadences, beats, and attitude that seemed to draw equally from Women's Music sheroes like Joan Armatrading and Bernice Johnson Reagon; the fighting power of reggae greats like Peter Tosh and Bob Marley; the full-throated, the earnest elegance of folk icon Odetta; Johnny Cash's Man in Black outlaw spirit; and a little bit of Sting's smoothness, *Tracy Chapman* tells stories of everyday lives where injustices were named, and the complexity of survival was explored feelingly, through storytelling. "Fast Car," "Behind the Wall," and "She's Got Her Ticket" make up a trilogy of women's struggles against domestic violence, each exploring a different outcome: narrow escape, continued harm, transcendence. In "Behind the Line," Chapman sings of the segregation and raced-based riots that have scarred cities and towns for the past two hundred years; in "Mountains o' Things," she steps into the mind of a greedy capitalist who seeks to blunt his own loneliness with consumption, at the cost of others' lives; in "Talkin' 'bout a Revolution," she gives voice to the rise of people's movements around the world.

"Fast Car" tells a compelling story of yearning shaped by surviving intergenerational violence, and the ways that class, among other things, shapes and limits women's choices. The landscape of the song seems consummately American (the open road as a space of potential and reinvention; landing at the dead-end space of the supermarket as a checkout girl, with a bar and friends as the only escape). But unlike the white masculinity of Bruce Springsteen's storytelling, which covers some of the same territories, I didn't have to imagine myself as a white man to be transported into the song. I could imagine her lover as any gender, and I could imagine them as Black, or Latinx, or white. This is a product of

273

Chapman's powerful lyrics and embodied performances, including her ability to capture the inner thoughts of her heroes—their process of discovery.

This was the music that I needed at a time when I felt pressure to know everything before it was taught, where I felt the limits of others' assumptions of me most keenly. In graduate school, I often felt like an imposter. The elderly white professor in the first-year course that served as an introduction to graduate school confirmed my fear for me one day in my first semester, as I sat on the wide concrete steps of the English building, soaking up some sun before classes. Standing close, his baggy suit pants leg at my eye's view, he bent down to pat me on the head. "You're a wonderful young lady, Francesca," he said, smiling at me like one might smile at a pet. "But you may not belong in graduate school." Kay, the graduate program administrative assistant, a total badass who seemed to hold the keys to the kingdom of the English department, frequently confused me for Eleanor, the *other* Black girl in my year, a brilliant and wildly accomplished Alice Walker scholar. In this era, Affirmative Action opened doors while subtly reinforcing the contingency of the bargain.

I was the only Black Shakespeare nerd; a proud land grant State University graduate in the company of Ivies; an introvert training for a profession that demands that you, well, "profess." And I was queer, and until Tracy Chapman, I hadn't quite seen myself in the media around me. I was not white, not butch, not femme, sometimes fluid in who I fell in love with. I mean, I *felt* queer, but was I really? Despite some major girl crushes throughout my childhood and young adult life, a bit of flirtation and occasional sapphic footsy under the table at my favorite gay bar, and one memorable girl-on-girl bathroom make-out session, technically, I hadn't ever had sex with a woman.

Chapman herself has been a bit of an enigma, private about her sexual identity until her onetime romantic partner Alice Walker disclosed their relationship in the 1990s. But those of us with our gaydar activated knew what we knew. For many, "Fast Car" felt like a lesbian anthem, a desire to escape from small-town drudgery and heteronormative life. And in "For My Lover," on the second half of the album, she sang deliciously of an outlaw love. With the twang of Ed Black's steel guitar and Chapman's tough-girl contralto, the song moodily discloses the trials of a love that is deemed criminal and dangerous by society's standards:

Everyday I'm psychoanalyzed
For my lover, for my lover
They dope me up and I tell them lies
For my lover, for my lover.

This resolute trickster lover shares much in common with the LGBTQ folks, especially folks of color, who have been arrested, institutionalized, blacklisted, fired from their jobs, cast out of political organizations, and murdered for their gender expression, sexual desires, and choice of sexual partner in the twentieth (and twenty-first) century. But the narrator refuses a story of tragedy, willing to risk it all for love and "you, you, you, you, you." In this song, and in the other intimate final songs on the album, Chapman avoids explicitly gendered pronouns, in favor of "baby" and "you."

In the tension between the determination of the first songs on the album, and the more personal, veiled stories of love in the last ones, Chapman captured the flow of feelings that I felt, both hypervisible and invisible as a Black woman in a white space, and still in formation in my own identity—as blurred as that fuzzy image of Chapman on the album cover. What I needed was some space in-between, just to think. *Tracy Chapman* created that space of protection, confirmation, and contemplation as I figured out who I was, rather than just who others wanted me to be. *Tracy Chapman* for me dramatized the space on the verge of action, where desire begins to crystallize. That crystallization can absolutely happen in the moment of singing, when I was all alone in my room, matching my voice to Chapman's as she digs into those last lines of each song.

Listening to *Tracy Chapman*, I found the power of uncertainty as both a space of discovery and perhaps a destination in itself. In the company of her music, perhaps I could both know what I know and be open to the flux at the heart of queer identity.

Later that summer, when I came back home to Chicago for school break, I told my mother that I was queer at the International House of Pancakes in Boystown, Chicago's gay neighborhood, where she lived. My mother, who knew me better than anyone, told me, "I already knew. I was waiting for you to tell me."

—Francesca Royster, *"Turning the Tables*: Records That Changed Our Lives," 2022 (excerpt)

a Tori Story

by: Dame Darcy

PANDORA LITERALLY RAN AWAY WITH THE CIRCUS.

PERFORMING AS A FIRE BREATHER AND ACROBAT WHEN I MET HER.

SHE BROUGHT SO MUCH MAGIC TO MY LIFE, AND INTRODUCED ME TO BESTIES I HAVE TO THIS DAY.

That Summer WE WERE MERMAIDS AT THE PARADE ON CONEY ISLAND

Six short years later, PANDORA DIED YOUNG. AND WHILE ALL HER FRIENDS WERE IN THE GRIEVING PROCESS I WAS CONTACTED BY THE EDITOR OF THE IMAGE COMICS COMPILATION...

Comic Book Tattoo. HE WAS TORI'S FRIEND AND ASKED ME TO DRAW A COMIC OF HER SONG, PANDORA'S AQUARIUM. NEIL GAIMAN AND I ARE COMICS PALS, HE'S A FRIEND OF TORI'S TOO, AND DID A FORWARD FOR THE BOOK, SO MAYBE THATS HOW I GOT CONNECTED?

But I'm still not sure?... AT THE TIME IT FELT LIKE THE SPIRIT OF PANDORA FACILITATED THIS, AND BROUGHT SOME LIGHT INTO MY LIFE THROUGH THE MOURNING.

We press Track One for the fifth time; we push to the front row of the venue; we hear ourselves reflected in uncanny detail by the songs of someone a million miles or a hundred years away. Sometimes, the boost we get from an artist comes from their example in life, instead of their sound on wax. We feel heard, we see something to strive for, and we keep going.

SWEET INSPIRATION

Sister Rosetta Tharpe

On a Bridge Called Rosetta's Voice

As a very young child growing up in Detroit I pieced together my own liberation theology. From Sunday School and Vacation Bible School songs and hymns ("Jesus Loves Me This I Know," "He's Got the Whole World in His Hands"). From the Bible text my father quoted far more often than any other (Romans 8:31: "If God be for us, who can be against us?"). From recordings of spirituals my aunt played on the hi-fi in the dark of the early morning (Rosetta Tharpe's "Didn't It Rain" and "This Train").

I wove these texts together to create a profoundly protective shield that would evolve over time. My youngest childhood self could come to no other conclusion but to believe that the two primary forces I understood to be against me—people opposed to civil rights and my mother—were the devil.

Little girl me wasn't worried about the devil. Jesus loved me and he had the whole world in his hands.

I was worried for my abusive mother, and for Lester Maddox, who I was told over and over again stood at the schoolhouse door with a hatchet in his hands waiting, I deduced, to behead Black girls just like me who wanted to get an education. And I was worried about the white policeman holding a leash of a German Shepherd lurching at a brave Black boy.

I knew my mother, the policeman, and Lester Maddox were all headed to the fiery pits of hell, where they would drink burning lava and scream as their throats were scorched. I knew that even if Maddox chopped off the brown girl's head, seconds later she would be in heaven on a cloud drinking milk and honey at the welcome table telling Black King Jesus just what Lester Maddox did. My theology kept me soul-safe, if not body-safe.

When I was sixteen I was raped. I was no longer soul-safe. "Lord help me make another day." I prayed that prayer, and God sent me the memory of Rosetta Tharpe's voice and then a Sister Rosetta Tharpe album.

After great trauma, *sane* is something you rebuild on the daily. Over the years there is one psyche work song I have come to love more than all the others.

If I started to lose my memory and I lost the most precious truth last, the final thing I would remember is I love my daughter. And the second to last thing I would remember would be a little portable record player and Rosetta Tharpe, gospel's first superstar, coming for to save me when I thought no one else was coming. And she came riding a song called "This Train."

"This train is a clean train"—the first line of my favorite Rosetta Tharpe song, seems simple but it isn't. After telling us that the train is bound for glory, she makes a true list of who can't ride the train: liars, false pretenders, backbiters. After a riveting guitar break she follows the true list with a false list. My father's family loved popular music. They bought hi-fis, singles, and albums, and they frequented the show bars and concerts, and they had told me that Rosetta winked while singing "the train doesn't pull winkers"; mimed shooting craps while singing it didn't pull crap shooters; mimed throwing back a shot of whiskey just before or after singing it didn't pull whiskey drinkers; pushed her tongue into the side of her cheek just after singing, "this train don't pull tobacco chewers." It was a joke even a kid could get with her family exuberantly describing the gestures, how Rosetta joked all the way through the chorus while singing the train didn't pull jokers.

By the end of the song we know Rosetta's train is a "her" and it is a clean train but not the way most folks define clean. Rosetta's train is a clean train because it is true, because it is authentic, because it hauls everybody *but* the liars, false pretenders, and backbiters. Sin is not pleasure; it's lying about identity.

That promise lifted me. Rosetta was the train and she had had good and bad in her. To be clean was to own one's complexity and contradictions and wrap them in the performance of sensual beauty.

On a bridge called Rosetta's voice I moved from trauma to transcendence. As I got older and YouTube was invented, I got to see Rosetta's "This Train" gestures with my own eyes. I was still building sane every day, but now I didn't just have Rosetta's voice, I had the sight of her, of her hands playing her guitar, her unashamed sweat, but best, her audacious sound that carried me back to passion when I was quit of it, a hundred different times.

I am not the only one she came for. Rosetta, she never forgot the Southern rural audience. She started singing in a church in Chicago, she played in Detroit, but the autoworkers and the urban numbers players were not her cornerstone. She played for those who got left back South, for twentieth-century cotton pickers and housemaids, women who had nothing but a church and a radio when they woke up in the morning with the task of making a sane day.

What she did for those women worked for me in very different circumstances. I was as materially privileged a brown daughter as a twentieth-century Negro could be. If the details of my trauma are no longer relevant, and the details are no longer relevant, some of the thanks goes to Rosetta.

How many women have said some version of this to me about Sister Rosetta? "The sun returned to my backdoor on the growl in her voice, chasing out the trouble in my mind." Or, that after she was diagnosed with "the sugar," diabetes, and appeared onstage in a wheelchair following a circa 1970 amputation, they had whispered, "Lord, didn't I cry when they cut off her leg. I love her song 'Trouble In Mind.'" That gets said. It just doesn't get reported. I'm reporting it.

And I'm reporting this: Soon after she lost her leg to complications of diabetes, Rosetta was dead. Sweet Marie Knight was not afraid of her friend's dead body. Rosetta's favorite costar brushed Rosetta's hair and painted Rosetta's face for the funeral. Everybody says Rosetta looked more beautiful than she had looked in years.

Some folks say they were lovers. Some say they were not. I say the duets they sang were more than the equivalent of making love. Marie Knight was sandwiched by powerful women. Mahalia Jackson brought Marie up to sing on her stage. Rosetta was in the audience and took her to Decca records. Then they made those saving sides.

Sister Rosetta Tharpe sold tickets to her 1951 wedding in Griffith stadium. It was over fifteen thousand tickets and people paid $1.50 to $4.00 to see her husband promise to honor and obey her. The saddest witness? Marie Knight. Her protégé and duet partner.

Rosetta inspired my audacious plan to move to Nashville and be a country songwriter as a way of supporting my ambitions to be a novelist. She was a fountain of ambitious business plans that made art possible.

And she inspires the blurring of certain lines. Rosetta always had her foot on some chalk line and was smearing it. She loved singing gospel songs in bars surrounded by chorines with few clothes. That wasn't something she tolerated—that was something she savored. Even when it was all mixed up with poverty and exploitation. She knew how to find and focus on the sugar in the chord, and the way she sang and strummed, that focus inspired other women to find what sweet might be in the bitter of life.

After I was raped I didn't forget or even want to forget what happened to me. I wanted to organize it so it didn't disorganize me. I cleaned my mind like some women clean houses, one room at a time, singing along to music when I could, and nothing worked better than singing to Rosetta as she strong strummed her big guitar. How many of us say this, "On a bridge called Rosetta's voice I crossed drowning waters, and took pleasure in doing it!" How? I heard Rosetta! Her sound is pleasure. Her syllables wise. Don't matter what's been inside this body. This is a clean train.

On the train that is Rosetta's voice I took a long ride that ended far away from my girlhood theology. I no longer believe in literal heaven, though it once saved my life to believe it. I no longer believe in literal hell or the devil, though it saved my life to believe it. I do believe in love and witness and God as love. Rosetta's "Didn't It Rain" is the Rosetta song that lights my life brightest now.

"Didn't It Rain" is a song of witness, and it is a song of memory. The rain isn't falling now. But it fell hard. It fell long. And you withstood it.

In 1919 Harry Burleigh, a formally educated Black composer and church musician, published the first known printed version of "Didn't It Rain" as "Oh, Didn't It Rain." Before the music and lyrics he offered a short essay on "Negro Spirituals," acknowledging that he had received the song and left his mark on it, but not written the song. Burleigh's mark was a kind of European classicism, but a

European classicism that perceived the profound significance of the underlying text, writing, "the cadences of sorrow invariably turn to joy, and the message is ever clear manifest that eventually deliverance from all that hinders and oppresses the soul will come, and man—every man—will be free." Burleigh said nothing about every woman, nothing about every child. It took Rosetta to do that.

There is a YouTube video of Rosetta singing "Didn't It Rain" outdoors at the defunct Wilbraham Road railway station in England on May 7, 1964, a few days after my fifth birthday. The performance is shockingly brilliant. Rosetta strides daintily—that seems a contradiction in terms but she embodies just that very contradiction—onto the platform wearing an immense tailored coat, with bejeweled collar. She wears stylish, pointy-toed high heels with a V-shaped cut out of the vamp. Her slim ankles as powerful as her large body. Her large body as beautiful as her slim ankles. Her hair styled intentionally or fortuitously in a style that echoes and rhymes with the Beatles' hairdos. Eric Clapton, Jeff Beck, Keith Richards, and Brian Jones, who are all said to have attended the show, would have noticed that.

I noticed this: Rosetta was audible witness to infant injuries. Her "Didn't It Rain" transforms the Burleigh song, the commonly known version sung by Mahalia Jackson and taught in the Sunday schools, into something significantly secular.

Burleigh's lyric is relatively simple, drawing heavily on a single Bible verse, Genesis 7:4, that becomes the first line of his lyric, "Fo'ty days, fo'ty nights when de rain kept afallin'." His lyric is centered on judgment and threat—in response to the rain, "de wicked climb de tree," but they know the rain is coming for them and they will be drowned. They know escape is futile. When I was a girl and heard Burleigh's version of the song, when I sang that song at vacation Bible School at the same time Rosetta was singing in London, I imagined wealthy planters climbing magnolia trees trying to escape the sin of slavery—with judgment in the form of rain coming—and only those on the ark with Noah, the good but afflicted people, would be saved.

This week, in 2019, watching the YouTube video of Rosetta Tharpe playing electric guitar, rhythm, and lead, accompanying herself more brilliantly than Eric Clapton could have accompanied her, my sixty-year-old self hears something different.

Rosetta performs as a woman complete in herself. She is question and answer. She is call and response. She is audible witness that the rain came, the pain came, it was long and it was hard, it was survived.

Listening to Rosetta now I hear: Childhood is over. Power and voice are grown-ass claimed. Here on earth. By Rosetta's human hands chording and slashing on guitar. By human voice speaking to human audience.

The time to be emboldened by the promise of a future celestial judgment is over. People overlook it, but Rosetta improvised upon and altered the lyrics she was given. She leaves out the references to climbing trees. Her version is not centered on God's vengeance. It is centered on a woman's witness. "I know it rained. You know it rained." She added words to "Didn't It Rain" that don't exist in the conservative Burleigh version. She returns to the Bible, but to one of the most life-on-earth-centered stories in the Bible. She talks about David, the smaller person with less power, winning over the human giant Goliath. To further turn the song toward battles and bodies in this world, she references the "heat of the day," the time when Black folks worked without equal pay, or without pay at all, enslaved, without signing toward the fires of hell.

When Rosetta rewrites, guitar slashes, scat sings, and bellows her way into and through "Didn't It Rain," she infuses it with irony and that thing that sustains me, eclipsing beauty. You cannot endure the rain with the gumption to jibe with Rosetta's version of "Didn't It Rain" and remain a child forever.

I love Mahalia Jackson, who recorded a fine version of "Didn't It Rain" in 1954. Her version is all about promising the bad will be punished. Rosetta's recorded version, released in 1948, is about something altogether else; it's about the pleasure of seizing sound, making sound, receiving sound.

We know, Rosetta knows, drowning rains, pain and shame, come in this world. And listening to Rosetta we learn: if we are vigorous we find the will to float through rain on lifebuoys of witness, syncopation, sound, and song that is Rosetta's heaven on earth. And if you want a taste of that, you can sing along, clap along, dance along, too.

—Alice Randall, *Turning the Tables*, Season 3,
"Eight Women Who Invented American Popular Music," 2019

Aretha Franklin

4. I NEVER LOVED A MAN THE WAY I LOVE YOU
Aretha Franklin (ATLANTIC, 1967)

In the universe of popular music, this album exploded like a brand new sun. It took Aretha Franklin eleven songs to shift the canon of AM radio away from the realm of girlish glee to the cataclysms of womanly love. *I Never Loved a Man* connected with Black and white audiences and became the biggest commercial success of her building career. On this Atlantic Records debut, Franklin trucks confidently in the desires of a modern-day woman. In a word, she's "real"—plainspoken and passionate, without guile or undue glamour. The album has funky rhythms, of course. And horns. And some of the most memorable hooks in popular music. Franklin's reimagining of the Otis Redding single "Respect" is now on the National Recording Registry of the Library of Congress, reportedly as a feminist anthem. But the song is also redolent of Black consciousness and pride. And yet, it's Franklin's renderings of vulnerability in love that make the album universal. The title track was her first million-seller. She also wrote or co-wrote some of the best-known songs of her career for the release, including "Baby, Baby, Baby" and "Dr. Feelgood." For better or worse, each song here sounds like she lived it. Producer Jerry Wexler called the famously private Franklin "Our Lady of Mysterious Sorrows."

—Gwen Thompkins, WWNO, *Turning the Tables*,
"The 150 Greatest Albums Made by Women," 2017

Skeeter Davis: The Patron Saint of Female Artists Who Fall Between the Cracks

Summertime in '83, the last time I took LSD
But listening to Patsy Cline
And Skeeter Davis really blew my mind

   —"Summer of My Wasted Youth," Amy Rigby

Ask the general public who Patsy Cline was and most will have some idea: lush country songbird, she had the full biopic treatment; died early enough to leave a concise impression.

But Skeeter Davis? A singular artist who came along early and stayed for decades; the patron saint of female artists who fall between the cracks—too pop for country, too country for pop—Skeeter Davis gamboled through musical styles and associations like she changed her hairstyle and clothes, always remaining her unique self. Throw in a few marriages—the second to a straight arrow member of the country music establishment, the third to the bass player of an unclassifiable band—and an unchecked affection for Jesus and you have a life story too sprawling for film or streaming series.

The sound of a girl singing with herself was what drew me to her "End of the World" single when I was a kid. That and the undeniable heartbreak in the spoken, final half-verse:

Why—does the sun go on shining?
Why—does the sea rush to shore?

Skeeter Davis, born Mary Frances Penick to a Kentucky farmer and an often-depressed mother, first scored hits in the 1950s as one-half of the Davis Sisters. She and best friend Betty Jack sang with an eerie familial blend, sisters of the soul. In Skeeter's openhearted tell-all *Bus Fare to Kentucky*, she describes the two teenagers cutting their thumbs and pressing them together to seal the deal with blood. Their biggest hit was built on one of those head-spinning country phrases so simple you have to think twice to grasp its meaning: "I Forgot More Than You'll Ever Know About Him." Skeeter and Betty sounded like a single voice doubled, until Skeeter would leap into the perfect harmony that was one of her gifts. When a tragic post-gig car accident took Betty Jack's life, it was hard for Skeeter to go on—harmony singing was where she felt the most at home.

Nashville guitarist and producer Chet Atkins solved that problem by creating a sound to put her at ease, double-tracking her voice, a novel idea back then. Over a dozen singles in as a solo artist, her recording "End of the World" was picked up by New York radio DJ Scott Muni and sold a hundred thousand records in a week. It was as if listeners could feel the absence of Betty Jack or anyone they'd ever lost in the grooves of the record. Written by Arthur Kent and lyricist Sylvia Dee, the hurt in the song went deeper than the mere loss of romantic love. The ache in Skeeter's delivery was so real it split the world in two, life carrying on while the singer's own voice echoed the keen of loneliness.

"End of the World" was the first-ever single to crack the Top 10 and Top 5 on all four *Billboard* charts at once. Skeeter lit up the charts again and again through the 1960s and into the '70s. She lost favor in Nashville but continued performing and was rediscovered by eclectic rock band NRBQ in the 1980s. Their joint album *She Sings, They Play* had the warm magic of her early efforts. She and Joey Spampinato, the group's bass player, fell in love and married in 1987.

In 1999, I slipped backstage at the Grand Ole Opry House at Opryland. It was a little like being in a high school locker room. Meeting the fans was part of the gig for country stars. I saw a trim blond woman in a long velvet dress like you might wear to a Renaissance fair. Her smile was as wide and sweet as on her album cover photos.

"Skeeter! I'm such a fan, I put your name in one of my songs," I said.

"Are you from New York?" she asked. That voice with the catch in it was for real. We talked about Nashville and rock musicians. And relationships. I could see how maybe she was a little too much: for Joey, for Nashville. She went to her locker and brought out a children's book she'd written and signed it to me. Then she gave me her phone number. In the next room, Garth Brooks was locking eyes with anyone brave enough to look his way. He was the biggest star in country music at the time, just as Skeeter had been at one point. Now she was—as she had always been—just herself.

A few months later, I watched Skeeter take the stage at the Ryman Auditorium. The Opry had returned to the Mother Church, the place it first found its audience— and I felt that pull, the one that brought me to Nashville in the first place: a love of country music and the people who created it. Skeeter projected her humor and gentle spirit into a microphone and up into the balcony so that we all felt humbled and exalted at the same time.

Back in my rented house, I wrote a song based on what Skeeter had told me about the breakup of her marriage, one I hoped I could get her to sing on. I left a message on her answering machine, asking if she might be up for coming to the studio. I didn't know she had been diagnosed with the cancer that would kill her a few years later. I just figured she was busy.

I eventually recorded the song, harmonizing with myself. I could feel Skeeter just over my shoulder, smiling that smile too big to categorize.

—Amy Rigby, musician, *Turning the Tables* contributor

A Different
Kind of Outlaw

In the middle of the night, the breast pump suction starts to sound like a beat. It's a slow one, but still a burning, repetitive thump that is so coolly rhythmic it sings as you struggle to keep your eyes open and head up: swish, slosh, swish, slosh, over and over again. There are different speeds and therefore different songs, a mixtape of motherhood exhaustion just for you. Swish, slosh, swish, slosh. It is one of the most solitary sounds you'll ever hear, which makes sense, because in some ways early motherhood is the most solitary thing you'll ever do, even though the whole idea was to never be alone again.

This is because so many moments in early parenthood feel as if they are unique to you and your own set of original, embarrassing failures: the first baby nail you cut too short so it bleeds, the first night you are so exhausted you can't actually sleep, the swaddle you can never secure. You are certain that this happens to no one else but you, or that no one understands. You've never been more certain, so you must not have been made for this. I must not have been made for this.

I wasn't sure I wanted to be a mother when I was growing up; my female role models, which primarily comprised musicians like Liz Phair, Fiona Apple, and Ani DiFranco, were greeted either with hesitancy or dismissiveness when they had children (Phair, DiFranco) or with confusion when they never did (Apple). Once a female artist became a mother, everything was colored by that transition whether they liked it or not. Every album was "an album influenced by parenthood," even if the songs were about sleeping with strangers at a bar down the street, and press coverage shifted to questions about whether the baby was going on the tour bus or not, and, wow, it must be so hard to balance nighttime feedings and studio sessions. There was no room to be dimensional, and I wanted to have dimensions.

I realized though, in my early thirties, that I also very badly wanted a baby. A family. It took until then to understand that my views of motherhood, especially mothers who were also artists and writers, had been dictated to me by everyone but the women themselves. I gave birth to my first child, a son, in 2013. It was a high-risk pregnancy followed by a traumatic birth and a beautiful baby, and then seemingly endless lonely nights to the squeak-song of that breast pump, the only music that seemed to make sense.

I first heard of Margo Price not long after I moved to Nashville from New York in early 2012—she would frequently pop up at gigs around town, mostly with her band at the time, Buffalo Clover. A mutual friend, over coffee while my six-month-old son was in daycare, even made a suggestion: "You should get to know Margo," she said. "She's a mom like you." In a different, less vulnerable state, I may have taken that as an insult, but this time, I was open. I paid attention. I didn't need a friend as much as I needed my experiences molded back to me in a way that made sense, just as much as I needed to completely shatter the cage I'd built around the idea of motherhood. I started to listen to Price, but I watched her, too.

I watched the way that Price writes and talks about motherhood—how it feels intentional, her choices specific. She shares from a place of deep, unfathomable loss and unapologetic love, and from a personal truth unafraid of whether it goes along with the convention of what it means to be a mother—or a rock star, for that matter. Nothing was or is too "mothery" for her: being pregnant onstage, sharing a photo nursing with a couple of mammoth plastic Jumperoos in the background, a matchy-matchy family photo or futile attempts to keep the kids out of frame during a quarantine-era Zoom call. But nothing is too non-mothery either. She released a song about orgasms and female pleasure written after she was done having babies (sex for sex's sake, how taboo of a thing to do if you've already birthed your brood); she hops behind the drum set on tour in a barely there sequin bodysuit, her naked legs keeping rhythm. It's the idea of "dimensional" I'd always looked for, without ever sacrificing humanity, normalcy, fun, or even the mundane. Not "doing it all," because no one can, no mother can. Just being every part of herself.

Price was already a parent when she released her solo debut, *Midwest Farmer's Daughter*, in 2016. She was raising her son, Judah, and sang about the pain of losing his twin, Ezra, on the album's six-minute opener, "Hands of Time." It's a country ballad for the ages written as only a mother could, with no traces of the domesticity and allegiance that I found far too often in the genre and beyond—she had babies at home, but the yearning inside of her for something more, something bigger, something less cruel, was squarely hers to own. No one in town wanted the LP except for Jack White's Third Man Records, and I have no doubt that was due in part to the fact that a woman in her thirties with a child at home is not the strongest selling point.

"It's hard to be a mother, a singer, and a wife," Price sings on "Wild Women," the same person who I later watched scream "I want to see you come" onstage at the Ryman Auditorium. Price gets called "outlaw country" a lot, and I understand why: the music she makes doesn't conform to the machinery of Nashville and Music Row. It's the easiest way to describe it all.

But I see her as a different kind of outlaw. A mother, a singer, a wife, a wild woman, unafraid to be it all and show it all, against convention, against the rulebook, along for the ride with us, when we're alone in the dark with nothing but a breast pump and a sleeping baby. It shows up in her life, and it shows up in her songs.

Because maybe the real outlaws are the mothers, mothering in plain view.

—Marissa R. Moss, *Turning the Tables* contributor

76. STAND BY YOUR MAN
Tammy Wynette (EPIC, 1969)

There's a generation of feminists who might know *Stand by Your Man* and its title song primarily by an infamous 1992 interview Hillary Clinton gave in support of her husband's first presidential bid. There's a generation before that, though, who know the album for its perceived affront to the women's movement of the 1960s and 1970s. But if Tammy Wynette's focus on domestic life ran counter to many women's aspirations, it gave voice to many others who could identify with what they heard. The songs on *Stand by Your Man* exemplified the way Wynette centered the personal heartaches that women suppress in order to care for loved ones: the burden of holding an imperfect marriage together, the strength summoned to comfort a child whose father's walked out, the difference between a weekend fling and a commitment that lasts through the weekday routine. This album also portended Wynette's role in shaping the lush countrypolitan style with which Nashville infiltrated the pop charts into the '70s. And while sweeping strings weren't yet supplanting steel guitar, *Stand by Your Man*'s crossover-friendly backing choirs and tearful evocation of middle-class hardiness ushered it into the mainstream.

—Rachel Horn, NPR Music, *Turning the Tables*,
"The 150 Greatest Albums Made by Women," 2017

294

Tammy Wynette
by Maggie Thrash

Your Good Girl's Gonna Go Bad!

TAMMY WYNETTE
A good country record

"My first love is country music. I don't feel that I could ever be anything other than country—that's all I ever want to be and I'm perfectly happy being a country music singer, but I do enjoy other kinds of music. Ray Charles is just one of my favorites.

If I come off with a good country record, I always hope—as much as I think all the artists hope—that it will be a big crossover record. But I don't aim in that direction. I want a good country record, one that hopefully will sell good and will be a number-one record, and if it crosses over, I'm just very lucky and very thankful that they played it—but I don't aim in that direction. I just appreciate it if it happens.**"**

—NPR's *Voices in the Wind* with Bill Barbar, 1975

Review: boygenius, *the record*

On *the record*, the first full-length album by the supertrio of songwriters Lucy Dacus, Julien Baker, and Phoebe Bridgers, boygenius honors how friendship shapes our very sense of self.

———————

Friendship is not the backdrop for *the record*, or merely context for its creation. It's why and how this album was made. More than just the topic of many of these songs, friendship is the spark that animates its deepest inquiries and the force that grounds its existential questions about how we care for each other, why we choose each other, and how this kind of closeness can transform us. Perhaps that sounds like terrain usually reserved for romance, but these *are* love songs. In a *Rolling Stone* profile Bridgers describes writing that first boygenius EP that way: "It was not *like* falling in love," she says, "it *was* falling in love." You can hear a reverence for friendship when Dacus sings, "It feels good to be known so well" on the standout single "True Blue." Or in the video for "Not Strong Enough," composed of footage they shot of a day spent together at an amusement park—making each other laugh, posing for goofy photos, falling asleep on each other's shoulders. Or in the touching last line of "Leonard Cohen," another Dacus-led song dedicated to her band mates: "I never thought you'd happen to me."

—Marissa Lorusso, NPR Music, 2023 (excerpt)

boygenius

LUCY DACUS
Defined by friends

66 Friendship is something that I think about a lot. My life is defined by my friends. It's the thing that my life is. I feel like there's maybe some good media about friendships, but not a ton. Romance also has typical touchstones, whereas every friendship is so unique. I kind of feel like there's even more there to play with. So why aren't people doing it [making art about friendship]? It doesn't feel like a hack subject. The way that I've been writing a lot of love songs recently and I feel myself being like, this is overplayed or this isn't profound in the slightest, but I can pick any one of my friends and write something that is just completely unique to them. 99

—*Weekend Edition* with Miles Parks, 2023

Robyn Is the 21st Century's Pop Oracle

There is this moment, about a minute and a half into the music video for Robyn's flawless 2010 single "Call Your Girlfriend," that gives us a quintessential glimpse, something just shy of a thesis, of the Swedish pop star. In it, she's doing a highly aerobic choreographed dance in an empty warehouse, performing to the camera, which is capturing it in a single, continuous shot; the song she's singing is premised largely on passing caring and hard-won advice about getting over a breakup to a woman through the man she is seemingly stealing from her. The song foregrounds the feelings of the two women; the romance with the new dude is somewhere in the backseat.

As Robyn is laying this drama, she's meeting our gaze by staring intently back at us through the camera; she's pacing through stuttering rhythmic moves, her severe silvery-white bowl cut motionless throughout. She's fully clothed in a long-sleeve sweater, leggings, and candy pink platform oxfords. She prances backward and with a rough somersault, unfurls herself, cheek to the floor. She humps the ground in a way that recalls both Prince and a cartoon caterpillar while intoning the line "Tell her that I give you something you never even knew you missed." The camera does not zoom in on her body; it does not grant the reassurance a close-up of Robyn's smiling or seductive face would provide. Robyn then rolls away on the floor in her Muppet-y sweater. She's not here to seduce us in all the hackneyed ways that are so familiar. She's here to give us something we never even knew we missed.

Since early on in her two-decade-plus career as a pop artist, the popular line has always been that even though Robyn has the perfect voice and songs that fit seamlessly amid the bland and the bold of the American pop Top 40, she's never quite broken through, because something is *off*. She's *too* Euro, *too* cool, *too* weird— but that insistent "too" reveals the unspoken rules: we demand pop star girls to be less; to be vessels for our desire, not confidently expressing the complexity of their own; to be malleable, not showing up with an auteur's vision. They are supposed to be writhing, glistening tits-up on the floor, not log-rolling away in a sweater. She sings on 2005's "Who's That Girl":

Who's that girl that you dream of?
Who's that girl that you think you love?
Who's that girl, well I'm nothing like her
I know there's no such girl

In blunting the fantasy girl with the real, it's not that Robyn isn't (fill in the blank) enough, but rather, *she's everything.*

The reductive reasoning about Robyn also misses the way her image and music have been so instructive for both her fans and the artists who came in her wake. She's an artist in control of her work, a soft-butch cool-girl who served us a dreamy possibility beyond the rigid binaries, who adapted pop's dance floor language into something that served her own dreams. Her complexity is a kind of permission: leaving the major label climate after a decade of nursing stardom to start her own label (Konichiwa Records) and make the music she wanted to make, taking long multiyear stretches between releasing her albums, being a constant collaborator (Neneh Cherry, the Knife, Röyksopp), making EPs and mini-albums as is her wont. She has conducted her career with continual centering on independence, on what makes sense and suits her, rather than on any sort of industry convention or pacing. She's a teen pop star who has gotten only more interesting and assertive with age, an artist who is not ducking out, now, at thirty-nine. She's served as an icon for weird girls, queer artists, and nonbinary folks who are the innovators behind some of the best pop music (and its boldest experiments) of the past few years: Lorde, Perfume Genius, Carly Rae Jepsen, Alma, SSION, and Charli XCX chief among them.

Her image and her independence continue to matter, but her songs are what have gained salience in recent years. While thematic echoes of "Dancing on My Own" show up in Lorde's "Green Light" (the young singer performed on *Saturday Night Live* last year with a framed portrait of Robyn), the spiritual endowment of, particularly, Robyn's post-2005 work feels especially prescient. The songs of *Robyn* and the three-part *Body Talk* endure musically, and the emotional range in them still feels revelatory—a relief even. She created dance floor anthems that stack hooks with anger ("Don't Fucking Tell Me What to Do," "Dancing on My Own"), alienation ("None of Dem"), resistance ("Fembot"), sorrow ("Missing U"), and cynicism ("Love Kills") as much as they broach romance. Historically, the dance floor has been a safe space, a nightlong utopia of lust and freedom and carefree self-expression. In 2018, it's all the more necessary. But the reality is that we need music that brings—and allows for—so much more: for songs that assure us that yes, music is the place where we can come in our frightened loneliness. Even in the darkness of our mourning, our confusion and sadness, Robyn assures, again and again, that the disco ball will still shine on us.

—Jessica Hopper, *Turning the Tables*, Season 2,
"25 Most Influential Women+ Musicians of the 21st Century," 2018

Diana Ross:
A Sparrow's Legacy

Her petal-soft soprano revolutionized pop. Her business acumen served as a blueprint for Beyoncé's. Her unabashed attitude developed a template for Mariah Carey, Whitney Houston, and Madonna to embrace: a diva who knew her value and held others to the same responsibility. Her shoulders carried Motown to the bank, rewriting the definition of success for Black musicians. Throughout the course of her dynamic five-decade career, Ms. Diana Ross invented the contemporary girl group, the crossover hit, and positioned Black popular music as the cultural touchstone of music for the twenty-first century.

In March 1997, the hip-hop world mourned the Notorious B.I.G. only months after losing Tupac. With their murders, many considered the genre also dead in the water. Enter that year's song of the summer: the Bad Boy Records platinum hit "Mo Money Mo Problems." Returning to the genre's disco roots, Diddy produced an up-tempo beat for Biggie to posthumously deliver a masterpiece in lyricism. Even though the song is often remembered as the braggadocio of men swinging their flashy chains around, its emotional core lies in Ms. Ross's sampled signature battle cry: "I'm coming out!"

In 1980, the veteran Ms. Ross had reaffirmed her eminence in the form of her eleventh album, *Diana*. After running into three drag queens dressed up as her in a nightclub bathroom, disco legend Nile Rodgers pulled from James Brown's "Say It Loud—I'm Black and I'm Proud" to write *Diana*'s centerpiece, "I'm Coming Out." "The time has come for me to break out of this shell," she sings, welcomed by a triumphant horn fanfare. Infinitely charismatic, Ms. Ross had lent her voice to a growing liberation movement, an unintentional contribution that would become an intentional staple of queer pride.

In a similar vein, "Mo Money Mo Problems" arrived at a crucial time in hip hop, helping Black culture propel itself out of the underground into global primacy—on the coattails of an iconic queer anthem. Spilling from open windows, starting the block party, living on through remix after remix, no one could escape Ms. Ross's triumphant soprano. Her voice sent Biggie off and opened a new door in hip hop as a result.

That iconic voice has long been an accompaniment to history. Born in Detroit during a second wave of Black migration, Ms. Ross grew up alongside a city in the midst of cultural rebirth. In 1960, she convinced Smokey Robinson to bring her, Florence Ballard, Mary Wilson, and Betty McGlown for an audition at Motown Records. Initially, Berry Gordy turned the girls away. Undeterred, they showed up at Motown every day to offer background vocals and claps. Four years later, the Supremes' first No. 1 hit, "Where Did Our Love Go," was a smash breakout. The group went on to release twelve No. 1's within five years, a reign that included five consecutive chart toppers and established Motown as an internationally successful Black enterprise notable for integrating the airwaves. Amidst race riots, the end of segregation, and an emerging Black Power movement, Diana Ross and the Supremes sang for young America, creating a profitable market that transcended both class and race.

Her eye-on-the-prize ambition, her singular, genre-flexible determination, made Ms. Ross an international superstar capable of reinventing her sound time and time again, and also ushered in a new vanguard of music—one with Black women in leading roles for the first time. Her voice reverberated through history, creating debts on behalf of musicians who owed her everything without having to study her. The new millennium's indulgence in commercial hip hop, contemporary R&B, and nu-disco funk has Ms. Ross to thank. With her voice, Ms. Ross delivered promises. She dared to dream of grander tomorrows and in doing so, sang alongside generations to come.

—LaTesha Harris, NPR Music, *Turning the Tables* contributor

95. ¿DÓNDE ESTÁN LOS LADRONES?
Shakira (SONY, 1998)

Shakira's luggage was once stolen at the airport in Bogotá, Colombia. The loss, which included a trove of lyrics in one of the suitcases, left her devastated and shook. But the incident also fueled the inspiration for what would be her next album, *¿Dónde Están los Ladrones?* (Where Are the Thieves?). While it's partially inspired by the robbery, the album hints toward the political corruption and mistrust Colombian society held toward its own government. As a follow-up to her success with *Pies Descalzos*, Shakira produced every song on her fourth studio record while experimenting with new pop and rock arrangements. She certainly made the most of a bad situation: the imaginative songs of *¿Dónde Están los Ladrones?*, brimming with Shakira's witty and brutally honest wordplay, cemented her place in the alternative Latin rock canon. Some Shakira fans see this album as her last piece of work in this genre before crossing over into the English-speaking market with her following record *Laundry Service*, which ignited cultural conversations about Shakira's authenticity. Yet as a half-Colombiana, half-Salvadoreña young girl, I never saw other young *mujeres* from my countries in the media doing what they loved. Shakira, and this album, represented embracing my "otherness" and owning it unapologetically.

—Jessica Diaz-Hurtado, NPR, *Turning the Tables*,
"The 150 Greatest Albums Made by Women," 2017

SHAKIRA
Too strong and too powerful

❝ I was never able to join my school choir, because there was this music teacher who thought my voice was too strong and too powerful, and it wouldn't fit right in the rest of the choir. It was formed by very white voices. That's how you call the voices of children, you know, in Spanish—voices that haven't developed yet, and that sound very light and soft and beautiful. My voice was strong, and I wanted to sing out loud, and he didn't think that I was the right choice. . . . I take pop music very seriously. And I try to give the best I can give through my music and always improve and always learn, because I think that that's the only way you don't get bored with what you're doing. 🗨🗨

—*Morning Edition* with Juan Forero, 2007

MARIAH CAREY
I think that was my lesson

In 2006, uber diva Mariah Carey talked about her 2005 album *The Emancipation of Mimi*, which was thought of as a "comeback" album after a series of personal and professional trials.

🗨🗨 I think I wouldn't have been blessed with such a phenomenal success of this album if it were about anger right now for me, you know what I mean? I had to go through a situation where people did write me off, because people do tend to believe whatever they read, whatever they see in the papers. And I used to be one of those people, until I experienced what it can be like to go through something that's really deep and really kind of intense. And to go from that and to just be creative and to make an album, and to not lose faith in myself, I think was my lesson. 🗨🗨

—*News & Notes* with Ed Gordon, 2006

Gangsta Boo, "Where Dem Dollas At"

Gangsta Boo is the Queen of Memphis and the First Lady of Hypnotize Minds, Prophet Posse, and Three 6 Mafia. She is the original "fucking lady": horrorcore, smoke, mosh pits, and boss shit. Whenever she enters the room of a track, the whole of femme Memphis enters with her. No song exemplifies this consistently dynamic and breathtaking character of Boo's presence more than "Where Dem Dollas At." The song's architecture is reflective of her distinct ability to command a royal Southern court; the city's premier producers, DJ Paul and Juicy J, sampled a popular Memphis song "Sho Nuff," originally produced by Memphis native and son of the Bar-Kays' bassist, Jazze Pha. Its insistent title query, chanted by a chorus of Boo's dubbed voice, is punctuated by a sample of one of her own lines from her featured verse on Indo G's "Remember Me Ballin'." That she can sample herself— "I'm chiefin' heavy understand me, baby, this Gangsta Boo"—and chant a demand for the location of the cash is an explicit recognition of her power and significance as a formidable rapper in an all-men music collective in the 1990s South.

"Where Dem Dollas At" is the template for cash-as-women's-agency that reverberates throughout subsequent women rappers' work, from Trina to Megan Thee Stallion to Cardi B, as laborers in the music industry. The enduring question of the song is what Gangsta Boo, as well as frequent collaborator La Chat, is owed for her trailblazing work as a tenaciously deft lyricist better than most of her men counterparts. In an industry where women's increased presence as artists rarely translates into increased power, compensation, or control, "Where Dem Dollas At" is a reminder of where we have been, just how far we have to go, and how we need to keep chanting the questions until we get the answers we deserve.

—Zandria F. Robinson, NPR Music's *The South Got Something to Say: A Celebration of Southern Rap*, 2020

77. AALIYAH
Aaliyah (BLACKGROUND/VIRGIN AMERICA, 2001)

For her third and final act, Aaliyah made her strongest and most important offering. Her very tragic and untimely death shortly after the release of this self-titled album made it difficult and haunting for most people to listen to. But *Aaliyah* is a revelation that projects an effortlessly cool aesthetic coupled with the actual vulnerability that comes with being cool. The compositions on the forward-thinking album, most by Stephen Garrett (Static Major), were complex and futuristic, much more so than any other R&B records released at the time, and the way Aaliyah perfectly embodied Garrett's songwriting is astounding. You'd never think that she didn't write these songs herself. On this album, Aaliyah continued the legacy of soprano singers like Minnie Riperton and Mariah Carey and simultaneously set the stage for artists like Kelela and Solange to emerge. In the process, *Aaliyah* became a catalyst and bridge that created a smooth transition from '90s style R&B into modern alternative R&B.

—Stasia Irons, KEXP, *Turning the Tables*, "The 150 Greatest Albums Made by Women," 2017

Returning to Lady:
A Reflection on
Two Decades in
Search of Billie Holiday

In all honesty, when, as a child, I discovered Billie Holiday, I was looking for my father. After his death, I sought him in all the things I knew he loved, especially books and music. I listened. I read. In Lady's voice I heard something beyond what I sought of him: I heard the seeking itself. In her voice there was the longing, the yearning that I felt but had not the words to express. To long for something you will never have, to aspire for a destination you will never reach—that is what I heard in Billie Holiday's voice. In her sound there is a quiet depth, an interiority that is nonetheless reaching, aspiring. Where will she land? It is always someplace unexpected, perhaps not where she was headed, but, oh the journey there, and the place itself, is beautiful—not because it satiates, but precisely because it doesn't.

When, as an adult, I wrote about her in *If You Can't Be Free, Be a Mystery: In Search of Billie Holiday*, she was the object of my desire and longing. I wanted desperately to treat her well, to refuse previous portrayals that lingered too long on the tragedy and too little on the genius. I turned away from the torch songs, the ones that are quite literally about longing, to the hip, sassy, flirtatious ones: the buoyant "No Regrets" and "Them There Eyes" of her youth; the grown woman versions of "Billie's Blues," "Fine and Mellow," or the defiant "Strange Fruit." Listen closely to the version of "No Regrets" recorded in 1936 and you hear a woman who

Billie Holiday
by Jazmin Anita

hasn't lived long enough to have regrets anyway. In these songs there is a biography, one that acknowledges the struggle that was her life, but that reminds us of the many ways she fought, defiantly, and at times with militancy: "Before I be your dog / I'll see you in your grave." She did not shout or yell; she didn't need to. The clarity, the full-on stare of those statements and those to whom they are directed know better than to cross her.

But to attend to Lady closely is to be haunted by her voice, to always return to it. Listen and you will hear her everywhere: in restaurants, bars, soundtracks and in the voices of emerging jazz and pop artists. And, that haunting suggests, you haven't finished, you need to listen more: Did you hear what you thought you heard? Listen again: seek out later versions and contexts of the tune you thought you knew. Joni Mitchell, who claims Billie Holiday as one of her most formative influences, shares this insight about Lady Day: "Billie Holiday makes you hear the content and intent of every word she sings—even at the expense of her pitch or tone. Billie is the one that touches me deepest." Like Toni Morrison's *Beloved*, she touches us deep "on the inside." Her voice is an invitation to listen to your own interior voices as well.

In the years following the publication of my book about her, I returned to Lady only sporadically. I had ingested so much of her, I felt I needed to breathe, I needed to exhale her. When I did return, it was to "You're My Thrill." Mitchell recorded this one in tribute to Billie on her own album of standards. There is a raw eroticism to 1949's "You're My Thrill," a wanting and desire so intense as to frighten. Is this all-encompassing desire only for a lover? Might it also be for the momentary bliss, the all-too-brief, ever-evasive peace brought on by heroin? ("Where's my will, why this strange desire?") I want here to at least acknowledge that possibility.

In truth, I initially turned to Billie Holiday, and continued to turn to her, because of what I heard in her but also because I had questions about addiction. I knew and loved people who struggled with various forms of substance abuse. It was the mid-'70s and heroin was back with a vengeance in my working-class Black community; it would soon be supplanted by crack. I had family members who fell prey to both. In the days before Narcan and safe spaces to shoot up and calls for the humane care of addicts, in the days before the face of opioid addiction was white, addicts were hunted, arrested, stigmatized, and treated like shit. And in our family, in our community, their struggles were known but whispered about. No one wanted to bring attention to them, least of all the addicts themselves. This was especially the case with heroin addiction. We neither named nor talked about it. It was a loud secret. There it was, out there, waiting. Was it waiting for me?

In the loud silence, in the quest and questioning, Lady provides answers. Later, because I did not want to join the chorus of those who seemed overly consumed with Lady the junkie, I focused my attention on how poorly she was treated by the authorities and the tabloids. Indeed. She had suffered the same fate of other poor Black addicts, perhaps more so because of her fame. She was arrested on her death bed for possession and use. Her secret was open.

Billie Holiday neither denied nor evaded the fact of her addiction. In all of her adult life, there are two constants: her music and her habit. And she spoke openly of each. She spoke about the difficult dance of kicking the habit, only to pick it up again. But she does more than that. In a first-person piece, attributed to her but said to have been written by William Dufty (who also wrote *Lady Sings the Blues*),

309

she talks matter-of-factly about her addiction, without shame. "MAYBE I NEEDED HEROIN TO LIVE" she exclaims in the tabloid piece, recently republished in the very valuable *Billie Holiday: The Last Interview and Other Conversations*. I didn't deal with this version of Holiday in my own book. I don't recall consciously choosing not to, but this Holiday is a Holiday of refusal, refusing even my own attempts to present an alternative version of her life. This one isn't the kick-ass, genius woman instead of the tragic addict. This one is the kick-ass, genius, Black woman who makes no excuses for her addiction. Who explains the logic and the why of it. Who is neither apologetic nor ashamed. She notes her parents, neither of whom ever indulged in drug use, died at much younger ages than she: "Heroin not only kept me alive—maybe it also kept me from killing." Who am I to say this isn't true?

Holiday closes the interview with, "I hold no regrets and I carry no shame." I didn't read this when I was first searching for answers in her life and her voice. I wish I had. There is a finality here. This is a destination, an unexpected landing: to come to the end with neither regret nor shame.

—Farah Jasmine Griffin, *Turning the Tables*, Season 3, "Eight Women Who Invented American Popular Music," 2019

DIONNE WARWICK
I've learned from the very best

❝ Well, I'm very comfortable being who I am, and that's very important, I think. And I think I've learned from the very best in our industry, the icons of music and those that are in film, as well. When you sit and you watch a Marlene Dietrich walk onstage or Carol Burnett walk onstage or Lena Horne walk onstage, you know that's how you've got to walk onstage, and that's the way you're supposed to look when you walk onstage. So that's it. ❞

—*Talk of the Nation* with Neal Conan, 2010

2. THE MISEDUCATION OF LAURYN HILL
Lauryn Hill (RUFFHOUSE/COLUMBIA, 1998)

Lauryn Hill *by* Rashida Chavis

The Fugees struck gold in the late 1990s with albums like *The Score*, a feat that also made their resident wordsmith, Lauryn Hill, a household name. But when Hill went out on her own two years later and dropped her debut, the neo-soul masterpiece *The Miseducation of Lauryn Hill*, she schooled everyone all over again in new and necessary ways. In it, Hill refuses to shy away from topics often left unspoken, injecting classroom love lesson interludes and hard-hitting lyrics about how money changes people in the banger "Lost Ones." Then there's the cautionary tale "Doo Wop (That Thing)," a bold song that unpacked sexual politics and not only scored Hill two Grammys, but also earned her the distinction of becoming the first woman since Debbie Gibson (with 1988's "Foolish Beat") to have a song that she simultaneously wrote, recorded, and produced soar to the top of the *Billboard* charts. And that's just one song on *The Miseducation of Lauryn Hill*. The album, rife with Hill's biting rhymes and sharp turns of phrase, is a wonder from start to finish, from her smoldering duet with fellow R&B superstar Mary J. Blige "I Used to Love Him" to the unapologetic, plucky "To Zion," in which Hill details how people discouraged her from having a child in order to further her career:

But everybody told me to be smart
"Look at your career," they said

"Lauryn, baby, use your head"
But instead I chose to use my heart.

It's further proof that, yes, women absolutely can—and will continue to—have it all.

—Paula Mejia, *Turning the Tables*,
"The 150 Greatest Albums Made by Women," 2017

QUEEN LATIFAH
It's okay to try something new

"Oh, man, I got plenty of stuff to say. I mean, I still have a bunch of records that I've recorded through the years since that last album came out. I kind of—I guess I might have thought that someone else would have came along and took the reins. And, you know, not that I was looking for someone to take my place, but I surely expected that, you know, when Lauryn Hill came out, that there would be other people who came out and kind of said something. I don't think anybody has really said a whole lot consistently about a lot of substantial stuff. I mean, it's not like every one of my records was a message record. There was a lot of bragging and boasting in there, but at the same time, there was a lot of social consciousness and positivity wrapped in the guise of a hot record. I'm not saying don't make hardcore records, but let's get a balance. Let's support artists who are really challenging themselves musically and blending the genres and, you know, doing different things. That's the only way you really expand the music and let kids who are in love with hip hop know that it's okay to try something new. How else do you think you would get a Lauryn Hill? If she didn't take a chance on the music and do it differently, if the Fugees didn't do it differently, it never would have happened."

—*Tell Me More* with Michel Martin, 2007

1. BLUE
Joni Mitchell (REPRISE, 1971)

After nearly fifty years, *Blue* remains the clearest and most animated musical map to the new world that women traced, sometimes invisibly, within their daily lives in the aftermath of the utopian, dream-crushing 1960s. It is a record full of love songs, of sad songs; but more than that, it is a compendium of reasonable demands that too many men in too many women's lives heard, in 1971, as pipe dreams or outrageous follies. "All I really, really want our love to do / is to bring out the best in me and in you, too," Mitchell sang to an elusive partner on the album's first track. That line, like so many of the melodic and lyrical gestures throughout *Blue*, is simple, but so radical. With the counterculture collapsing under the weight of its machismo-driven mythologies, women pushed forward with calls to imagine genuine equality in real life—in the private places where love and art are made. *Blue* articulates that demand and its effects more clearly than any other work of art. Musically, it reflects Mitchell's belief in what she's called "the feminine appetite for intimacy," with her nearly naked guitar playing, Appalachian dulcimer, and occasional piano dominating the mix. Yet its rhythms and unexpected flights of melody also reveal Mitchell's movement toward the deeper improvisational waters of jazz, a sonic illustration for her love of crossing lines, the "white lines of the highway" or the generic ones of the recording studio. Lyrically *Blue* communicates both the cool of Joan Didion and the rawness of Sylvia Plath and reminds us that emotional writing is powerful only when it is punishingly precise. The way Mitchell made the album was also revolutionary: she produced the sessions herself, directing a small band that included rival/peers like James Taylor (one of several lovers honored and exposed by her observations) and Stephen Stills. Mitchell would travel much farther on the lonely road she identifies in "All I Want," but *Blue* is her crossroads, where she bests her devils and invents a mode of expression that every singer-songwriter must master, but none can truly imitate.

—Ann Powers, NPR Music, *Turning the Tables*,
"The 150 Greatest Albums Made by Women," 2017

Erykah Badu *by* Asiah Fulmore

AFTERWORD
by Marissa Lorusso

everal years ago, the poet Eileen Myles joked that if "the poetry world celebrated its female stars at the true level of their productivity and influence, poetry would wind up being a largely female world, and the men would leave." To actually appreciate the role women have played in shaping the past, present, and future of the art, Myles implies, is a potentially horrifying prospect for those who have traditionally been in power. They wouldn't be able to stand it. They'd pack up shop.

I don't know if the same would happen in the music world. But I do know that taking women's music seriously—really seriously; really reckoning with what it takes to create beautiful, challenging, thoughtful, messy, honest music under the conditions of patriarchy—can be momentous, life-changing work. I know that because of the book you're holding in your hands, and the many voices, perspectives, ideas, and questions it represents.

When I first heard Ann Powers, the cofounder of *Turning the Tables*, describe her initial idea for this project—a list of the 150 greatest albums made by women, created to challenge the typical boys' club of best-ever album countdowns—it felt revolutionary and quietly earth-shattering to me. I was new to NPR Music, having just graduated from being one of the team's interns; soon after, I'd become a permanent member of the *Turning the Tables* team, a position I held (with great pride!) for many years. Ann's proposition felt like a bold, indisputable way to assert how much music by women matters: to argue that you could, in fact, tell the entire story of popular music in this country solely through the work of women musicians.

Because women's art is so routinely undervalued—by pundits and critics, on the *Billboard* charts and in sales figures, in major industry awards and in scholarly literature—it felt like a revelation to bring together a group of women critics, scholars, listeners, and journalists for this enormous celebration of women's musical accomplishments.

I didn't realize it at the time, but when we started working on *Turning the Tables*, we were joining a wave—a groundswell of discussions about questioning the classics and challenging traditional ideas about what constitutes the very best of anything. Almost a decade ago, the #OscarsSoWhite hashtag galvanized conversation about how picks for the "best" films of the year ignored pivotal work by filmmakers of color. The racial justice protests across the United States in the summer of 2020, which refocused attention on the Black Lives Matter movement, included reckonings about the ways Black writers, thinkers, and artists are routinely left out of mainstream canons and curricula. In the mid-aughts, the #MeToo movement's revelations about the ubiquity of sexual violence led to discussions about whose perspectives and experiences are taken seriously, in Hollywood and elsewhere. This debate about greatness is happening all the time, in smaller ways, too; open any social media app right now and spill a single opinion about a work of art *you* love—I guarantee that someone, somewhere, will tell you that their favorite is superior.

But what really struck me, right from the very beginning of the project that would eventually lead to this book, was the fact that it wasn't just a way to replace one canon with another. We didn't simply want to prove that music by women is *just as good* as music by men—to try to go toe-to-toe with the Beatles or Biggie or Miles and prove that for every classic album of theirs, we could provide a record by women that was equally crucial. Instead, the project was a means to question the very framework by which greatness gets defined—and then, to fill that framework with so much paradigm-shifting, era-defining, boundary-breaking art that the whole thing collapsed, so that we could start to build something entirely new.

Because the more we worked on our first list—and everything that came after—the more we encountered and reencountered one simple fact: canons are inherently exclusionary. A list, after all, can have only a set number of items. That means, too, that there's a limit on how many voices can be part of the discussion.

But aren't those things true only if we believe that a canon needs to be a static, stable thing—something we all agree on, something that's meant to represent everyone? This project felt like a chance, instead, to picture a world beyond those assumptions. What if we agreed instead that the depth and breadth of women's accomplishments in music couldn't actually ever be collected in a single list? That one "best-of" compilation couldn't ever, actually, represent everyone? What would that look like?

It would mean finding ways to dig into these questions, over and over—by re-creating this project, year after year, and finding new ways to keep asking new questions about history, greatness, and gender. Like in our second season, focused on the women and nonbinary artists shaping the sound of the twenty-first century, where we asked: What does it mean to create a canon in real time—to try to correct the record *before* history is set in stone? Or our celebration of eight women who laid the foundation for popular music in the early twentieth century that considered: How do artists' legacies get created—and how can we tell stories about history that don't privilege outstanding individuals by marginalizing the communities of which they were a part? When we commissioned essays about particularly life-changing albums, we wondered: How do we, as listeners, decide what is important to us—and what's the difference, anyway, between "important" and "important to us"?

It would mean continually acknowledging that so many people have been left out of mainstream canons, for so many reasons—gender, yes, but also race, and class, and geography, and disability, and language; access to (or assumptions about!) gear or technology or an audience—reasons that have nothing to do with sheer musical quality. It would mean seeking out those alternate histories; if we didn't find them, it would mean imagining them together. And it would mean actively celebrating and inviting disagreement—being thrilled when other writers, fans, and listeners took it upon themselves to make their own *Turning the Tables*-style lists to rebut ours, or to honor their local scenes or favorite genres.

It would mean challenging our own preconceived notions, too. We've watched as recent conversations about gender have evolved rapidly in the mainstream—especially around the increasing visibility of transgender and nonbinary identities, queerness, and gender nonconformity—and between each era of *Turning the*

Tables, we considered how our project should best reflect gender diversity. Championing women's history has immense value, of course—but that process looks different when you reckon with the ways that the gender binary itself can be a source of oppression, or how the category of "womanhood" can be used as a weapon of exclusion against trans and gender-nonconforming people.

These conversations feel especially vital right now. In 2022, a Gallup poll found that one in five American members of Generation Z—the generation born between 1997 and 2003—identify as part of the LGBTQIA+ community; that same year, singers Sam Smith and Kim Petras became the first openly nonbinary and transgender artists, respectively, to earn a *Billboard* No. 1 hit. But the very next year, state legislatures across the US introduced a record number of anti-drag and anti-trans bills, with some states—including Tennessee—passing laws that many argue would effectively criminalize public musical performance by transgender artists. And outside of legal marginalization, trans and nonbinary artists are far too often left out of traditional pop canons, while simultaneously being responsible for much of pop's most visionary work. (The music of the late electronic producer SOPHIE, the trans punk pioneer Laura Jane Grace, and the bounce icon Big Freedia come immediately to mind, just to name a few recent examples. And that's not to mention the impact of contemporary trans and nonbinary music journalists; JJ Skolnik and Sasha Geffen, both of whom have contributed to *Turning the Tables*, are some of the most incisive and thrilling critics working today.)

Our attempts at inclusion haven't always gotten it right. When we added a plus sign to the end of the word "women" in our list of "The 200 Greatest Songs by 21st-Century Women," for example, to signify a wider range of marginalized genders, some in our audience—including some trans and nonbinary readers—told us they found the move thoughtless and misguided. It was an important perspective, and a useful reminder of the importance of staying open to critique. In that way, even our missteps have emphasized to us that the work of asking these questions, of considering new perspectives, of handing over authority to other voices—of acknowledging failures and missed opportunities, of finding new ways to correct the record: *this*, actually, has been the true joy of this project. The goal was never to set one truth in stone forever. It was instead to imagine "music

318

history as a huge continuing conversation," as Ann says in the Introduction to this book.

That conversation isn't happening without resistance; power doesn't shift hands quite so easily. A study by the Annenberg Inclusion Initiative found that, for all the songs on the *Billboard* Hot 100 between 2012 and 2022, women comprised only 12.8 percent of the songwriters and 2.8 percent of the producers. The study also found that at the Grammys, only 13.9 percent of nominees in the major categories were women. And technology isn't solving the problem. It might seem like the infinite access afforded by the streaming era would render the old gatekeepers irrelevant; in reality, though, it's not so simple. Reporting by writer Liz Pelly, who has contributed to *Turning the Tables*, has shown the way that streaming playlists—a major way that people listen to and discover music—usually heavily favor male artists; then, when the play count for those men goes up, the algorithm assumes that's all listeners want to hear and proposes even *more* men to listen to!

Sometimes, it feels like we can scream about the underrated genius of Diamanda Galás all we want, or preach endlessly about how women like Sister Rosetta Tharpe invented rock and roll and women like Delia Derbyshire and Suzanne Ciani pioneered electronic music, or make an infinite playlist of the women who revolutionized jazz, but if the powers that be don't consider their stories valuable, worthwhile, or—god forbid—"Marketable," we'll likely get another dozen biopics about the Rolling Stones or scholarly deep dives into Bob Dylan instead. Awards will keep being given to male artists, producers, songwriters; men will stay at the top of the charts. Maybe a few outstanding women will break through—getting sprinkled into mainstream Top 10 lists or breaking a streaming record here and there.

Our canons may never replace the conventional wisdom. But we never wanted this project to become a new set of gatekeepers anyway. (We aren't, for example, trying to bring to life a version of Eileen Myles's hypothesis wherein all the men leave!) The goal is more space, more voices, more stories. For me, one of the most rewarding parts of working on *Turning the Tables* has been learning to shift my lens on the past, present, and future—looking away from the traditional models of "greatness" and looking toward other stories instead. The rich collection of voices

319

in this book are all part of that mission. They are a correction to the historical record; a means of making the importance of music by women feel unassailable, from the dawn of popular music through to the most groundbreaking work of today. And they're a jumping-off point for infinite new, future canons—each of which will deserve to be built, and broken, and turned into inspiration for a new set of ideas yet again.

Elizabeth Fraser, Cocteau Twins,
by Mayya Agapova

THE 150 GREATEST ALBUMS MADE BY WOMEN (2017)

1. *Blue*, Joni Mitchell
2. *The Miseducation of Lauryn Hill*, Lauryn Hill
3. *I Put a Spell on You*, Nina Simone
4. *I Never Loved a Man the Way I Love You*, Aretha Franklin
5. *Supa Dupa Fly*, Missy Elliott
6. *Lemonade*, Beyoncé
7. *Horses*, Patti Smith
8. *Pearl*, Janis Joplin
9. *Back to Black*, Amy Winehouse
10. *Tapestry*, Carole King
11. *Coat of Many Colors*, Dolly Parton
12. *Baduizm*, Erykah Badu
13. *Like a Prayer*, Madonna
14. *Whitney Houston*, Whitney Houston
15. *Where Did Our Love Go*, The Supremes
16. *Rumours*, Fleetwood Mac
17. *Control*, Janet Jackson
18. *Car Wheels on a Gravel Road*, Lucinda Williams

19. *Amor Prohibido*, Selena
20. *Presenting the Fabulous Ronettes Featuring Veronica*, The Ronettes
21. *Rid of Me*, PJ Harvey
22. *Diamond Life*, Sade
23. *Amazing Grace*, Aretha Franklin
24. *Coal Miner's Daughter*, Loretta Lynn
25. *Little Plastic Castle*, Ani DiFranco
26. *CrazySexyCool*, TLC
27. *Little Earthquakes*, Tori Amos
28. *Nina Simone Sings the Blues*, Nina Simone
29. *Jagged Little Pill*, Alanis Morissette
30. *21*, Adele
31. *Exile in Guyville*, Liz Phair
32. *Post*, Björk
33. *All Hail the Queen*, Queen Latifah
34. *Private Dancer*, Tina Turner
35. *Parallel Lines*, Blondie
36. *Nightclubbing*, Grace Jones

95. *¿Dónde Están los Ladrones?*, Shakira

96. *Hard Core*, Lil' Kim

97. *Daydream*, Mariah Carey

98. *Yeah Yeah Yeah Yeah*, Bikini Kill

99. *Fearless*, Taylor Swift

100. *It's My Way!*, Buffy Sainte-Marie

101. *Touch*, Eurythmics

102. *Sound & Color*, Alabama Shakes

103. *Enta Omri (You Are My Life)*, Umm Kulthum

104. *Come Away with ESG*, ESG

105. *The Glamorous Life*, Sheila E.

106. *Tragic Kingdom*, No Doubt

107. *Leader of the Pack*, The Shangri-Las

108. *Imagination*, Gladys Knight & the Pips

109. *Transgender Dysphoria Blues*, Against Me!

110. *Platinum*, Miranda Lambert

111. *The Litanies of Satan*, Diamanda Galás

112. *Mercedes Sosa en Argentina*, Mercedes Sosa

113. *Young, Gifted and Black*, Aretha Franklin

114. *Rumor Has It*, Reba McEntire

115. *La Pareja*, La Lupe and Tito Puente

116. *On How Life Is*, Macy Gray

117. *I Love Rock 'n' Roll*, Joan Jett and the Blackhearts

118. *I Feel for You*, Chaka Khan

119. *Cut*, The Slits

120. *Rapture*, Anita Baker

121. *Hejira*, Joni Mitchell

122. *The Scream*, Siouxsie and the Banshees

123. *The Changer and the Changed*, Cris Williamson

124. *No Secrets*, Carly Simon

125. *Tidal*, Fiona Apple

126. *A Song for You*, Carpenters

127. *Sister*, Sonic Youth

128. *Deep Listening*, Pauline Oliveros, Stuart Dempster, Panaiotis

129. *Broken English*, Marianne Faithfull

130. *Wild and Peaceful*, Teena Marie

131. *I Thought About You—Live at Vine St.*, Shirley Horn

132. *I Am Shelby Lynne*, Shelby Lynne

133. *Fanny Hill*, Fanny

134. *A Seat at the Table*, Solange

135. *The B-52's*, The B-52's

136. *Yoko Ono/Plastic Ono Band*, Yoko Ono/Plastic Ono Band

137. *50 Gates of Wisdom (Yemenite Songs)*, Ofra Haza

138. *Heaven or Las Vegas*, Cocteau Twins

139. *All Over the Place*, The Bangles

140. *Come Away with Me*, Norah Jones

141. *Ys*, Joanna Newsom

142. *My Life*, Iris DeMent

143. *Body Talk*, Robyn

144. *Last Splash*, The Breeders

145. *Moussolou (Women)*, Oumou Sangaré

146. *Flaming Red*, Patty Griffin

147. *Dolmen Music*, Meredith Monk

148. *The Mosaic Project*, Terri Lyne Carrington

149. *Songs in A Minor*, Alicia Keys

150. *The Roches*, The Roches

Salt-N-Pepa

THE 200 GREATEST SONGS BY 21ST-CENTURY WOMEN+ (2018)

1. M.I.A., "Paper Planes"
2. Yeah Yeah Yeahs, "Maps"
3. Beyoncé, "Single Ladies (Put a Ring on It)"
4. Amy Winehouse, "Back to Black"
5. Alabama Shakes, "Hold On"
6. Lorde, "Royals"
7. Sharon Jones & the Dap-Kings, "100 Days, 100 Nights"
8. Alicia Keys, "Fallin'"
9. Brandi Carlile, "The Story"
10. Peaches, "Fuck the Pain Away"
11. Janelle Monáe, "Tightrope" (ft. Big Boi)
12. Solange, "Cranes in the Sky"
13. Lana Del Rey, "Video Games"
14. Hurray for the Riff Raff, "Pa'lante"
15. Nicki Minaj, "Super Bass"
16. Mitski, "Your Best American Girl"
17. Florence and the Machine, "Dog Days Are Over"
18. Grimes, "Oblivion"
19. Beyoncé, "Formation"
20. Adele, "Rolling in the Deep"
21. Carly Rae Jepsen, "Call Me Maybe"
22. Kacey Musgraves, "Follow Your Arrow"
23. Amy Winehouse, "Rehab"
24. Rihanna, "Umbrella"
25. Cardi B, "Bodak Yellow"
26. Miranda Lambert, "Gunpowder & Lead"
27. Kesha, "Praying"
28. Norah Jones, "Don't Know Why"
29. Lady Gaga, "Bad Romance"
30. Rhiannon Giddens, "At the Purchaser's Option"
31. Against Me!, "Transgender Dysphoria Blues"
32. SZA, "The Weekend"
33. Courtney Barnett, "Avant Gardener"
34. Carrie Underwood, "Before He Cheats"

35. The Knife, "Heartbeats"

36. Bomba Estéreo, "Soy Yo"

37. Paramore, "Misery Business"

38. St. Vincent, "Cruel"

39. Valerie June, "Workin' Woman Blues"

40. Rihanna, "We Found Love"

41. Kelly Clarkson, "Since U Been Gone"

42. Esperanza Spalding, "I Know You Know"

43. Taylor Swift, "Blank Space"

44. Lizzo, "Good as Hell"

45. Anaïs Mitchell, "Why We Build the Wall"

46. Azealia Banks, "212" (ft. Lazy Jay)

47. Avril Lavigne, "Complicated"

48. Beyoncé, "Crazy in Love" (ft. Jay-Z)

49. Robyn, "Dancing On My Own"

50. Downtown Boys, "Monstro"

51. Feist, "1234"

52. Vanessa Carlton, "A Thousand Miles"

53. Cecile McLorin Salvant, "Monday"

54. Margo Price, "Hands of Time"

55. tUnE-yArDs, "Powa"

56. Nelly Furtado, "I'm Like a Bird"

57. Lady Gaga, "Born This Way"

58. Adele, "Someone Like You"

59. Little Big Town, "Girl Crush"

60. Ivy Queen, "Quiero Bailar"

61. Broken Social Scene, "Anthems for a Seventeen Year-Old Girl"

62. M.I.A., "Bad Girls"

63. Katy Perry, "Teenage Dream"

64. Waxahatchee, "Bathtub"

65. Shakira, "Hips Don't Lie" (ft. Wyclef Jean)

66. Sia, "Chandelier"

67. Grouper, "Heavy Water/I'd Rather Be Sleeping"

68. Nicki Minaj, "Feeling Myself" (ft. Beyoncé)

69. Xenia Rubinos, "Mexican Chef"

70. Blu Cantrell, "Hit 'Em Up Style (Oops!)"

71. India.Arie, "Video"

72. Regina Spektor, "Us"

73. Icona Pop, "I Love It" (ft. Charli XCX)

74. Sharon Van Etten, "Every Time the Sun Comes Up"

75. Jill Scott, "Golden"

76. Rihanna, "Bitch Better Have My Money"

77. ANOHNI, "Drone Bomb Me"

78. Natalia Lafourcade, "Hasta la Raíz"

79. Gretchen Wilson, "Redneck Woman"

80. Joanna Newsom, "Peach, Plum, Pear"

81. Jenny Lewis, "Just One of the Guys"

82. Corrine Bailey Rae, "Put Your Records On"

83. Young M.A., "OOOUUU"

84. Pink, "Don't Let Me Get Me"

85. Ibeyi, "River"

86. Matana Roberts, "All Is Written"

87. Sylvan Esso, "Coffee"

88. Evanescence, "Bring Me to Life"

89. FKA twigs, "Two Weeks"

90. Caroline Shaw, "Partita for 8 Voices"

91. The Moldy Peaches, "Anyone Else but You"

92. Fea, "Mujer Moderna"
93. HAIM, "The Wire"
94. Eve, "Let Me Blow Ya Mind" (ft. Gwen Stefani)
95. Noura Mint Seymali, "Ghlana"
96. EMA, "California"
97. Ludicra, "Clean White Void"
98. SOPHIE, "Lemonade"
99. Ana Tijoux, "1977"
100. Maggie Rogers, "Alaska"
101. Shovels & Rope, "Birmingham"
102. Janelle Monáe, "Pynk"
103. Beyoncé, "Countdown"
104. Princess Nokia, "Tomboy"
105. Thao & the Get Down Stay Down, "We the Common"
106. Babymetal, "Gimme Chocolate!!"
107. Gwen Stefani, "Hollaback Girl"
108. Pistol Annies, "Bad Example"
109. Angel Olsen, "Shut Up Kiss Me"
110. Santigold, "L.E.S. Artistes"
111. Mary Halvorson Octet, "Away with You (No. 55)"
112. Estelle, "American Boy" (ft. Kanye West)
113. Flor De Toloache, "Dicen"
114. Laura Marling, "Rambling Man"
115. The Internet, "Girl" (ft. Kaytranada)
116. First Aid Kit, "My Silver Lining"
117. Jean Grae and Blue Sky Black Death, "Threats" (ft. Chen Lo)
118. Big Freedia, "Azz Everywhere"
119. Tanya Tagaq, "Uja"
120. Miley Cyrus, "Wrecking Ball"
121. G.L.O.S.S., "G.L.O.S.S. (We're from the Future)"
122. Kali Uchis, "Tyrant"
123. Tegan and Sara, "The Con"
124. Amerie, "1 Thing"
125. Priests, "And Breeding"
126. Andra Day, "Rise Up"
127. Julia Wolfe, "Anthracite Fields: IV. Flowers" (ft. Bang on a Can All-Stars & Choir of Trinity Wall Street)
128. Hop Along, "Tibetan Pop Stars"
129. Joanna Newsom, "Sapokanikan"
130. Elizabeth Cook, "Heroin Addict Sister"
131. Jlin, "Black Origami"
132. Ciara, "Goodies"
133. Gossip, "Standing in the Way of Control"
134. Maren Morris, "My Church"
135. Big Thief, "Mary"
136. Mon Laferte, "Pa' Dónde Se Fue"
137. Jazmine Sullivan, "Bust Your Windows"
138. Micachu & the Shapes, "Golden Phone"
139. Moor Mother, "Deadbeat Protest"
140. Jenny Hval, "That Battle Is Over"
141. Taylor Swift, "You Belong with Me"
142. Cooly G, "He Said I Said" (ft. Aaron Carr)
143. Mala Rodríguez, "Yo Marco el Minuto"
144. Jamila Woods, "Blk Girl Soldier"
145. Nicole Mitchell, "Shiny Divider"
146. Metric, "Help I'm Alive"

147. Imogen Heap, "Hide and Seek"
148. Rilo Kiley, "Portions for Foxes"
149. Sky Ferreira, "Everything Is Embarrassing"
150. Arooj Aftab, "Lullaby"
151. Fever Ray, "Seven"
152. DJ Sprinkles, "House Music Is Controllable Desire You Can Own"
153. Lily Allen, "Smile"
154. Holly Herndon, "Chorus"
155. Mortals, "View from a Tower"
156. Julien Baker, "Sprained Ankle"
157. Terri Lyne Carrington, "Mosaic Triad"
158. Mary Gauthier, "Mercy Now"
159. Sarah Kirkland Snider, "Penelope: The Lotus Eaters"
160. The Band Perry, "If I Die Young"
161. Carly Rae Jepsen, "Run Away with Me"
162. Cristina Pato, "Muiñeira for Cristina"
163. Windhand, "Black Candles"
164. Amara La Negra, "Poron Pom Pom"
165. Tweet, "Oops (Oh My)" (ft. Missy Elliott)
166. I'm With Her, "I-89"
167. Daymé Arocena, "Mambo Na' Mà"
168. René Marie, "Dixie/Strange Fruit"
169. Brandy Clark, "Hold My Hand"
170. Kelis, "Milkshake"
171. Fatima Al Qadiri, "D-Medley"
172. Juana Molina, "Eras"
173. Jhene Aiko, "The Worst"

174. Abigail Washburn, "City of Refuge"
175. A-WA, "Habib Galbi"
176. Victoire, "Cathedral City"
177. Light Asylum, "A Certain Person"
178. Noname, "Diddy Bop"
179. Laura Mvula, "Father Father"
180. Sara Bareilles, "Love Song"
181. St. Vincent, "Digital Witness"
182. Idina Menzel, "Let It Go"
183. Jorja Smith, "Blue Lights"
184. Khia, "My Neck, My Back (Lick It)"
185. Ms. Dynamite, "Dy-Na-Mi-Tee"
186. Torres, "Sprinter"
187. Anna Thorvaldsdottir, "In the Light of Air—Luminance"
188. KING, "The Greatest"
189. McCrary Sisters, "Train"
190. Phoebe Bridgers, "Smoke Signals"
191. Ashley McBryde, "Girl Goin' Nowhere"
192. Emel Mathlouthi, "Kelmti Horra"
193. Allison Miller's Boom Tic Boom, "Otis Was a Polar Bear"
194. Lizz Wright, "Hit the Ground"
195. Buika, "Mi Niña Lola"
196. La Insuperable, "Damelo" (ft. Chimbala)
197. Kaki King, "Playing with Pink Noise"
198. Demi Lovato, "Cool for the Summer"
199. Rapsody, "Black & Ugly"
200. Lori McKenna, "Humble & Kind"

SZA *by* Asiah Fulmore

TURNING THE TABLES CONTRIBUTORS, 2017–2023

Adia Victoria

Aggi Ashagre

Alex Ariff

Alex Ramos

Alex Vazquez

Ali Tonn

Alice Randall

Alisa Ali

Alisha Lola Jones

Alisha Sweeney

Alison Fensterstock

Alison Jones

Alyson Hurt

Alyssa Edes

Amanda Petrusich

Amelia Mason

Amy Miller

Amy Rigby

Anastasia Tsioulcas

Andrea Swensson

Ani DiFranco

Ann Powers

Anne Litt

Annie Bartholomew

Annie Zaleski

April Ledbetter

Asiah Fulmore

Audie Cornish

Beca Grimm

Beth Winegarner

Briana Younger

Brittney McKenna

Bruce Trujillo

C. V. Grier

Carina del Valle Schorske

Caroline Randall Williams

Carrie Courogen

Caryn Rose

Catalina Maria Johnson

Catherine Zhang

Cheryl Pawelski

Cheryl Waters

Christina Cala

Christina Lee

Cindy Howes

Ciona Rouse

Claire Lobenfeld

Colin Marshall

Constance Miller

Cyrena Touros

Dame Darcy

Daphne Brooks

Dawnie Walton

Deb Vargas

Deborah Paredez

Dee Dee Bridgewater

Desiré Moses

Dwan Reece

Elena See

Elizabeth Blair

Elizabeth Nelson

Emily Abshire

Emily Bogle

Emily Lordi

Erin MacLeod

Faith Pennick

Farah Griffin

Farrah Skeiky

Francesca Royster

Gabrielle Bell

Gayle Wald

Geeta Dayal

Gemma Watters

Gwen Thompkins

Harmony Holiday

Hazel Cills

Hilarie Ashton

Hilary Hughes

Holly George-Warren

Holly Gleason

Ilana Kaplan

Isabel Zacharias

Jacob Ganz

Jamie Ludwig

Jayna Brown

Jazmin Anita

Jenn Pelly

Jenny Gathright

Jess Rotter

Jessi Whitten

Jessica Diaz-Hurtado

Jessica Gentile

Jessica Hopper

Jessica Wilkerson

Jessie Scott

Jewly Hight

Jill Sternheimer

JJ Skolnik

Jolie Myers

Joni Deutsch

Joni Tevis

Jude Rogers

Judith Tick

Judy Berman

Julianne Escobedo
Shepherd

Julyssa Lopez

Kaia Kater

Karen Tongson

Katherine St. Asaph

Katie Presley

Katie Simon

Keanna Faircloth

Kelly Link

Kelly McCartney

Kelly McEvers

Keryce Chelsi Henry

Kiana Fitzgerald

Kim Junod

Kim Kelly

Kim Mack

Kim Ruehl

Kristen Kurtis

Laina Dawes

Lara Pellegrinelli

LaTesha Harris

Laura Snapes

Laura Sydell

Lauren Bentley

Lauren Migaki

Lauren Onkey

Leah Donnella

Leslie Ureña

Lily Moayeri

Linda Fahey

Lindsay Kimball

Lindsay Zoladz

Lior Phillips

Lisa Famiglietti

Lisa Lagace

Liz Pelly

Loren DiBlasi

Lori Selke

Louise Brown

Luke Medina

Lyndsey McKenna

Maggie Brennan

Maggie Thrash

Margaret Farrell

Margaret Flatley

Margo Price

Maria Sherman

Marisa Arbona-Ruiz

Marissa Lorusso

Marissa R. Moss

Maureen Mahon

Mayya Agapova

Melissa A. Weber

Melissa Hmelnicky

Melissa Locker

Michele Myers

Michelle Mercer

Mina Tavakoli

Mito Habe-Evans

Monika Evstatieva

Namwali Serpell

Natalie Weiner

Neda Ulaby

Nickolai Hammar

Nicole Rifkin

Niki Walker

Nina Corcoran

Nina Gregory

Noah Caldwell

Paige McGinley

Paula Mejia

Phil Harrell

Rachel Horn

Rachel Martin

Ramtin Arablouei

Rashida Chavis

Raye Zaragoza

Rebecca Bodenheimer

Rita Houston

Rund Abdelfatah

Ruth Saxelby

Saidah Blount

Samantha Silver

Sarah Handel

Sarah Kerson

Sarah Wardrop

Sasha Geffen

Shana L. Redmond

Sheli Delaney

Sherry Rayn Barnett

Sidney Madden

Sophie Kemp

Sowmya Krishnamurthy

Stasia Irons

Stefanie Fernández

Suraya Mohamed

Suzy Exposito

Sydnee Monday

Talia Schlanger

Tammy Kernodle

Tanya Ballard Brown

Terri Lyne Carrington

Theresa Kereakes

Tift Merritt

Tom Cole

Tracy Fessenden

Zoë Madonna

CREDITS & PERMISSIONS

Grateful acknowledgment is given to the following for the use of their work in this publication:

Music notes used throughout © pingebat/stock.adobe.com.

Record used throughout © MAXSHOT_PL/stock.adobe.com.

Texture used throughout © Bowonpat/stock.adobe.com.

Pages iii: Barbara Lynn at the New Orleans Jazz and Heritage Festival, 1977. Photo by Chris Strachwitz, courtesy of the Arhoolie Foundation.

Pages v, 66, 248, 321, 324: Halftone stars © Md/stock.adobe.com.

Pages v, 241, 267: Illustrations by Jess Rotter.

Pages vi: Lydia Mendoza in San Antonio, Texas, 1975. Photo by Chris Strachwitz, courtesy of the Arhoolie Foundation.

Pages ix, 32, 152, 159, 206, 276–77: Illustrations by Dame Darcy.

Page x: Group portrait of various female hip hop groups and performers, New York, New York, late 1980s. Photo by Janette Beckman/Getty Images.

Pages xv, 46, 213, 295: Illustrations by Maggie Thrash.

Pages 1, 35, 57, 89, 111, 141, 163, 197, 229, 261, 279: background texture © Nikola/stock.adobe.com; circle swirls © kazy/stock.adobe.com; ink blot illustration © TANATPON/stock.adobe.com.

Page 2: Bessie Smith in 1936. Photo by Carl Van Vechten, courtesy of the James Weldon Johnson Collection in the Yale Collection of American Literature, Beinecke Rare Book and Manuscript Library. © Carl Van Vechten Trust.

Page 10: Dolly Parton at Symphony Hall, Boston, MA, 1972. Photo by Henry Horenstein.

Page 15: Willie Mae "Big Mama" Thornton, at the American Folk Blues Festival, October 1965. Photo by Chris Strachwitz, courtesy of the Arhoolie Foundation.

Pages 20, 79, 122, 177: Illustrations by Nicole Rifkin.

Pages 23, 147: Illustrations by Gabrielle Bell.

Page 28: Mahalia Jackson with Duke Ellington, 1954. Photo by Myron H. Davis, courtesy of The William Russell Jazz Collection at The Historic New Orleans Collection, acquisition made possible by the Clarisse Claiborne Grima Fund, MSS 520.3281.

Page 36: The Staple Singers performing at Wattstax, Los Angeles Memorial Coliseum, on August 20, 1972. Photo by Michael Ochs Archives/Getty Images.

Pages 48, 311: Illustrations by Rashida Chavis.

Page 54: Nina Simone at the Village Gate, 1971. Photo by Sherry Rayn Barnett.

Pages 58, 66, 142, 264: Illustrations by Margaret Flatley.

Page 70: Beyonce Knowles, Michelle Williams, and Kelly Rowland of Destiny's Child, May 15, 2005, at the Oslo Spektrum in Oslo, Norway. Photo by Frank Micelotta/Getty Images.

Page 82: Debbie Harry in Berkeley, CA, 1978. Photo by Theresa Kereakes.

Page 89: Woman silhouette © babkinasvetlana/stock.adobe.com

Page 90: Joan Jett, December 9, 2013, in Hollywood, California. Photo by Christopher Polk/Getty Images for Clear Channel.

Pages 91–109: Woman folio art © babkinasvetlana/stock.adobe.com; Rope folio art © WinWin/stock.adobe.com.

Page 93: Cyndi Lauper at the Beverly Theatre in Beverly Hills, CA, February 1, 1984. Photo by Sherry Rayn Barnett.

Page 97: Celia Cruz at Hammersmith Odeon, London, UK, July 10, 1986. Photo by David Corio/Redferns.

Page 106: Lizzo performing in Baltimore, MD, July 25, 2019. Photo by Farrah Skeiky.

Page 112: Patti Smith in Los Angeles, 1976. Photo by Theresa Kereakes.

Page 118: Etta James at the New Orleans Jazz and Heritage Festival, 1979. Photo by Michael P. Smith, © The Historic New Orleans Collection, 2007.0103.2.249.

Page 121: Whitney Houston performs at the Canadian National Exhibition in Toronto, August 22, 1986. Photo by Ron Bull/*Toronto Star* via Getty Images.

Pages 136–37: Tina Turner and the Ikettes performing in New Orleans, 1970. Photo by Michael P. Smith. Gift of Master Digital Corporation, © The Historic New Orleans Collection, 2011.0307.11.

Pages 143–61: X folio art © SergeyBitos/stock.adobe.com.

Page 149: The Raincoats rehearsing in West London, 1979. Photo by Janette Beckman/Redferns.

Pages 155, 202, 308: Illustrations by Jazmin Anita.

Page 160: Diamanda Galás on stage at the Patronaat in Haarlem, Netherlands, on 18th November 1988. Photo by Frans Schellekens/Redferns.

Page 164: St. Vincent at the 9:30 Club in Washington, DC, March 1, 2014. Photo by Farrah Skeiky.

Page 168: Sheila E. opens for Prince at the Summit, January 10, 1985. Photo by Steve Campbell/*Houston Chronicle* via Getty Images.

Page 170: Suzanne Ciani in the recording studio in Soho, New York City, 1970s. Photo by Lloyd Williams.

Page 173: Missy Elliott at Hit Factory New York, 16 October 1998. Photo by David Corio/Redferns.

Page 174: Alice Coltrane, 1970. Photo by Echoes/Redferns.

Page 189: Roberta Flack, 1971. Photo by Anthony Barboza.

Page 197: Globe art © miloje/stock.adobe.com.

Page 198: Joni Mitchell, 1983. Photo by Laurie Lewis.

Pages 207, 314, 329: Illustrations by Asiah Fulmore.

Page 227: Gal Costa in Cannes, January 1973. Photo by Gilbert TOURTE/Gamma-Rapho via Getty Images.

Page 229: Cats © SlothAstronaut/stock.adobe.com.

Page 230: Carole King on stage in London, 1972. Photo by Michael Putland/Getty Images.

Page 248: Queen Latifah in New York City, March 1990. Photo by Janette Beckman/Getty Images.

Page 252: Loretta Lynn in Branson, Missouri, 1976. Photo by Stephanie Chernikowski/Michael Ochs Archives/Getty Images.

Page 262: Mary J. Blige at China Club in New York City, 1992. Photo by Al Pereira.

Page 280: Rosetta Tharpe, c. 1957 at Leeds City Town Hall, Leeds, West Yorkshire, England. Photo by Terry Cryer.

Page 287: Aretha Franklin sings in the Atlantic Records studio during "The Weight" recording session on January 9, 1969, in New York City. Photo by Michael Ochs Archives/Getty Images.

Page 297: boygenius (Lucy Dacus, Julien Baker, and Phoebe Bridgers) perform an NPR Tiny Desk Concert in 2018. Photo by Camerona Pollack/NPR.

Page 320: Illustration by Mayya Agapova.

Pages 321–23, 325–32: background texture © Nikola/stock.adobe.com.

Page 324: Sandra "Pepa" Denton, Deirdre "Spinderella" Roper, and Cheryl "Salt" James, the hip-hop group Salt-N-Pepa in New York, 1988. Photo by Janette Beckman/Getty Images.